CATO
SUPREME COURT
REVIEW
2002 — 2003

⟨ CATO ⟩
SUPREME COURT
REVIEW
2 0 0 2 — 2 0 0 3

ROGER PILON
Publisher

ROBERT A. LEVY
Associate Editor

JAMES L. SWANSON
Editor in Chief

TIMOTHY LYNCH
Associate Editor

CENTER FOR CONSTITUTIONAL STUDIES

CATO
INSTITUTE
Washington, D.C.

ISBN I-930865-52-X

Printed in the United States of America.

Cover design by Elise B. Rivera.

Cato Institute
1000 Massachusetts Ave., N.W.
Washington, D.C. 2000I
www.cato.org

Contents

FOREWORD

Substance and Method at the Court

Roger Pilon

The Cato Institute's Center for Constitutional Studies is pleased to publish this second volume of the *Cato Supreme Court Review*, an annual critique of the Court's most important decisions from the term just ended, plus a look at the cases ahead—all from a classical Madisonian perspective, grounded in the nation's first principles, liberty and limited government. A year ago, on September 17, Constitution Day, we released the inaugural volume of the *Review* at a gala conference, "The Supreme Court: Past and Prologue," held at the Cato Institute. The conference was followed by the first annual B. Kenneth Simon Lecture in Constitutional Thought, given by Douglas H. Ginsburg, chief judge of the United States Court of Appeals for the District of Columbia Circuit. Judge Ginsburg's lecture, "On Constitutionalism," could not have been better suited for the occasion. It is the lead article in this volume of the *Review*.

With that, we hope to have begun a tradition. This year, too, the *Review* will be released at a Constitution Day conference on the Court's recent and coming terms. And this year's lecture in honor of the late Ken Simon, who passed away this summer, will also be devoted to a basic, timeless theme that was dear to Ken, "The Indivisibility of Personal and Property Rights: A View from the Founding." The lecture will be delivered by Walter E. Dellinger III, acting solicitor general under President Clinton. And it will appear as the lead article in next year's volume of the *Review*.

Both lectures treat fundamental, substantive subjects, focusing on why it is we have constitutional government in the first place. James Madison, like the rest of the Founders, understood that the purpose of government is to secure property. But he conceived of that term broadly, as did America's philosophical father, John Locke: "Lives, Liberties and Estates, which I call by the general Name, *Property*."

It is to secure such basic, substantive rights, the Declaration of Independence tells us, that governments are instituted among men. Unfortunately, with the rise and dominance of majoritarian process, that fundamental point has too often been obscured as the pursuit of policy has overtaken adherence to principle. One aim of this *Review* is to direct attention to that problem.

But there are other ways, too, in which we can lose sight of the substantive purpose of government. One is through a change in judicial methods, the methods employed by the branch of government charged with being the "bulwark of our liberties," as Madison put it. As I argued in last year's Foreword, "Restoring Constitutional Government," the structure of the Constitution suggests certain basic constitutional questions. First, is the governmental action authorized by the Constitution or by a state constitution? And second, if so, are the means employed necessary and proper—that is, could the authorized end be realized without those means; and do they violate either enumerated or unenumerated rights? A court that followed such a method would not go far wrong, constitutionally.

Unfortunately, the methods of the modern Court have been drastically altered by the New Deal's constitutional revolution, and not for the better. Today, except when governmental actions implicate "fundamental" rights, which are nowhere distinguished in the Constitution, the presumption of individual liberty implicit in question one has been replaced by a presumption of constitutionality in favor of the government. Thus, the burden is on the individual to defend his liberty, not on the government to defend its action. That switch is conceptually simple, however, compared with what has happened to question two. The word "necessary" in the Constitution's Necessary and Proper Clause was long ago lost, in *McCulloch v. Maryland* (1819), replaced by "appropriate," which of course does not mean the same thing. But regarding rights (and the scope of "proper"), if the governmental action implicates "fundamental" rights, the government must have a "compelling interest" if it is to win and its means must be "narrowly tailored" to that interest. That is the methodology of "strict scrutiny." "Mid-level" or "heightened scrutiny" is applied when somewhat "lesser" rights are at issue—in cases involving gender discrimination, for example, as opposed to racial discrimination, which is subject to a strict scrutiny test. With mid-level scrutiny the government must have an "important interest" and its means must be "substantially related" to that interest.

Then there are even lesser rights—property, contract, and the rights at issue in "ordinary commercial transactions," for example. To pass constitutional muster, governmental actions implicating those rights need only be "rationally related" to some "conceivable interest" of the government. Thus the "rational basis" test.

Nobody, including those on the Court, knows what any of that really means—certainly not the layman who tries to make sense today of "constitutional law." We've had cases in which four levels of judicial scrutiny have been articulated—*e.g., Turner Broadcasting Sys., Inc. v. FCC* (1994). More recently, Justice Ruth Bader Ginsburg hinted at a level of scrutiny between "mid-level" and "strict" when she spoke of the government's justification in gender discrimination cases as having to be "exceedingly persuasive" (*U.S. v. Virginia Military Academy* (1996)). And just this term, in *Lawrence v. Texas,* Justice Sandra Day O'Connor wrote that when laws exhibit a desire to harm a politically unpopular group, the Court has applied "a more searching form of rational basis review" to strike them down. Is that "more searching" form equivalent to "mid-level" review, or something just below it?

Interestingly, the issue of judicial methodology arose in the two most prominent cases before the Court this term, which is why it is featured in this Foreword. In the two University of Michigan affirmative action cases, *Gratz v. Bollinger* and *Grutter v. Bollinger,* involving racial and ethnic discrimination, the Court purported to apply strict scrutiny, but the dissent complained that there was nothing strict about the scrutiny the Court applied. In *Lawrence,* the Texas sodomy case handed down three days later, on the Court's last day in session, it appears that the Court simply abandoned its post-New Deal levels-of-scrutiny approach.

The articles that follow discuss those issues more fully, but a note or two would be in order here as well. In summary, the Court in *Grutter* invoked strict scrutiny to find, first, that Michigan's Law School had a "compelling interest" in having a diverse student body; and, second, that the race-conscious admissions policy the law school followed toward that interest—"a highly individualized, holistic review of each applicant's file, giving serious consideration to all the ways an applicant might contribute to a diverse educational environment"—was "narrowly tailored" to serve the interest. Not so, said dissenting Justice Clarence Thomas. Before this decision the

Court had allowed racial discrimination by the government only for national security and remedial purposes, neither of which was at issue here, he argued; and strict scrutiny precludes the kind of deference the *Gratz* and *Grutter* Court gave to the university in determining that diversity is a compelling state interest. Moreover, added Chief Justice William Rehnquist in his separate dissent, the "critical mass" of minority students the law school sought to admit was nothing but a thinly disguised scheme for proportional representation.

As I argue in my essay, however, the two sides at bottom are at war over "strict scrutiny" and its application. Yet the very idea of "compelling state interest" sits uncomfortably in our constitutional order. If the idea means anything at all, it is entailed in a power that may be constitutionally authorized to a government. If, however, it is a separate policy goal that some may think "compelling," it is a mere value judgment; there is no principle at issue; and it is no surprise that justices differ about what interests are or are not "compelling." As for "narrowly tailored," when coupled with such an interest, it is an even more inscrutable idea, reducing to a series of subjective indicia. In the end in *Grutter*, interests trump rights, policy trumps principle, and that is the end of principle. But the deeper problem lies in the Court's methodology, which makes little sense when one presses it in a case like this. Indeed, it is hardly an accident that the case generated so many opinions.

Turning to *Lawrence*, in the run-up to the case there was much debate among lawyers about whether the Court would treat homosexuals as a "suspect class," discriminated against historically, and apply strict scrutiny to the Texas statute criminalizing homosexual sodomy, or whether some lesser level of scrutiny would be applied, including the rational basis test. As Randy Barnett discusses in his essay, the Court cut through that debate, and through scrutiny theory itself, to chart a much simpler, more constitutionally credible course. At the extremes of the modern view, the Court had two choices. It could have found that there was a "fundamental" right to engage in homosexual sodomy, then insist that the state show that its statute overriding that right was narrowly tailored to serve a compelling state interest. But there were no precedents for finding that the right was "fundamental." Indeed, the Court had upheld a similar statute only 17 years earlier. Alternatively, the Court could have applied the rational basis test, presumed the constitutionality of the statute, and then insist that Lawrence show that there was no rational nexus between the statute and some conceivable state interest.

The Court did neither. It spoke simply of liberty—presuming, in effect, that Lawrence had a right to do what the statute forbade. The Court then asked the state to justify the statute—in other words, the burden was on the state to justify its restriction, not on Lawrence to justify his liberty. The state spoke of morality. The Court found, under the circumstance, that that reason was insufficient to restrict Lawrence's liberty. In a nutshell, that was the end of it. There was no need to talk about "fundamental" and "nonfundamental" rights, or different levels of state "interest," or different degrees of fit between means and ends. None of that made any sense in this case, if it makes sense in any case. Methodologically, *Lawrence* was a breath of fresh air.

And so we are left with the question of whether *Lawrence* is like the train ticket that is good only for this train on this day, or whether it will have legs for future cases. It is hard to imagine that the Court will abandon the methodology that has shrouded its work in mystery for more than six decades, not least because those methods have served the political agenda of the New Deal that is with us still today. Under modern methods, certain political and personal liberties get exquisite attention from the courts, while property rights and economic liberties are relegated to the status of a "poor relation" in the Bill of Rights, as Chief Justice Rehnquist once put it. At the same time, it is hard to imagine that the Court can much longer pretend that there is not something seriously wrong—to say nothing of extra- or even unconstitutional—in the methodology it has used since the New Deal Court invented it from whole cloth in the late 1930s. The far simpler and far more straightforward methodology the Constitution itself suggests would encourage the Court away from subjective policy and toward objective principle. That alone recommends it for a nation founded in principle and in the idea, in particular, that judicial methods should serve substantive ends—and that substance, in America, is liberty.

Introduction

This is the second volume of the *Cato Supreme Court Review*, an annual publication that examines the most significant opinions of the Supreme Court of the United States. Each year the *Review* will publish essays covering ten to fifteen cases from the Court's most recent term. The volume that you hold in your hands includes cases from the term beginning in October, 2002, and ending in late June, 2003.

In three ways, the *Cato Supreme Court Review* is unlike any other publication that follows the Court. First, it is timely. Indeed, this volume is the first in-depth review of the 2002 October Term—published less than three months after the Court handed down its final decisions on June 26, 2003. Each year's *Review* will appear on Constitution Day—September 17—soon after the term ends, and shortly before the next term begins on the first Monday in October.

Second, because the Constitution is not the exclusive domain of lawyers and judges, we asked our contributors to write articles that will appeal to a diverse and large audience. Although the *Review* is of course a "law" book, in the sense that it is about the Court and the Constitution, we intend it not only for lawyers but also for journalists, editors, broadcasters, publishers, legislators, government officials, professors, students, and all citizens interested in their Constitution and the Court's interpretation of it.

Third, and most important, the *Cato Supreme Court Review* has a singular point of view, which we do not attempt to conceal. I confess our ideology at the outset: This *Review* looks at the Court and its decisions from the classical Madisonian perspective, emphasizing our first principles of individual liberty; secure property rights; federalism; and a government of enumerated, delegated, and thus limited powers.

October Term 2002 was a vintage one for the Court and produced a number of major decisions involving first principles, including *Lawrence v. Texas, Grutter v. Bollinger*, and *Gratz v. Bollinger*. In his

1

Foreword to this volume Roger Pilon discusses Randy Barnett's article on *Lawrence* and his own piece on *Gratz* and *Grutter*. The Court also issued noteworthy opinions on the First Amendment, intellectual property, punitive damages, campaign finance, federalism, and property rights.

Thomas Goldstein considers the term's major "non-decision" *Nike v. Kasky*, in which the Supreme Court appeared poised to resolve some of the uncertainty regarding the definition of, and constitutional protection afforded to, "commercial speech." The *Kasky* case arose from Nike's public response—in editorials, letters to the editor, newspaper interviews, and the like—to allegations that its contract factories in Southeast Asia were essentially "sweatshops." A California trial court dismissed a suit brought by a consumer against Nike on First Amendment grounds, but a bitterly divided state supreme court reversed.

Goldstein addresses the First Amendment issues that remain unresolved because the U.S. Supreme Court changed its mind and, after briefing and oral argument, dismissed the case. He argues that the California ruling is indefensible as a matter of basic First Amendment principles. Although the Supreme Court has articulated several tests for identifying "commercial speech," Nike's statements are protected under any definition. Nike's discussion of overseas labor conditions is prototypical speech on matters of public importance. Goldstein therefore urges lower courts not to follow the California ruling.

In *Virginia v. Black* a divided Court overturned a state statute that outlawed cross burning. The Court concluded that sometimes the First Amendment protects cross burning, but when done to intimidate others, cross burning is a "particularly virulent" form of conduct that can be banned. In my essay I agree that the Court was right to affirm that the First Amendment protects symbolic speech, that cross burning is a type of such speech, and that the Virginia statute that banned it was unconstitutional.

But in holding that cross burning with the intent to intimidate can be proscribed, the Court drew no bright line rule to distinguish between protected and unprotected speech, engaged in content-based discrimination, and chilled protected expression. The opinion was a confusing combination of majority and plurality votes, concurrences in the judgment, partial and full dissents, and arguments about whether cross burning was speech in the first place. The justices achieved consensus on but one issue: that the burning of a cross merits unique treatment by the Court. That view might serve as the limiting principle that will restrain the Court in proscribing other forms of offensive or threatening speech. But even if thus limited, *Virginia v. Black* raises profound questions about the very purpose of the First Amendment and the circumstances under which individuals can be protected from offensive or threatening expression or conduct.

First Amendment lawyer and Cato adjunct scholar Robert Corn-Revere writes that the Supreme Court's decision in *United States v. American Library Association* represents a significant missed opportunity for the Court to clarify how the First Amendment should apply to publicly funded expressive institutions. In that case a divided Court upheld federal funding conditions set forth in the Children's Internet Protection Act that require the use of content filters to block pornographic images on Internet access terminals in public libraries. Corn-Revere writes that the various rationales used in the plurality, concurring, and dissenting opinions highlight the difficulties in applying the First Amendment to restrictions on public institutions created for the purpose of disseminating speech. As a result, the precedential value of the *American Library Association* decision is questionable, and it raises the possibility of further as-applied challenges to the law.

The Supreme Court's decision in *Eldred v. Ashcroft*, upholding the Sonny Bono Copyright Term Extension Act, left the public waiting another twenty years for full access to many works of music, film, and literature that were about to enter the public domain. It also left the legal community without the hoped-for guidance on the scope of the Copyright Clause or on the tension between the Copyright Clause and the First Amendment. Instead, the Court placed heavy emphasis on past congressional practice in retroactively extending copyright terms without fully explaining how such retroactive extensions could be reconciled with the text and structure of the Constitution. Erik S. Jaffe takes issue with the Court's reliance on the questionable legal adage that a "page of history is worth a volume of logic" and argues that greater attention to first principles of constitutional interpretation makes retroactive copyright term extensions highly suspect. A history of congressional disregard for the limits of the Constitution, he contends, is no substitute for the Copyright Clause's requirement that Congress act to "promote the Progress of Science" through grants of exclusive rights for "limited Times." Similarly, Jaffe argues, the fact that copyrights in general can be reconciled with the First Amendment is no substitute for specific First Amendment scrutiny each time Congress expands copyright protection and thus increases copyright's burden on the freedom of speech.

This year's punitive damage case, *State Farm v. Campbell*, is about a lot more than punitive damages. That's why Robert A. Levy's article discusses such diverse topics as judicial activism, substantive due process, state long-arm jurisdiction, and choice-of-law rules. Fundamentally, *State Farm* is about whether punitive damage reform and federalism can coexist. Levy harmonizes the views of some conservatives who want to rein in runaway punitive damage awards with the views of other conservatives who find no federal judicial power to do so. Elaborating on the Scalia and Thomas dissents in *State Farm*, Levy traces the controversy over the Court's substantive due process jurisprudence and offers recommendations to restore sanity in the punitive damages arena while honoring traditional notions of federalism.

If First Amendment scholars agree on anything, it is that the Amendment must protect political speech. Yet in recent years, political speech has come to be more heavily regulated than commercial speech or internet pornography. How has that come about? Bradley A. Smith argues that *Federal Election Commission v. Beaumont* epitomizes the intellectual confusion and lack of political understanding underlying the Supreme Court's complex reading of campaign finance law. Smith writes that the Court, with little thought, has defined fundamental elements of our democratic system as "corrupt." In so doing, the Court has provided leeway to legislatures to suppress disfavored speech and harass disfavored groups. Recent decisions, culminating in *Beaumont*, indicate that the Court is prepared to accept still more regulation of political speech. Smith suggests that challengers to the recently enacted "McCain-Feingold" campaign finance law may find the case has already been decided against them.

Jim Bond's article on *Nevada v. Hibbs* poses two provocative questions. First, does *Hibbs* clarify the Court's sovereign immunity jurisprudence? Probably not, says Bond. By backpedaling from recent cases that refused to abrogate state immunity, *Hibbs* may have raised more questions than it answered. Second, Bond asks whether sovereign immunity has been effective in curbing federal power. The political left, to its dismay, says "yes," and welcomes the partial about-face in *Hibbs*. The right is split. Conservatives applaud the pre-*Hibbs* opinions, warning that federal authority is unrestrained. Libertarians, concerned about state violations of individual rights, prefer to confine immunity to the express text of the Eleventh Amendment. Bond's view is that the dispute may be "Much Ado about Nothing," because sovereign immunity has done little to curtail federal power and voters can abrogate immunity if they wish. In the previous volume of the *Cato Supreme Court Review*, Cato's Robert A. Levy argued the libertarian position. He was no less concerned than Bond about overarching federal authority, but he urged a frontal assault via the enumerated powers doctrine rather than a backdoor remedy that immunized rights violations. Our readers might be interested in contrasting the two articles.

It is no accident that the Bill of Rights lists the Right to Property along with other rights such as the Right to Free Speech and the Right to Free Exercise of religious liberties. In 1795, nearly a decade before *Marbury v. Madison*, the Court declared: "The preservation of property then is a primary object of the social compact." As one prominent liberal law professor, Laurence Tribe, acknowledges— albeit in a footnote—many "of the Framers believed that preservation of economic rights was the *central* purpose of civil government." Nearly a half century ago, the Supreme Court advised that the Takings Clause was designed to bar government from forcing some people alone to bear public burdens that, in all fairness and justice, should be borne by the public as a whole. The founders would embrace that principle. According to Ronald D. Rotunda, it is less clear if they would embrace the result in *Brown v. Legal Foundation of Washington*. That case allows the state to take as its own the interest earned from the trust accounts of clients who hire lawyers and deposit money with them for safekeeping.

Rotunda argues that the five to four majority in *Brown* wrote its decision narrowly and in such a way as to give back that which it, at first, appeared to take away. The majority concedes that the government cannot take the principal (which belongs to the owners of that principal) unless it pays just compensation. Nor can the government take the interest, except under the peculiar facts of this case, where the Court found that the value of the money taken was worth zero to the owners of the principal. The opinions are drafted narrowly and suggest that five members of the majority along with all four dissenters would not approve a program governing "Interest on Lawyers' Trust Accounts" that did not, as a legal and factual matter, contain all the caveats found in the majority opinion. The majority invites further attacks on IOLTA programs as the technology apportioning interest improves.

Finally, in a look ahead to the forthcoming October Term 2003, Michael A. Carvin identifies the cases of greatest interest—including the long awaited Bipartisan Campaign Reform Act argued on September 8, 2003 and *Locke v. Davey*, an intriguing religion clause case with broad implications—and the principles at stake.

I thank our contributors for their generous participation: There would be no *Cato Supreme Court Review* without them. I thank my colleagues at the Cato Institute's Center for Constitutional Studies, Roger Pilon, Timothy Lynch, and Robert A. Levy for valuable editorial contributions; David Lampo for producing and Elise Rivera for designing the *Review*; research assistant Elizabeth Kreul-Starr for valuable work in preparing the manuscripts for publication; Brooke Oberwetter, and interns Tyler Andrews, Michael McClellan, Sarah McIntosh, and Matthew Tievsky for additional assistance. Finally, I thank our readers for their generous comments and encouragement upon the publication of last year's inaugural volume.

We hope that this volume, and those to come, chart a journey of the Court toward a jurisprudence grounded on first principles. But we aspire to do more than document the Court's progress. We want the *Cato Supreme Court Review* to be more than a weathervane, merely reflecting the direction of the wind. Instead, we hope that these essays, and those in past and future volumes, influence, at least in some small way, how the wind blows. Our goal is to reanimate the principles laid down more than two centuries ago in the Declaration of Independence and the Constitution and to apply those principles today to the cases and controversies that come before the Supreme Court of the United States. In so doing we aim to resurrect the spirit of another age when, long before they were eclipsed by the rise of the modern regulatory and redistributive state, the natural rights of liberty and property superseded the will of government and of men. With continuing optimism for the task ahead, we present the second volume of this *Review*.

James L. Swanson
Editor in Chief

On Constitutionalism

*Honorable Douglas H. Ginsburg**

As we are gathered here to celebrate the inauguration of a new journal devoted to the Constitution and its interpretation, this is an appropriate occasion to remind ourselves of some basic principles of our Constitution and of constitutionalism more generally. I begin with an observation so fundamental, so straightforward and obvious, that it could be controversial only in the most elite law schools. That observation, to which I will devote considerable attention, is that ours is a written Constitution. When I say ours is a written constitution, I refer, of course, to the actual Constitution, the Constitution of the United States, the document reprinted in this little pamphlet in my hand. I do not refer to the legion of Supreme Court decisions interpreting the Constitution, applying it to particular factual situations, and in many cases providing us with an extended exegesis on its meaning. Those decisions are not the Constitution; as a practical matter, they are reasonably reliable guides to its application in future cases, but they are not the Constitution itself. To maintain otherwise is to ascribe to the Supreme Court a doctrine of infallibility it has never claimed for itself.

Because our own Constitution looms large in our conception of what the word "constitution" means, it has become uncommon now to see the word used in its underlying sense, as referring to the natural structure of a thing. That was the sense in which the Founders could complain, in the Declaration of Independence, that King George and others had "combined to subject us to a jurisdiction foreign to our constitution and unacknowledged by our laws." So you see, we had a constitution before anyone had undertaken to

*Chief Judge, United States Court of Appeals for the District of Columbia Circuit. These remarks, the first annual B. Kenneth Simon Lecture in Constitutional Thought, were delivered at the Cato Institute on September 17, 2002. The author acknowledges the assistance of his law clerks, Michael F. Williams and John H. Longwell, in preparing these remarks.

write it down, indeed before we had declared our independence. In modern American political discourse, however, "constitution" means, first and often last, a code of super-laws. That the Framers did give us such a code—a written constitution—has special consequences for how our government should work.

The Nature and Advantages of Our Written Constitution

From antiquity, people have committed to writing the rules designed to govern their affairs. A most basic reason for preferring a written to an oral record has been to facilitate communication across time. The spoken word, being ephemeral, is subject to mistake or misstatement in its retelling; when precision is important, people memorialize their intentions in writing. A will is a familiar as well as a venerable example. For centuries the common law has encouraged that a testament be drafted, executed, and administered in accordance with strict procedural formalities to ensure that the true intentions of the deceased may be ascertained and followed after— sometimes long after—his demise. Both to reduce the danger of fraud and to minimize the probability of error, we have long learned to prefer the written word.

The usefulness of a written document is not, of course, limited to situations in which the lawgiver—and a testator is, within his sphere, a lawgiver—can no longer speak. The law also encourages the use of written agreements—contracts—particularly when significant time may pass between formation of the contract and performance of its terms. Although the contract normally need not carry the drafter's instructions from the tomb in the manner of a will, it can address a related problem arising from communication across time. The intentions and preferences of a person entering into an agreement may change as his circumstances change, and it would be both unfair and inefficient to allow a contracting party opportunistically to avoid the consequences of a bargain upon which another may reasonably have relied. A court may analyze a written contract to discern the mutual intentions of the parties, and to give effect to their promises and expectations as of the time of their agreement. Whereas the problem addressed by a written will is evidentiary, the written contract addresses problems both evidentiary and behavioral.

A statute, another form of written law, accomplishes a similar goal. One advantage of a statute over common law is that (putting to one side the possibility of inartful drafting) there should be little question what a statute requires of those to whom it is addressed. Just as a contract creates private law between the parties, a statute constitutes an agreement of a public sort among the legislators and between the government and its citizens. Legislators and the executive are democratically accountable to the public for the laws they enact, and the courts take care that the statute not operate differently from what the governed reasonably had understood. It was these aspects of written law—immutability and notice—that prompted Hammurabi to publish his Code (ca. 1780 B.C.), and that later prompted the Roman Consuls to issue the Twelve Tables (ca. 450 B.C.), even though they were only codifying customary law for the young Republic.

There is a rich literature, read by all educated men at the time of the framing of our Constitution, that envisioned contract—that is, an agreement freely entered—as the ideal if not the actual foundation of all legitimate government, indeed as the foundation of society itself. In these Enlightenment conceptions of the social contract, Rousseau and Montesquieu, Hobbes and Locke, imagine each citizen voluntarily ceding to all others, or to the polity, or to a particular leader, the unrestrained liberty of a state of nature in exchange for the security necessary to the tranquil enjoyment of life, especially security in one's property. John Locke, the most influential social contract theorist in the North American colonies, was an Englishman, and his thinking clearly reflected his experience under the British constitution.

At the time Locke published his Second Treatise of Government in 1690, few governments in the world could assert a more just claim to having struck the proper balance between freedom and security—to have arrived at the proper replication of the social contract—than His Majesty's Government at London. To be sure, Holland in the seventeenth century was a crucible of individualism, religious pluralism, and economic liberty; and Spain had combined mercantilism and monarchy to extend its influence across the continents. Although the English enjoyed neither the freewheeling laissez faire of the Dutch nor the Spaniards' flow of tribute from colonies rich in gold and slave labor, it was the rights of Englishmen—and particularly the right to be represented in the councils of government—that the Americans wanted, demanded, and finally took up arms against their King to secure.

9

The Framers, of course, rejected the idea of monarchy for their new union. More important for our topic is their rejection of the unwritten British constitution. That constitution is more accurately described as uncodified, for large parts of it are in fact written, starting with Magna Carta (1215). The British Constitution comprises the 800-year accretion of organic statutes, such as the Act of Settlement (1701); laws and customs concerning the composition of the Parliament; political conventions; case law; and commentary; all founded upon the supremacy of Parliament and the rule of law.

The American Framers really had no choice but to produce a written constitution, in order solemnly and credibly to assure the states—large and small, free and slave—that their conflicting interests would be accommodated, and their continuing sovereignty respected. Thus, the Constitution not only established the roles and functions of the national government: legislative, executive, and judicial, separated in keeping with the teachings of Montesquieu, Locke, and Blackstone. It also specifically enumerated the powers of each branch, identified those matters for which national authority would supplant state authority, and attended to such administrative matters as succession and apportionment. A common misconception holds that only with the later addition of the first ten amendments, the Bill of Rights, did the Constitution include guarantees of individual liberties. As Madison pointed out during the debates over ratification, "the Constitution proposed by the Convention contains . . . a number of such provisions," including the prohibition of ex post facto laws, the availability of habeas corpus, and the right to a jury trial in the state where the crime was committed.[1] And within two years, of course, the Bill of Rights itself was added to the document.

Because the Framers bequeathed us a written constitution, it behooves us to review the advantages and disadvantages that come with that legacy. As with wills, contracts, and statutes, our Constitution should provide a durable statement of what the basic law is; of what the Framers would communicate could they still do so; of the bargain our ancestors struck, and we implicitly assumed, as part of our American heritage; of how our Government should work and of the constraints upon its actions.

---

[1] THE FEDERALIST No. 84 (James Madison).

One of our nation's most influential jurists, Chief Justice John Marshall, assessed the virtues of the written Constitution in his seminal opinion in *Marbury v. Madison*.[2] Recall that John Adams, the lame-duck President and a Federalist, had nominated William Marbury to be a justice of the peace in the District of Columbia, and the Federalist-dominated Senate had confirmed him. That was on March 3, 1801, just one day before the presidency and control of the Senate shifted to the Democratic Republican Party, which had prevailed in the election of November 1800. President Thomas Jefferson, upon entering office a few days later in March, found that Marbury's commission had not been delivered and he refused to send it. Marbury filed suit in the Supreme Court of the United States to compel James Madison, Jefferson's Secretary of State, to deliver the commission so that Marbury could take office and draw his pay.

Chief Justice Marshall transformed this seemingly mundane dispute over one man's entitlement to an inferior post into the authoritative statement of what the judiciary is to do when faced with a conflict between the Constitution, on the one hand, and a statute and an executive action on the other. You see, Marbury, invoking an Act of Congress conferring jurisdiction upon the Supreme Court to issue a writ of mandamus to a "person[ ] holding office under the Authority of the United States," sought a writ directing Madison to deliver the commission. The Court held Marbury was entitled to his commission and the Secretary of State could be directed by a writ of mandamus to deliver it, but then concluded the Supreme Court could not issue the writ because that would be an exercise of original, rather than appellate, jurisdiction, and Article III confined the original jurisdiction of the Supreme Court to a limited class of cases—not including Marbury's. As such, there was a conflict between the jurisdiction the Congress had granted to the Court and that which the Constitution permitted. Chief Justice Marshall took the occasion to announce "that a law repugnant to the constitution is void; and that courts, as well as other departments are bound by that instrument." As Professor Susan Low Bloch has observed:

> This was a masterful opinion. Only by asking the questions in the order he used, with jurisdiction last, and by creatively finding a conflict between Section 13 of the Judiciary Act

<hr>

[2]*Marbury v. Madison*, 5 U.S. 137 (1803).

and Article III of the Constitution, could Marshall assert the judicial power to review acts of both the legislative and the executive branches without ordering anyone to do anything—and thereby avoid the risk of defiance.[3]

And therein lies the origin of judicial review—the power of a court to declare invalid an act of the legislature or of the executive—as a necessary concomitant of a written constitution. Marshall's reasoning, however well-accepted, is not without its difficulties. He wrote:

> Certainly, all those who have framed written constitutions contemplate them as forming the fundamental and paramount law of the nation, and consequently, the theory of every such government must be, that an act of the legislature, repugnant to the constitution, is void.[4]

This theory, which Marshall later described as "essentially attached to a written constitution,"[5] avoids neatly the question who decides whether a law is indeed repugnant to the Constitution.[6]

That said, judicial review is with us still, and *Marbury v. Madison* is a foundation-stone of our legal system, built as it is upon a written constitution. And Chief Justice Marshall's observations about the reason for enacting a written constitution are of great relevance to our topic:

> That the people have an original right to establish, for their future government, such principles as, in their opinion, shall most conduce to their own happiness, is the basis on which the whole American fabric has been erected. . . . The powers of the legislature are defined and limited; and that those limits may not be mistaken or forgotten, the constitution is written.[7]

---

[3] *The Marbury Mystery: Why Did William Marbury Sue in the Supreme Court?*, 18 CONST. COMMENT. 607, 610–611 (2001).

[4] *Marbury*, 5 U.S. at 176.

[5] *Id.*

[6] *See* 1 LAURENCE H. TRIBE, AMERICAN CONSTITUTIONAL LAW 210–11 (3d ed. 2000).

[7] *Marbury*, 5 U.S. 175–76.

A written constitution is not without its arguable disadvantages. Indeed, the virtues of such a document—its immutability, its constraint upon government action—could become drawbacks when rapid action is necessary or desirable.[8] Moreover, a written Constitution imposes upon judges the difficult task of interpreting and applying the text to circumstances that could not have been imagined by the Framers. What role for the First Amendment in regulating the airwaves?[9] Is using thermal imaging technology to penetrate the walls of a home a "search"?[10] That these questions are difficult, however, does not mean we should give them short shrift and capitulate to those who either do not conceive or care not to apprehend how the constraints of a written Constitution protect our liberty.

Regardless whether one prefers the constrained government bequeathed by the Framers or an activist, more freewheeling government like that of the contemporary United Kingdom, there can be no question about what our Constitution established. It is a written document. It carefully enumerates and circumscribes the powers and duties of each branch of the national government, of the national government in relation to the states, and of both with respect to individuals. And because that is what we have, and what federal judges swear to uphold and defend, we ought to be faithful to it and, as we are sworn to do, decide cases "agreeably to the Constitution and laws of the United States," and thus preserve the advantages of having a written constitution.

Fidelity to the Written Constitution

To be faithful to our written Constitution, a jurist must recognize and respect the limiting nature of its terms. Granted, what a term such as "due process" requires in a particular circumstance is not always clear. Nevertheless, there should be no question at all about whether a 34-year-old or a naturalized citizen may become President of the United States. That the terms giving rise to most questions of constitutional meaning lie somewhere between inherent ambiguity and mathematical certainty is no excuse from the duty of fidelity

---

[8]*But cf.* Kennedy v. Mendoza-Martinez, 372 U.S. 144, 160 (1963) (the Constitution is "not a suicide pact").

[9]*E.g.*, Red Lion Broadcasting Co. v. FCC, 395 U.S. 367, 386–90 (1969).

[10]*See* Kyllo v. U.S., 533 U.S. 27 (2001).

13

to the text. Rather, to be faithful to the written Constitution a jurist must make it his goal to illuminate the meaning of the text as the Framers understood it.[11] To be sure, there will be disagreements even among principled jurists whose only goal is fidelity to the text, but with the aid of historical sources such disagreements will be confined to the ordinarily narrow and determinate zone within which competing constructions of a word or phrase are reasonable.

Through most of the history of the Republic, judges were faithful in their subservience to the text of the Constitution. That is not to say that fidelity to the text was a uniform and consistent practice at the Court. Consider the *Dred Scott* case,[12] in which the Court for the first time in the 56 years since *Marbury* invalidated an Act of Congress. The Congress had enacted the Missouri Compromise in 1820, prohibiting slavery in the Louisiana Territory north of Missouri. Scott's previous owner had taken Scott from Missouri to a territory in which slavery had been outlawed by the Compromise and then back to Missouri, where the owner sold Scott to Sandford. Scott brought an action in federal court seeking his freedom, claiming that he became a free man by virtue of his presence in the territory where the Congress had outlawed slavery. The Court held that the Congress was without power to divest Scott's previous owner of his property interest in Scott, and hence the Missouri Compromise was void.

What is striking about the decision is its apparently willful obtuseness in ascertaining what the Constitution requires. In observing that the "right of property in a slave is distinctly and expressly affirmed in the Constitution,"[13] the Court cited provisions of the Constitution that did not carry the weight of that idea.[14] And that

---

[11] *But cf.* Lawrence v. Texas, 123 S. Ct. 2472, 2484 (2003) ("Had those who drew and ratified the Due Process Clauses of the Fifth Amendment or the Fourteenth Amendment known the components of liberty in its manifold possibilities, they might have been more specific. They did not presume to have this insight. They knew times can blind us to certain truths and later generations can see that laws once thought necessary and proper in fact serve only to oppress. As the Constitution endures, persons in every generation can invoke its principles in their own search for greater freedom").

[12] Dred Scott v. Sandford, 60 U.S. 393 (1857).

[13] *Id.* at 451.

[14] The Court cited clauses reserving to the states the right to import slaves until 1808 and requiring states to return escaped slaves, Dred Scott, 60 U.S. at 411, 451–52, neither of which establish an individual's right of property in a slave so as to override state or federal law denying recognition of such a right.

is only the most infamous example of the opinion's violence to the principle of faithful interpretation of the written Constitution. Even more egregious was its limitation of the provision giving Congress power "to dispose of and make all needful rules and regulations respecting the territory . . . of the United States" (Article IV, § 3) to apply only to property ceded to the national government by the states in the aftermath of the Revolution, not to property, such as the Louisiana Territory, obtained from a foreign nation.[15]

Despite sporadic departures like *Dred Scott*, respect for the text of the Constitution was the norm from *Marbury* through the first third of the twentieth century. But the Great Depression and the determination of the Roosevelt Administration placed the Supreme Court's commitment to the Constitution as written under severe stress in the 1930s, and it was then that the wheels began to come off.

Among the powers granted to the Congress in the Constitution is the power "[t]o regulate commerce . . . among the several states."[16] From early in the history of the Republic, this authority was recognized to extend to articles in commerce among the states, while jurisdiction over health, safety, or other exercises of the police power was reserved exclusively to the states.[17] The Clause was deemed broad enough, therefore, to allow regulation not only of ferries and railroads that transported goods in interstate commerce,[18] but also of ancillary facilities, such as stockyards, described as "a throat through which the current [of commerce] flows."[19] The power did not encompass regulation of child labor, however, because "the use of interstate transportation was [not] necessary to the accomplishment of harmful results."[20] Desirable though a prohibition upon child labor may have been, therefore, the Congress was without power to enact it. A contrary result would have allowed the Congress to regulate almost anything pursuant to its power over interstate commerce, regardless whether the subject regulated was within the police power of the states.

---

[15] *Id.* at 432–42.
[16] U.S. Const. art. I, § 8.
[17] Gibbons v. Ogden, 22 U.S. 1 (1824).
[18] Shreveport Rate Cases, 234 U.S. 342 (1914).
[19] Stafford v. Wallace, 258 U.S. 495 (1922).
[20] Hamer v. Dagenhart, 247 U.S. 251 (1918).

During the 1930s, President Roosevelt proposed and the Congress enacted New Deal legislation in the teeth of the Court's prior decisions explicating the limits of the written Constitution. In effect, the President and the Congress dared the Court to strike down laws with strong popular support. Then President Roosevelt announced, after his landslide victory in 1936, his plan to "pack" the Supreme Court—that is, in the name of efficiency, to add another seat to the Court for each active justice over the age of 70, which would have given him six additional appointments. The Court-packing plan was voted down overwhelmingly by the Senate, but until then the threat of some change in the composition of the Court must have added to the strain placed upon the Justices' adherence to their announced understanding of the Constitution. After all, the power of the sword of Damocles is not that it falls, but that it hangs.

It was under the threat of the Court-packing plan that the Justices decided *NLRB v. Jones & Laughlin Steel Corp.*,[21] upholding the power of the Congress to require employers to recognize and bargain with unions representing their employees. The Court's loose reasoning appears entirely too familiar from our contemporary perspective: strikes and other labor strife burden interstate commerce; therefore, employer-employee relations are subject to the power of the Congress to regulate interstate commerce.

In context, however, it is clear that the decision was a stark break from the Court's precedent. Whereas the Court had previously determined that the national government could not intrude upon the police power of the states by proscribing child labor, it now threw open the door to national regulation of employment relations—and much more. Not only interstate commerce but anything that affects interstate commerce came within the reach of the Congress. Indeed, not until *United States v. Lopez* in 1995 did the Court find another federally regulated subject beyond the reach of the Commerce Clause, and that was the possession near a school of a gun that was not shown to have moved in interstate commerce.[22]

I have singled out the Court's interpretation of the Commerce Clause not because it is extreme but because it is illustrative. To take another example, the Constitution carefully separates legislative

---

[21] NLRB v. Jones & Laughlin Steel Corp., 301 U.S. 1 (1937).

[22] United States v. Lopez, 514 U.S. 549 (1995).

and executive powers. "All legislative powers herein granted shall be vested in a Congress of the United States,"[23] whereas "[t]he Executive Power shall be vested in a President of the United States of America."[24] From that clear demarcation the Court had once inferred there must be a limit upon the ability of the Congress to delegate lawmaking functions to the executive branch. By delegating its legislative function the Congress avoids political accountability—therein lies the appeal of delegation—and frustrates the Framers' purpose in separating governmental powers. Accordingly, in the years before *Jones & Laughlin* the Supreme Court invalidated delegations of legislative power that contained no "intelligible principle to which the person or body authorized to take action is directed to conform."[25] After the watershed New Deal cases expanding the reach of the Congress through the commerce power, however, the Court never again found an Act of Congress, however open-ended, to violate the Non-Delegation Doctrine.[26]

Not only structural constraints in the written Constitution have been disregarded; even precepts within the Bill of Rights have been blinked away. The Takings Clause of the Fifth Amendment, which provides that the Government may not take private property except for a public use, and then only if it pays just compensation, provides no protection against a regulation that deprives the nominal owner of most of the economic value of his property.[27]

At the same time that the Court redacted the textual limits upon the authority of the Congress to regulate, it has interlineated the Constitution with new rights, which is to say new limits upon government, of its own devising. In so doing, the Court acts as a council of revision with a self-determined mandate. Its decisions are frankly legislative in character: invalidating acts of the national and state legislatures on grounds that are not to be found in the Constitution, and on its own initiative placing new obligations upon the federal

---

[23] U.S. CONST. art. I, § 1.

[24] U.S. CONST. art. II, § 1.

[25] Panama Refining Co. v. Ryan, 293 U.S. 388 (1935).

[26] Whitman v. American Trucking Associations, 531 U.S. 457, 474–75 (2001).

[27] Cf. Lucas v. South Carolina Coastal Council, 505 U.S. 1003, 1018 (1992) ("[W]hen the owner of real property has been called upon to sacrifice *all* economically beneficial uses in the name of the common good, that is, to leave his property economically idle, he has suffered a taking").

and state governments. However one might approve of the Court's decisions as matters of policy, they have only the merest pretense of comporting with the Constitution as it was written.

Consider the Court's 1965 pronouncement of a constitutional right to privacy in *Griswold v. Connecticut*.[28] A long-neglected state statute made unlawful the use of "any drug, medicinal article, or instrument for the purpose of preventing conception."[29] The Planned Parenthood League of Connecticut and several physicians challenged the law as infringing upon their clients' privacy. Of course, the Constitution is not silent on the topic of privacy. The Fourth Amendment establishes a specific, but limited right

> of the people to be secure in their persons, houses, papers, and effects, against unreasonable searches and seizures.[30]

This constitutional limitation upon government being insufficient by itself to the task at hand, the Court invalidated the statute for invading what it perceived to be "the zone of privacy created by several fundamental constitutional guarantees," to wit:

> The right of association contained in the penumbra of the First Amendment[;]
> The Third Amendment in its prohibition against the quartering of soldiers "in any house" in time of peace without the consent of the owner[;]
>
> The Fourth Amendment[;]
>
> The Fifth Amendment [which] in its Self-Incrimination Clause enables the citizen to create a zone of privacy which government may not force him to surrender to his detriment[; and]
>
> The Ninth Amendment [which] provides: "The enumeration in the Constitution, of certain rights, shall not be construed to deny or disparage others retained by the people."[31]

---

[28]Griswold v. Connecticut, 381 U.S. 479.

[29]*Id.* at 480.

[30]U.S. CONST. amend. IV.

[31]*Griswold*, 381 U.S. at 484.

Thus, while a jurist devoted to the Constitution as written might conclude that the document says nothing about the privacy of "intimate relation[s] of husband and wife,"[32] and thereby remits the citizenry to the political processes of their respective states, the Court managed to find a multitude of sources for such a right, albeit not in mere words but in the imagined "penumbras" and "emanations" from various tangentially relevant clauses.[33]

Griswold is not an aberration. Just last year the Court determined that, because most states do not allow the execution of a mentally retarded murderer, those that do are inflicting a cruel and unusual and, therefore, unconstitutional punishment.[34] This is as frankly a legislative decision as the Court has ever rendered. It has nothing to do with the constitutionality of capital punishment and everything to do with the Justices' personal senses of decency. My quarrel, mind you, is not with the policy the Court adopted in this or any of the cases I have mentioned—on which I express no view—but with the Court's making such choices for us, notwithstanding the lack of any sound basis in the Constitution for doing so.

The question remains whether this freewheeling style of constitutional decisionmaking, in which the document itself plays only a cameo role, is to be a permanent feature of constitutional law, or whether we can regain the virtues of a written constitution. If history is any guide, then reform is not likely to spring from any branch of the federal government.

If renewed fidelity to the Constitution as written is possible—and I think it is—then it will come only through a change in the legal culture. The ranks of scholars and judges advocating greater fidelity to constitutional text is still small but it is growing. Scholars are attending more to the original meaning of at least some of the clauses of the Constitution instead of focusing exclusively upon the Court's prior decisions. I daresay there has been more study of the Commerce Power and the Non-Delegation Doctrine in the last 10 years

---

[32] *Id.* at 482.

[33] *Id.* at 484. What is worse, there was an argument from the text of the Constitution available to a Court intent upon striking down the Connecticut statute. Judge Posner has suggested that the role of the Catholic Church in the survival of the statute should have raised concerns under the Establishment Clause. *See* RICHARD A. POSNER, SEX AND REASON 326 (1992).

[34] Atkins v. Virginia, 536 U.S. 304 (2002).

than in the prior half-century. Like archaeologists, legal and historical researchers have been rediscovering neglected clauses, dusting
them off, and in some instances even imagining how they might
be returned to active service. As the new legal scholarship gains
acceptance, and students are exposed to the competing vision it
represents, they will as lawyers begin to present more textual arguments, some of which may eventually win acceptance in the courts.

The career of the Second Amendment provides a contemporary
glimpse of this process. For two decades a cadre of textually minded
law professors bemoaned the short shrift given to the right arguably
conferred by the Second Amendment upon individuals—as opposed
to the "militia," now known as the National Guard—"to keep and
bear arms." Because academic lawyers so assiduously ignored its
text, Sanford Levinson of the University of Texas Law School dubbed
it "the embarrassing Second Amendment."[35] As new historical scholarship on the meaning of the Amendment gained acceptance, however, one of the least textually constrained members of the legal
academy, Professor Laurence Tribe, recently revised his treatise to
say that the Second Amendment does indeed protect the right of
the individual to bear arms.[36] And now let the litigation begin: With
criminal charges relating to simple possession of a firearm potentially subject to a constitutional defense, there can be little doubt
that defense lawyers will argue the Second Amendment and thereby
force the courts to sort out its implications for contemporary state
and federal regulation of firearms.

As you can see, the process of refocusing attention upon the text
of the Constitution depends crucially upon the generation and distribution of historically sound scholarship concerning the meaning of
the Constitution the Framers wrote. And on that note, I applaud the
Cato Institute for providing a new and surely destined to be influential forum for that scholarship—the Cato Supreme Court Review.

---

[35] Sanford Levinson, *The Embarrassing Second Amendment*, 99 YALE L.J. 637 (1989).

[36] *See* 1 LAURENCE H. TRIBE, AMERICAN CONSTITUTIONAL LAW 898–99 n.213, 901–02
n.221 (3d ed. 2000).

Justice Kennedy's Libertarian Revolution: *Lawrence v. Texas*

Randy E. Barnett

In *Lawrence v. Texas*,[1] the Supreme Court held unconstitutional a Texas law criminalizing sexual relations between persons of the same sex. That would be reason enough to consider the case a landmark decision. But to those schooled in post-New Deal "fundamental rights" jurisprudence, what was most striking about *Lawrence* was the *way* the Court justified its ruling. If the approach the Court took in the case is followed in other cases in the future, we have in *Lawrence* nothing short of a constitutional revolution, with implications reaching far beyond the "personal liberty" at issue here.

Contrary to how their decision was widely reported, the *Lawrence* majority did not protect a "right of privacy." Instead, quite simply, they protected "liberty." Breaking free at last of the post-New Deal constitutional tension between the "presumption of constitutionality," on one hand, and "fundamental rights," on the other, Justice Anthony Kennedy and the four justices who joined his opinion did not begin by assuming the statute was constitutional. But neither did they call the liberty at issue "fundamental," which the modern Court would have been expected to do before withholding the presumption of constitutionality from the statute. Instead, the Court took the much simpler tack of requiring the state to justify its statute, whatever the status of the right at issue.

To better appreciate the significance and the implications of this major break with the recent past, it will be useful to begin not with the case but with a brief history of this "presumption of constitutionality." Reflecting on *Lawrence* in that larger context will show the potential the decision has—and show too how it returns us, in a fundamental way, to our first principles as a nation.

---

[1] 123 S. Ct. 2472 (2003).

Constitutional Liberty Meets the "Progressive" Movement

At the end of the 19th century, as the so-called progressive movement grew in political strength, states passed statutes regulating
and restricting all manner of economic activity. At the same time,
"morals" legislation became more pervasive as well, although often
such laws were enacted under the rubric of "public health," a development the historian Ronald Hamowy has called the "medicaliza-
tion of sin."[2] All of this was part of an intellectual and political
movement to improve upon the result of private, personal, and
economic choices by aggressively using government power to
enhance the general welfare.

As that sort of legislation gained in popularity, the Supreme Court
resisted sporadically, striking down some but not all statutes restricting economic activities. *Lochner v. New York* was the most famous
of those cases.[3] There the Supreme Court struck down provisions
of a state statute limiting the maximum hours bakeshop employees
could work per week. The Court found the provisions violated the
"liberty of contract" between employees and employers that was
protected, it said, by the "liberty" portion of the Due Process Clause
of the Fourteenth Amendment. In other cases, the Court struck down
noneconomic legislation as well, such as state laws mandating
English-only education of children[4] or requiring parents to send
their children to public schools,[5] as arbitrary infringements of liberty.

In those cases the Court spoke simply of the liberty of the individual, then required the state to justify restricting that liberty. Not
surprisingly, given their political agenda, progressives bitterly criticized the Court's use of the Due Process Clause, especially in the
economic sphere, as thwarting the democratic political process. Yet
only a small fraction of progressive legislation was voided. Moreover, the Supreme Court did not categorically ban such statutes.
Rather, it merely required that the government justify its regulations.

---

[2] *See* Ronald Hamowy, *Preventive Medicine and the Criminalization of Sexual Immorality in Nineteenth Century America, in* ASSESSING THE CRIMINAL: RESTITUTION, RETRIBUTION, AND THE LEGAL PROCESS 33 (Randy Barnett & John Hagel III eds., 1977).

[3] 198 U.S. 45 (1905).

[4] Meyer v. Nebraska, 262 U.S. 390 (1923).

[5] Pierce v. Society of Sisters of the Holy Names of Jesus and Mary, 268 U.S. 510 (1925).

Indeed, the principal problem with the Supreme Court's jurisprudence during the Progressive Era was its lack of a coherent distinction between legislation upheld and legislation stricken. Had more statutes been found unconstitutional, the results would have been easier to explain.

Critics also claimed that those cases represented a revolutionary departure from the constitutional principles of the founding,[6] but their case was weak. They offered little persuasive historical evidence, and what evidence they presented ignored the structural changes wrought by the enactment of the Fourteenth Amendment. Needless to say, those critics paid no attention to the original meaning of that provision. Today, even some constitutional scholars sympathetic to economic regulation acknowledge the continuity between the principles of the founding and what the Progressive Era Supreme Court was trying to do in circumscribing state power via the Fourteenth Amendment.[7]

With the Great Depression and the New Deal, however, the focus shifted to progressive measures enacted at the national level. The Court struck down several of those measures as exceeding the powers of Congress under the Commerce Clause.[8] Yet eventually it reversed itself and upheld that legislation as constitutional. The story of that reversal is fascinating, but too complicated to summarize here. Suffice it to say that recent research has called into question the contention that the Progressive Era Court's jurisprudence was reversed only in 1937, under pressure of Roosevelt's Court-packing scheme, by the "switch in time that saved nine."[9] Rather, as early as the beginning of the 1930s, Hoover appointees (Hoover considered himself a progressive) softened the Court's constitutional objections

---

[6] *See, e.g.,* WALTON H. HAMILTON & DOUGLASS ADAIR, THE POWER TO GOVERN: THE CONSTITUTION—THEN AND NOW (1937). I respond to their historical claims in Randy E. Barnett, *The Original Meaning of the Commerce Clause,* 68 U. CHI. L. REV. 101, 130–132 (2001).

[7] *See especially* HOWARD GILLMAN, THE CONSTITUTION BESIEGED: THE RISE AND DEMISE OF LOCHNER ERA POLICE POWERS JURISPRUDENCE (1993).

[8] *See, e.g.,* Schecter Corp. v. United States, 295 U.S. 495 (1935).

[9] *See* BARRY CUSHMAN, RETHINKING THE NEW DEAL COURT: THE STRUCTURE OF A CONSTITUTIONAL REVOLUTION (1998). Cf., WILLIAM E. LEUCHTENBURG, THE SUPREME COURT REFORM: THE CONSTITUTIONAL REVOLUTION IN THE AGE OF ROOSEVELT (1995).

to progressive legislation, which had the effect of further undermining the coherence of the Court's earlier restrictive doctrines. Nevertheless, the final nail in the coffin of liberty did not come until the Supreme Court was thoroughly controlled by Roosevelt appointees in the early 1940s.

Enter the Presumption of Constitutionality

For present purposes it is significant that in 1931, years before the so-called Revolution of '37, Justice Louis Brandeis adopted a "presumption of constitutionality" when evaluating the exercise of state police powers. In *O'Gorman & Young, Inc. v. Hartford Fire Insurance Co.*, Brandeis wrote:

> The statute here questioned deals with a subject clearly within the scope of the police power. We are asked to declare it void on the ground that the specific method of regulation prescribed is unreasonable and hence deprives the plaintiff of due process of law. As underlying questions of fact may condition the constitutionality of legislation of this character, *the presumption of constitutionality* must prevail in the absence of some factual foundation of record for overthrowing the statute.[10]

Writing glowingly of this case in the *Columbia Law Review*, Walton Hamilton sang the praises of Brandeis's doctrinal maneuver—highlighting in the process the radical changes to come:

> The demand is to find an escape from the recent holdings predicated upon "freedom of contract" as "the rule," from which a departure is to be allowed only in exceptional cases. The occasion calls not for the deft use of tactics, but for a larger strategy. The device of presumptions is almost as old as law; Brandeis *revives the presumption that acts of a state legislature are valid and applies it to statutes regulating business activity*. The factual brief has many times been employed to make a case for social legislation; Brandeis demands of the opponents of legislative acts a recitation of fact showing that the evil did not exist or that the remedy was inappropriate. He appeals from precedents to more venerable precedents; *reverses the rules of presumption and proof in cases involving the*

[10]282 U.S. 251, 257–58 (1931) (emphasis added).

control of industry; and sets up a realistic test of constitutionality. It is all done with such legal verisimilitude that a discussion of particular cases is unnecessary; it all seems obvious—
once Brandeis has shown how the trick is done. It is attended
with so little of a fanfare of judicial trumpets that it might
have passed almost unnoticed, save for the dissenters, who
usurp the office of the chorus in a Greek tragedy and comment upon the action. Yet an argument which degrades "freedom of contract" to a constitutional doctrine of the second
magnitude is compressed into a single compelling
paragraph.[11]

As *O'Gorman* shows, well before the so-called Revolution of '37 the
Court was deferring to state legislatures. As the Brandeis quotation
suggests, initially the presumption of constitutionality could be
rebutted, at least in theory, by those objecting to a statute's constitutionality. By the 1940s, however, the presumption became irrebutta-
ble for all practical purposes, at least in the case of economic regulation. Thus, in the 1956 case of *Williamson v. Lee Optical,*[12] the Court
reversed a lower court that had held unconstitutional portions of a
state statute that made it unlawful "for any person not a licensed
optometrist or ophthalmologist to fit lenses to a face or to duplicate
or replace into frames lenses or other optical appliances, except upon
written prescriptive authority of an Oklahoma licensed ophthalmologist or optometrist."[13] The district court had held that such a
requirement was not "reasonably and rationally related to the health
and welfare of the people."[14] The law thus violated the Due Process
Clause by arbitrarily interfering with an optician's right to do
business.

Plainly, the trial court was not playing from the post-New Deal
playbook. It still believed that the presumption of constitutionality
was rebuttable. Thus, it had written:

---

[11]Walton H. Hamilton, *The Jurist's Art,* 31 Colum. L. Rev. 1073, 1074–75 (1931)
(emphases added) (footnotes omitted). Hamilton coauthored, THE POWER TO GOVERN,
discussed above, *supra,* note 6.

[12]348 U.S. 483 (1956).

[13]*Id.* at 485.

[14]Lee Optical of Oklahoma v. Williamson, 120 F. Supp. 128, 136 (1954).

It is recognized, without citation of authority, that all legislative enactments are accompanied by a presumption of constitutionality; and, that the court must not by decision invalidate an enactment merely because in the court's opinion the legislature acted unwisely. Likewise, where the statute touches upon the public health and welfare, the statute cannot be deemed unconstitutional class legislation, even though a specific class of persons or businesses is singled out, where the legislation in its impact is free of caprice and discrimination and is rationally related to the public good. *A court only can annul legislative action where it appears certain that the attempted exercise of police power is arbitrary, unreasonable or discriminatory.*[15]

No, not even then, as Roosevelt-appointee and former New Dealer Justice William O. Douglas[16] explained in his opinion for a unanimous Supreme Court, reversing the wayward district court.

[T]he law need not be in every respect logically consistent with its aims to be constitutional. It is enough that there is an evil at hand for correction, and that it might be thought that the particular legislative measure was a rational way to correct it. The day is gone when this Court uses the Due Process Clause of the Fourteenth Amendment to strike down state laws, regulatory of business and industrial conditions, because they may be unwise, improvident, or out of harmony with a particular school of thought.[17]

Justice Douglas's opinion made clear that when restricting liberty, the legislature need not have had good reasons. It is enough that it *might* have had good reasons:

The legislature *might* have concluded that the frequency of occasions when a prescription is necessary was sufficient to justify this regulation of the fitting of eyeglasses. Likewise, . . . the legislature *might* have concluded that one was needed

---

[15] *Id.* at 132 (emphasis added).

[16] Before his appointment to the Court to succeed Justice Brandeis, Douglas was Roosevelt's nominee to chair the Securities and Exchange Commission in 1937. Prior to his appointment to the Commission, Douglas was a professor at Yale Law School. Roosevelt reportedly came close to picking Douglas as his running mate in the 1944 election.

[17] 348 U.S. at 487–88.

often enough to require one in every case. Or the legislature *may* have concluded that eye examinations were so critical, not only for correction of vision but also for detection of latent ailments or diseases, that every change in frames and every duplication of a lens should be accompanied by a prescription from a medical expert. . . .[18]

Consequently, Justice Douglas concluded, "[w]e cannot say that the regulation has no rational relation to that objective and therefore is beyond constitutional bounds."[19] With *Lee Optical* as the norm, what then was left of judicial review?

Qualifying the Presumption of Constitutionality: The Theory of Footnote Four

As *Lee Optical* makes plain, post-New Deal deference to state legislatures and to Congress meant that courts simply would not guard against constitutional violations: "For protection against abuses by legislatures the people must resort to the polls, not to the courts,"[20] said Douglas. If applied consistently, this deferential attitude would obviously end the entire practice of judicial review. How then did the post-New Deal Court avoid that slippery slope? The answer is found in a single footnote that foreshadows the entire post-New Deal theory of judicial review and constitutional rights.

I allude, of course, to the famous Footnote Four of the 1938 case of *United States v. Carolene Products Co.*,[21] which concerned legislative restrictions on the sale of a milk substitute that competed with the products of dairy farmers.[22] In the text of his opinion, Justice Harlan Fiske Stone[23] strongly asserted the presumption of constitutionality.

---

[18] *Id.* at 477–88 (emphases added).

[19] *Id.* at 489.

[20] *Id.* at 488.

[21] 304 U.S. 144 (1938).

[22] *See* Geoffrey P. Miller, *The True Story of Carolene Products*, 1987 Sup. Ct. Rev. 397.

[23] Although a Coolidge appointee, Justice Stone was elevated to Chief Justice by President Roosevelt in 1941, the same year Stone authored the opinion of the Court in *United States v. Darby*, 312 U.S. 100 (1941). That opinion definitively expanded the powers of Congress under the Commerce and Necessary and Proper clauses in the same manner as the police power of states had been enlarged in 1937 in *West Coast Hotel v. Parrish*, 300 U.S. 379 (1937). The 5–4 decision in *West Coast Hotel*, in which the Court abstained from policing the limits of the police power of the states, was among the cases that led to 1937 being identified as the year of the New Deal constitutional revolution.

"[T]he existence of facts supporting the legislative judgment is to be presumed," he wrote,

> for regulatory legislation affecting ordinary commercial transactions is not to be pronounced unconstitutional unless in the light of the facts made known or generally assumed it is of such a character as to preclude the assumption that it rests upon some rational basis within the knowledge and experience of the legislators.[24]

Carolene Products is famous, however, for the footnote that immediately followed that passage,[25] which began as follows:

> There may be a narrower scope for operation of the presumption of constitutionality when legislation appears on its face to be within a specific prohibition of the Constitution, such as those of the first ten amendments, which are deemed equally specific when held to be embraced within the Fourteenth.[26]

The note goes on to add two more exceptions to the presumption of constitutionality—for laws that restrict the political process, and laws that are directed at "discrete and insular minorities."[27]

---

[24]Carolene Prods., 304 U.S. at 152.

[25]The fame of this footnote is illustrated by the fact it merits its own entry in THE OXFORD COMPANION TO THE SUPREME COURT OF THE UNITED STATES. See Dean Alfange, Jr., *Footnote Four*, in OXFORD COMPANION 306–07 (Kermit L. Hall et al. eds., 1992).

[26]*Id.* at 152 n.4.

[27]More fully, the text of the note reads:

> It is unnecessary to consider now whether legislation which restricts those political processes which can ordinarily be expected to bring about repeal of undesirable legislation, is to be subjected to more exacting judicial scrutiny under the general prohibitions of the Fourteenth Amendment than are most other types of legislation.
>
> Nor need we enquire whether similar considerations enter into the review of statutes directed at particular religious, . . . or national, . . . or racial minorities . . . ; whether prejudice against discrete and insular minorities may be a special condition, which tends seriously to curtail the operation of those political processes ordinarily to be relied upon to protect minorities, and which may call for a correspondingly more searching judicial inquiry.

Id. at 152–53 n.4 (citations omitted).

After *Carolene Products*, legislation was presumed to be constitutional unless one of the three exceptions in Footnote Four was satisfied, in which case the Court would give the statute "heightened scrutiny." Due to the indiosyncracies of the first eight amendments, this doctrinal maneuver allowed the court to uphold economic regulations, as in *Lee Optical*, while preserving judicial review of such "personal" freedoms as those of speech, assembly, and press. That the personal right to bear arms, explicitly mentioned in the Second Amendment, has not been judicially protected shows the ideological nature of this maneuver, as does the uneven protection of property rights, explicitly mentioned in the Fifth Amendment.

Ironically, in recent years judicial conservatives like Robert Bork and Raoul Berger have been among the most stalwart in their allegiance to the judicial philosophy of Footnote Four. For all the reverence they express toward the Framers of the Constitution, jurisprudentially speaking, they are unreconstructed Roosevelt New Dealers.

Enter the Unenumerated "Right of Privacy"

Until the 1960s, the Supreme Court was content for the most part to confine judicial review to policing most of the enumerated rights contained in the Bill of Rights, while deferring to legislative power in all other arenas. As just noted, this post-New Deal jurisprudence of (partial) restraint is today the holy grail of judicial conservatives. Their posture came about, in part, in reaction to *Griswold v. Connecticut*,[28] a case in which the Court considered the constitutionality of a state using its police power to ban not only the "personal" liberty to use contraceptives but also the "economic" liberty to sell and distribute them.

The *Griswold* Court struck down the statute for violating an unenumerated right it called the "right of privacy." The task of justifying this extension of judicial review to a right not specified in the Bill of Rights, for the first time since *Carolene Products*, fell to Justice Douglas, author of the *Lee Optical* opinion.[29] He did so by attempting

[28]381 U.S. 479 (1965).

[29]Douglas took pains to distinguish *Griswold* from *Lee Optical* and other cases rejecting the Due Process Clause jurisprudence of the Progressive-Era Court:

> [W]e are met with a wide range of questions that implicate the Due Process Clause of the Fourteenth Amendment. Overtones of some arguments suggest that *Lochner v. New York*, 198 U.S. 45, should be our guide. But we decline that invitation, as we did in *West Coast Hotel Co. v. Parrish*, 300 U.S. 379; Olsen v. Nebraska, 313 U.S. 236; *Lincoln Union v. Northwestern Co.*, 335 U.S. 525; *Williamson v. Lee*

to connect, however tenuously, this unenumerated right to those that are enumerated:

> The foregoing cases suggest that *specific guarantees in the Bill of Rights* have *penumbras, formed by emanations* from those guarantees that help give them life and substance. . . . Various guarantees create zones of privacy. The right of association contained in the penumbra of the First Amendment is one, as we have seen. The Third Amendment, in its prohibition against the quartering of soldiers "in any house" in time of peace without the consent of the owner, is another facet of that privacy. The Fourth Amendment explicitly affirms the "right of the people to be secure in their persons, houses, papers, and effects, against unreasonable searches and seizures." The Fifth Amendment, in its Self-Incrimination Clause, enables the citizen to create a zone of privacy which government may not force him to surrender to his detriment. The Ninth Amendment provides: "The enumeration in the Constitution, of certain rights, shall not be construed to deny or disparage others retained by the people."[30]

That was probably the best he could do to reach the result in the case while ostensibly staying within the prevailing constitutional theory of Footnote Four. On the one hand, had Douglas grounded the decision in "liberty" (which is mentioned in the text) rather than "privacy" (which is not), it would have risked undoing the strong deference to Congress and state legislatures that he and his fellow-New Deal justices had previously established.

On the other hand, by narrowly construing the unenumerated right being protected, Douglas ensured that procreative rights, and later abortion rights, would be viewed as special interest rights. Had those liberties been protected as aspects of a general right to liberty, rather than based on the more narrow right to privacy, they might

---

> *Optical Co.*, 348 U.S. 483; *Giboney v. Empire Storage Co.*, 336 U.S. 490.
> We do not sit as a super-legislature to determine the wisdom, need, and propriety of laws that touch economic problems, business affairs, or social conditions. This law, however, operates directly on an intimate relation of husband and wife and their physician's role in one aspect of that relation.

Id. at 481–82. Notice the rhetoric of "super-legislature" now associated with judicial conservatives.

[30] *Id.* at 484 (emphasis added).

have received broader support from those who wanted to see *their* favored liberties protected as well.

Douglas's choice also provoked the debate over "judicial activism" that remains with us to this day. Like the progressives decrying the Supreme Court that decided *Lochner,* judicial conservatives bitterly criticized the Warren Court for its deviation from the post-New Deal jurisprudence of Footnote Four. Indeed, Stanford law professor Gerald Gunther, no political conservative, paired *Griswold* with *Lochner* in his then-leading casebook in constitutional law.[31] Although his objective was to undermine the legitimacy of *Griswold,* it had the unintended consequence, among some, of causing a more sympathetic reconsideration of *Lochner.*[32]

Enter "Fundamental Rights" v. Mere "Liberty Interests"

Nevertheless, "emanations" and "penumbras" could not conceal the fact that the protection of an unenumerated right of privacy was outside the framework of Footnote Four. The beauty of the Footnote Four solution was that it cleanly limited judicial review to enumerated rights, while allowing government free rein in the economic sphere. The problem created by the unenumerated right of privacy, however, was that it now forced upon the Court the messy business of distinguishing those liberties, enumerated and unenumerated, that rebut the presumption of constitutionality from those that do not. The former it called "fundamental rights," while the latter were dubbed mere "liberty interests." But how to tell the difference?

Eventually the Court settled on limiting fundamental rights to those that were in its opinion "implicit in the concept of ordered liberty" and could be grounded in our "traditions and history." As Justice Byron White explained in *Bowers v. Hardwick,*[33] the 1986 decision that upheld a Georgia statute criminalizing sodomy, which *Lawrence* overturned:

---

[31] *See* GERALD GUNTHER, CONSTITUTIONAL LAW 570–646 (10th ed. 1975).

[32] I know of Professor Gunther's authorial intentions from private correspondence with him. In my first article on constitutional law, I credited him with having rehabilitated the doctrine of substantive due process, citing his casebook. He wrote to me protesting that he was appalled at the thought that his juxtaposition of the two cases might have had the opposite effect of what he was trying to achieve.

[33] 478 U.S. 186 (1986).

> Striving to assure itself and the public that announcing rights
> not readily identifiable in the Constitution's text involves
> much more than the imposition of the Justices' own choice
> of values on the States and the Federal Government, the
> Court has sought to identify the nature of the rights qualify-
> ing for heightened judicial protection. In *Palko v. Connecticut*,
> . . . it was said that this category includes those fundamental
> liberties that are "implicit in the concept of ordered liberty,"
> such that "neither liberty nor justice would exist if [they]
> were sacrificed." A different description of fundamental lib-
> erties appeared in *Moore v. East Cleveland*, . . . where they are
> characterized as those liberties that are "deeply rooted in
> this Nation's history and tradition." . . . See also *Griswold v.
> Connecticut.* . . .[34]

The outcome of that analysis depends almost entirely, however,
on how specifically you define the right being asserted. The more
specifically you define the liberty at issue—for example, a "constitutional right of homosexuals to engage in acts of sodomy"[35]—the
more difficult a burden this is to meet and the more easily the rights
claim can be ridiculed. Although "liberty" as a general matter is
obviously deeply rooted in our history and traditions, the specific
liberty to use contraceptives is not. Nor are many other liberties,
especially if unknown at the founding. Even liberties that existed at
the founding, like the liberty of self-medication, have not to date
been deemed "fundamental" by the Court.

Whenever a particular liberty is specified, therefore, it is always
subject to the easy rejoinder: "Just where in the Constitution does
it say that?" And that rejoinder is offered notwithstanding the plain
language of the Ninth Amendment: "The enumeration in the Constitution of certain rights shall not be construed to deny or disparage
others retained by the people."[36] With that background in mind, we
are now in a position to appreciate the potentially revolutionary
significance of the decision in *Lawrence v. Texas*.

---

[34]*Id.* at 191–92.
[35]*Id.* at 191.
[36]U.S. CONST. amend. IX.

Justice Kennedy's Crucial Switch from Privacy to Liberty

In the 1992 abortion rights case of *Planned Parenthood v. Casey*,[37] Justice Kennedy began to escape from the New Deal-era box in the part of the coauthored opinion that is commonly attributed to him.[38] He refused there to rest abortion rights on a "right to privacy," although that crucial move has been generally ignored. Instead, he rested those rights on liberty and explicitly on the Ninth Amendment:

> Neither the Bill of Rights nor the specific practices of States at the time of the adoption of the Fourteenth Amendment marks the outer limits of the substantive sphere of *liberty* which the Fourteenth Amendment protects. See U.S. Const., Amend. 9.[39]

Resting abortion rights on liberty, as opposed to privacy, was newsworthy, but little noticed. To this day, most scholars and public commentators still speak of the "right of privacy," not the "right of liberty." Until *Lawrence*, the question was whether this right to liberty would ever be seen again.

In *Lawrence v. Texas*, it has reappeared, with Justice Kennedy now writing for a majority of the Court (not including Justice O'Connor, who concurred only in the result), rather than as part of a mere trio in *Casey*. Liberty, not privacy, pervades this opinion like none other, beginning with the very first paragraph:

> *Liberty* protects the person from unwarranted government intrusions into a dwelling or other private places. In our tradition the State is not omnipresent in the home. And there are other spheres of our lives and existence, outside the home, where the State should not be a dominant presence. Freedom extends beyond spatial bounds. *Liberty* presumes an autonomy of self that includes freedom of thought, belief, expression, and certain intimate conduct. The instant case involves *liberty* of the person both in its spatial and more transcendent dimensions.[40]

---

[37] 505 U.S. 833 (1992).

[38] Justice Souter is credited with the discussion of stare decisis—properly ridiculed by Justice Scalia in his *Lawrence* dissent—and Justice O'Connor with the discussion of "undue burden."

[39] 505 U.S. at 848 (emphasis added).

[40] 123 S. Ct. at 2475 (emphasis added).

Other examples abound:

> We conclude the case should be resolved by determining whether the petitioners were free as adults to engage in the private conduct in the exercise of their *liberty* under the Due Process Clause of the Fourteenth Amendment to the Constitution.[41]

> There are broad statements of the substantive reach of *liberty* under the Due Process Clause in earlier [Progressive-era] cases, including Pierce v. Society of Sisters, 268 U.S. 510 (1925), and Meyer v. Nebraska, 262 U.S. 390 (1923); but the most pertinent beginning point is our decision in Griswold v. Connecticut, 381 U.S. 479 (1965).[42]

Justice Kennedy puts rhetorical distance between the decision in *Lawrence* and the right of privacy protected in *Griswold*: "The Court [in *Griswold*] described the protected interest as a right to privacy and placed emphasis on the marriage relation and the protected space of the marital bedroom."[43] Indeed, the "right of privacy" makes no other appearance in this opinion (apart from quotations from the grant of certiorari from a previous case discussing *Griswold*). In contrast "liberty" appears in the opinion at least twenty-five times.

Even Justice Kennedy's rejection of the argument from stare decisis rests on the centrality of liberty.

> In *Casey* we noted that when a Court is asked to overrule a precedent recognizing a constitutional liberty interest, individual or societal reliance on the existence of that liberty cautions with particular strength against reversing course. . . . The holding in *Bowers*, however, has not induced detrimental reliance comparable to some instances where recognized individual rights are involved.[44]

In *Lawence v. Texas*, therefore, liberty, not privacy, is doing all the work.

---

[41] *Id.* at 2476 (emphasis added).

[42] *Id.* (emphasis added).

[43] *Id.*

[44] *Id.* at 2483.

Justice Kennedy Employs an Implicit "Presumption of Liberty"

Lawrence is potentially revolutionary not only because it abandons a right to privacy in favor of liberty, but for another closely related reason: In the majority's opinion, there is not even the pretense of a "fundamental right" rebutting the "presumption of constitutionality." Justice Kennedy never mentions any presumption to be accorded the Texas statute.

More important, he never tries to justify the sexual liberty of same-sex couples as a fundamental right. Instead, he spends all of his energies demonstrating that same-sex sexual freedom is a legitimate aspect of liberty—unlike, for example, actions that violate the rights of others, which are not liberty but license. Not only does this take the Court outside the framework of Footnote Four, it also removes it from the framework of unenumerated fundamental rights that was engrafted upon it in the wake of *Griswold*. Until *Lawrence*, every unenumerated rights case had to establish that the liberty at issue was "fundamental," as opposed to a mere liberty interest.

Justice Scalia, in dissent, takes accurate note of all of this:

> Though there is discussion of "fundamental proposition[s]," . . . and "fundamental decisions," . . . nowhere does the Court's opinion declare that homosexual sodomy is a "fundamental right" under the Due Process Clause; nor does it subject the Texas law to the standard of review that would be appropriate (strict scrutiny) if homosexual sodomy were a "fundamental right." Thus, while overruling the outcome of *Bowers*, the Court leaves strangely untouched its central legal conclusion: "[R]espondent would have us announce . . . a fundamental right to engage in homosexual sodomy. This we are quite unwilling to do." 478 U.S., at 191. Instead the Court simply describes petitioners' conduct as "an exercise of their liberty"—which it undoubtedly is—and proceeds to apply an unheard-of form of rational-basis review that will have far-reaching implications beyond this case.[45]

In other words, with liberty as the baseline, the majority places the onus on the government to justify its statutory restriction.

---

[45] *Id.* at 2488 (Scalia, J., dissenting).

Although he never acknowledges it, Justice Kennedy is employing here what I have called a "presumption of liberty"[46] that requires the government to justify its restriction on liberty, instead of requiring the citizen to establish that the liberty being exercised is somehow "fundamental." In this way, once an action is deemed to be a proper exercise of liberty (as opposed to license), the burden shifts to the government.

All that was offered by the government to justify this statute is the judgment of the legislature that the prohibited conduct is "immoral," which for the majority (including, on this issue, Justice O'Connor) is simply not enough to justify the restriction of liberty. Why not? Here the Court is content to rest its conclusion on a quote from Justice Stevens's dissenting opinion in *Bowers*:

> Our prior cases make two propositions abundantly clear. First, the fact that the governing majority in a State has traditionally viewed a particular practice as immoral is not a sufficient reason for upholding a law prohibiting the practice; neither history nor tradition could save a law prohibiting miscegenation from constitutional attack. Second, individual decisions by married persons, concerning the intimacies of their physical relationship, even when not intended to produce offspring, are a form of "liberty" protected by the Due Process Clause of the Fourteenth Amendment. Moreover, this protection extends to intimate choices by unmarried as well as married persons."[47]

A stronger defense of this conclusion is possible.[48] A legislative judgment of "immorality" means simply that a majority of the legislature disapproves of this conduct. But justifying legislation solely on grounds of morality would entirely eliminate judicial review of legislative powers. How could a court ever adjudicate between a legislature's claim that a particular exercise of liberty is "immoral" and a defendant's contrary claim that it is not?

In practice, therefore, a doctrine allowing legislation to be justified solely on the basis of morality would recognize an unlimited police

---

[46] *See* RANDY E. BARNETT, RESTORING THE LOST CONSTITUTION: THE PRESUMPTION OF LIBERTY (Princeton, forthcoming 2004).

[47] Bowers, 478 U.S. at 216 (footnotes and citations omitted).

[48] And was offered to the Court in an amicus brief filed by the Institute for Justice, which I coauthored.

power in state legislatures. Unlimited power is the very definition of tyranny. Although the police power of states may be broad, it was never thought to be unlimited.[49]

Defending *Lawrence* from Judicial Conservatives

Given their grounding still rooted in post-New Deal constitutional jurisprudence, the responses of judicial conservatives (not to be equated with all *political* conservatives) are entirely predictable. Yet each fails upon critical inspection. Three such responses stand out.

First, judicial conservatives argue that all laws restrict some freedom; thus, requiring legislatures to justify to a court their restrictions on liberty would amount to giving judges an unbridled power to strike down laws of which they disapprove. But that is to equate "liberty" and "license," a mistake the Founders never made. Liberty is and always has been the *properly defined* exercise of freedom. Liberty is and always has been constrained by the rights of others. No one's genuine right to liberty is violated by restricting his or her freedom to rape or murder, because there is no such right in the first place.

That is not to say that the rightful exercise of liberty may never be *regulated*—or made regular (as opposed to prohibited outright).[50] It is only to say that, as Justice Kennedy implicitly acknowledges, the existence of a right to liberty places a burden on the government to justify any regulations of liberty as necessary and proper. Wrongful behavior that violates the rights of others may justly be prohibited without violating liberty rights—although "wrongful" is not the same as "immoral."

Second, and closely related, the *Lawrence* majority's position, judicial conservatives say, rejects any moral content of law. That is false. As was just explained, wrongful behavior that violates the rights of others may justly be prohibited without violating the liberty rights of

---

[49]See Randy E. Barnett, *The Proper Scope of the Police Power*, 79 Notre Dame Law Review (forthcoming).

[50]*See id.* I discuss the original meaning of the power "to regulate" in Randy E. Barnett, *The Original Meaning of the Commerce Clause.* 68 U. Chi. L. Rev. 101, 139–46 (2001); *id. New Evidence of the Original Meaning of the Commerce Clause*, 55 Ark. L. Rev. 847, 863–65 (2003).

others. Because it is usually (but not always[51]) immoral to wrongfully violate the rights of others, the entirely justified prohibition of wrongful behavior also necessarily prohibits much immoral behavior as well. But not all ostensibly immoral behavior is also unjust or wrongful, as Thomas Aquinas recognized when he wrote:

> Now human law is framed for a number of human beings, the majority of which are not perfect in virtue. Therefore human laws do not forbid all vices, from which the virtuous abstain, but only the more grievous vices, from which it is possible for the majority to abstain, and *chiefly those that are to the hurt of others, without the prohibition of which human society could not be maintained; thus human law prohibits murder, theft and the like.*[52]

To the claim that allowing legislatures to prohibit conduct solely because they deem it to be immoral is to grant legislatures an unlimited and therefore tyrannical power, judicial conservatives might respond that the police powers of states are to be constrained by their own constitutions and their own courts, not by federal judges. This response, if made, would be a non sequitur. On the one hand, if state constitutions grant their legislatures a "police power" that includes an unlimited power to prohibit private conduct solely because it is immoral—a dubious claim—that does not make the power any less unlimited or tyrannical. Nor in the face of such a constitutional grant of power would state judges be in any better position than federal judges to constrain their legislatures. If it is inappropriate for federal judges to restrict the asserted constitutional powers of state legislatures, it would be equally inappropriate for state judges to do so.

On the other hand, if the police power of states is not so unlimited and tyrannical as is being claimed, then it is not beyond the "judicial

[51] Under emergency situations it may not be immoral to act wrongfully to violate some rights of others. For example, it may not be immoral for a stranded camper to break into an empty cabin for shelter, though the act would still be wrongful and the camper would be liable for the trespass. *See* RANDY E. BARNETT, THE STRUCTURE OF LIBERTY: JUSTICE AND THE RULE OF LAW 169–72 (1998). The possible existence of these exceptional circumstances does not refute the normal case in which it is immoral or "bad" to act wrongfully or "unjustly" toward another.

[52] Thomas Aquinas, *Summa Theologica*, in GREAT BOOKS OF THE WESTERN WORLD (Robert Hutchins, ed., 1952), at 232a (emphasis added).

power" of either state or federal judges to hold state legislatures within their limits. Federal judges may do so, of course, only if they have jurisdiction to protect citizens' rights from violation by their own states. Although at the founding this power was lacking, the Privileges or Immunities Clause of the Fourteenth Amendment (which has effectively been folded into the Due Process Clause) gives the federal government such a power.[53] Judicial conservatives must read the Fourteenth Amendment very narrowly and ahistorically to deprive federal courts of this power of judicial review.

Finally, judicial conservatives repeatedly assert that there is no textual basis for the protection of a general right to liberty. Unlike "privacy," however, "liberty" is mentioned explicitly in the Due Process Clauses of both the Fifth and Fourteenth Amendments, so this is a much harder argument to sustain. The judicial conservative response is to argue that liberty may properly be restricted so long as "due process" is followed. As Justice Scalia wrote in his dissent: "The Fourteenth Amendment *expressly allows* States to deprive their citizens of liberty, so long as due process of law is provided."[54] This is textually and historically wrong.

Ever since the founding, "due process of law" has included judicial review to ensure that a law is within the proper power of a legislature to enact. Historical claims to the contrary are extraordinarily weak, relying exclusively (and ahistorically) on the seeming absence of an explicit grant of judicial power in the text. This fails to consider the original meaning of the "judicial power" reposed in the Supreme Court. An examination of the historical record leaves no doubt that the judicial power originally included the power to nullify unconstitutional laws—especially those that exceeded the power of the legislature.[55]

At the federal level, judicial review, which is part of the "due process of law," includes the power to nullify laws that exceed the

[53] *See* MICHAEL KENT CURTIS, NO STATE SHALL ABRIDGE: THE FOURTEENTH AMENDMENT AND THE BILL OF RIGHTS (1986). I discuss the original meaning and contemporary relevance of the Privileges or Immunities Clause of the Fourteenth Amendment at length in Barnett, *The Proper Scope of the Police Power, supra,* note 49, and in RESTORING THE LOST CONSTITUTION, *supra,* note 46, chapters 3 & 8.

[54] 123 S. Ct. at 2491 (Scalia, J., dissenting).

[55] For copious evidence supporting this historical claim, *see* RESTORING THE LOST CONSTITUTION, *supra,* note 46, chapter 6.

delegated powers of Congress. That is why the Supreme Court in *United States v. Lopez*[56] and *United States v. Morrison*[57] could properly strike down federal statutes that exceeded the power of Congress under the Commerce Clause. In addition, however, federal power is further constrained by the rights retained by the people—both those few that are enumerated and, as affirmed in the Ninth Amendment, those liberty rights that are unenumerated as well. At the state level, the Privileges or Immunities Clause of the Fourteenth Amendment prohibits states such as Texas from infringing the privileges or immunities of U.S. citizens. Those include both the liberty rights or "immunities" retained by the people, and the positive rights or "privileges" created by the Constitution of the United States. The "due process of law" includes federal judicial review to ensure that this constitutional restriction on the powers of states has not been transgressed.

Judicial conservatives move heaven and earth to excise the Ninth Amendment and the Privileges or Immunities Clause of the Fourteenth Amendment from the text of the Constitution because they think neither is definite enough to confine judges. That charge is only true, however, if one ignores the original public meaning of those provisions at the time of their enactment. Moreover, the Right's disregard of the text of the Constitution when it fails to support its vision of the "Rule of Law" is as much judicial "activism"—if one must use this phrase[58]—as the Left's disregard of text when it fails to support its vision of "Justice." In either case, judges are substituting for the text something they prefer—here, silence when the Constitution is in fact speaking eloquently.

Conclusion: A Remarkably Simple Ruling

In the end, *Lawrence* is a very simple, indeed elegant, ruling. Justice Kennedy examined the conduct at issue to see if it was properly an aspect of liberty (as opposed to license), and then asked the government to justify its restriction, which it failed to do adequately. The decision would have been far more transparent and compelling

---

[56] 514 U.S. 549 (1995).

[57] 529 U.S. 598 (2000).

[58] For my definition along with the reasons I have refrained from using this epithet in the past, see Randy E. Barnett, *Is the Rehnquist Court an "Activist" Court? The Commerce Clause Cases*, 73 U. COLORADO L. REV. 1275 (2002).

if Kennedy had acknowledged what was really happening (though perhaps that would have lost votes by other justices). Without that acknowledgment, the revolutionary aspect of his opinion is concealed and rendered vulnerable to the ridicule of the dissent. Far better would it have been to more closely track the superb amicus briefs of the Cato Institute, which Kennedy twice cited approvingly, and of the Institute for Justice.

If the Court is serious in its ruling, Justice Scalia is right to contend that the shift from privacy to liberty, and away from the New Deal-induced tension between the presumption of constitutionality and fundamental rights, "will have far-reaching implications beyond this case."[59] For example, the medical cannabis cases now wending their way through the Ninth Circuit would be greatly affected if those seeking to use or distribute medical cannabis pursuant to California law did not have to show that their liberty to do so was somehow "fundamental"—and instead the government were forced to justify its restrictions on that liberty.[60] While wrongful behavior (or license) could be prohibited, rightful behavior (or liberty) could be regulated, provided that the regulation was shown to be necessary and proper.

Although it may be possible to cabin this case to the protection of "personal" liberties of an intimate nature—and it is a fair prediction that that is what the Court will attempt—for *Lawrence v. Texas* to be constitutionally revolutionary, the Court's defense of liberty must not be limited to sexual conduct. The more liberties the Court protects, the less ideological it will be and the more widespread political support it will enjoy. Recognizing a robust "presumption of liberty" might also enable the court to transcend the trench warfare over judicial appointments. Both Left and Right would then find their favored rights protected under the same doctrine. When the Court plays favorites with liberty, as it has since the New Deal, it loses rather than gains credibility with the public, and undermines its vital role as the guardian of the Constitution. If the Court is true to its reasoning, *Lawrence v. Texas* could provide an important step in the direction of a more balanced protection of liberty that could find broad ideological support.

---

[59] 123 S. Ct. at 2488 (Scalia, J., dissenting).

[60] I should disclose that I represent clients in two such pending cases: *United States v. Oakland Cannabis Buyers Cooperative*, 532 U.S. 483 (2001) and *Raich v. Ashcroft*, 248 F. Supp. 2d 918 (N.D. Cal. 2003).

Principle and Policy in Public University Admissions
Grutter v. Bollinger
Gratz v. Bollinger

Roger Pilon

Twenty-five years ago the Supreme Court told us, in a 5–4 decision, that public universities could not use racial quotas in their admissions policies. That was the famous *Bakke* case involving the University of California/Davis Medical School.[1] This term, in another 5–4 decision, the Court told us that the University of Michigan Law School could take race into account in its admissions policies—but perhaps for only another 25 years.[2] Welcome to the world of anti-discrimination law.

The Constitution would seem to be clear on the matter: "No State shall . . . . deny to any person within its jurisdiction the equal protection of the laws."[3] Read naturally, that language appears to say that states must treat people as individuals, not as members of racial, ethnic, or other classes, to be treated differently because of those characteristics. Twenty-five years ago four justices, and a fifth for the most part, read the language that way, as prohibiting states from discriminating on the basis of race.[4] And four read it the same way

---

[1]Regents of Univ. of Cal. v. Bakke, 438 U.S. 265 (1978).

[2]Grutter v. Bollinger, 123 S. Ct. 2325, 2347 (2003).

[3]U.S. Const. amend. XIV.

[4]The Bakke Court split 4–4, with Justice Lewis Powell joining four other justices to announce the judgment of the Court that the University of California's admissions scheme was unconstitutional. Writing only for himself, however, Powell went on in dicta to argue that under certain circumstances, racial preferences in public university admissions might be constitutional. That lone opinion has served as the basis for much confusion in the intervening 25 years. *See* Michael E. Rosman, *Thoughts on Bakke and Its Effect on Race-Conscious Decision-Making*, 2002 U. Chi. Legal F. 45; Alan J. Meese, *Reinventing Bakke*, 1 Green Bag 2d 381 (1998).

this term. But things are not always as they seem in this most troubling area of our history and law. In fact, in the two so-called affirmative action cases before it this term, the Court split. While upholding the Law School's admissions scheme in *Grutter v. Bollinger*,[5] the Court in *Gratz v. Bollinger*[6] threw out the scheme employed by the University of Michigan's College of Literature, Science, and the Arts, ruling 6–3 that it was unconstitutional under the Equal Protection Clause of the Fourteenth Amendment.

Plainly, in this "split double header," as Justice Antonin Scalia put it,[7] the devil is in the details. But once those details emerge, does the Court's reasoning explain, much less justify, this outcome? And is that reasoning consistent with the Constitution? Let's start with the first principles of the matter. Against that background we'll then examine the reasoning in the two cases.

First Principles

The history of race relations in America is not pretty. From slavery through segregation to the more subtle forms of racism we see today, we've had to struggle to realize the American dream, and we're not there yet. Discrimination on other grounds has plagued us too—all the more reason to be clear about the principles at issue.[8]

We start, as in America we must, with the "higher law" of the Declaration of Independence, to which early abolitionists, Abraham Lincoln, Justice Harlan the elder, and Dr. Martin Luther King Jr., to name a few, all repaired for insight and inspiration. As that law found its way over time into the positive law of the Constitution, the Bill of Rights, and the Civil War Amendments, it spoke to a single idea—freedom. Not the "positive freedom" of the modern welfare state, but the simple, uncomplicated freedom to pursue happiness as one wishes, by one's own lights, restrained only by

---

[5] *Grutter*, 123 S. Ct. at 2347.

[6] Gratz v. Bollinger, 123 S. Ct. 2411 (2003).

[7] *Grutter*, 123 S. Ct. at 2349.

[8] I have discussed the issues that follow more fully in Roger Pilon, *Discrimination, Affirmative Action, and Freedom: Sorting Out the Issues*, 45 Am. U. L. Rev. 775 (1996).

the equal rights of others to do the same. That is the freedom that animated the civil rights movement from its inception.[9]

But a close look at that freedom yields conclusions that ring uncomfortably in the modern ear. For thus free, we may associate with anyone willing to associate with us—which means, of course, that we have a right *not* to associate, for any reason, good or bad, or no reason at all. As private individuals and organizations, that is, we have a right to discriminate, for any reason, which means there is no natural right against discrimination. And that right to discriminate—like the right to be free generally, from which it is derived—is grounded in the idea of sovereignty. Each of us is sovereign over himself and his actions, over what is his—in a word, over his property. Of course, we are also free to criticize those who exercise their freedom, including their right to discriminate, wrongly. But that's altogether different from denying them that right. There is all the difference in the world between defending the right to discriminate and defending the discrimination that flows from the exercise of that right. With perfect consistency we can defend the right while condemning its exercise. When warranted, decent people do that.[10]

Those fundamental principles concerning sovereignty apply in the public sector as well, but there they cut in the opposite direction when it comes to discrimination. For the public sector and the institutions that constitute it—public agencies, parks, universities, and so on—belong to all of us, or at least to the citizens of the jurisdiction at issue. Thus, just as we are sovereign, individually, over what is ours in the private sector, so too we are sovereign, collectively, over what is ours in the public sector.

But that raises immediately the problems of collective action and the competing principles that govern it. Since public institutions

---

[9] In the words of Dr. Martin Luther King Jr.:

> When the architects of our republic wrote the magnificent words of the Constitution and the Declaration of Independence, they were signing a promissory note to which every American was to fall heir. This note was a promise that all men would be guaranteed the unalienable rights of life, liberty, and the pursuit of happiness.

Martin Luther King Jr., "I Have a Dream" Speech at Lincoln Memorial (Aug. 23, 1963), reprinted in LEND ME YOUR EARS 497 (William Safire ed., 1992).

[10] *See* FLAG BURNING, DISCRIMINATION, AND THE RIGHT TO DO WRONG: TWO DEBATES (Roger Pilon ed., 1990).

spring from constitutions, state and federal, disagreements over running them should be settled in the first instance under constitutional provisions. But constitutions often speak very generally to such issues, if they speak at all, relegating them mostly to the political process—to the legislative arena. Yet the decisions that flow from that process must still respect the equal rights of each of us over what are, after all, our institutions—a matter to be policed in the judicial arena. In particular, equal protection means that government, because it belongs to all of us, cannot discriminate among us except as constitutionally authorized or, if a constitution is silent, on grounds that are narrowly tailored to serve the function of the institution.[11]

Unfortunately, there is no easy accommodation of the democratic and the equal-protection principles. On one hand, too great a deference to the democratic principle gives berth to majoritarian tyranny or, worse, to the capture of public institutions by skilled or well-placed minorities, as public-choice economists have amply shown.[12] On the other hand, a judiciary overly solicitous of equal protection, insisting on the right of each of us to control what is ours, invites the stalemate of the monopoly holdout. Neither result is acceptable. Both could be avoided from the start by leaving as much as possible, including education, in the private sector, where it can be carried out under the principles of private property and contract. But if the people in their public capacity are determined to conduct the many activities that today are conducted through public institutions, there must be some resolution of the inherent conflict, even if it can never be more than a second-best solution. That resolution must be mindful, however, of the nondiscrimination principle that informs equal protection: in particular, insofar as it is not constitutionally narrowed, collective ownership must be presumed to be for the benefit of all, equally. And neutral principles, generated behind a "veil of ignorance" about particular qualities, must ensure that.[13]

---

[11] Thus, to take an easy case, a public fire department may discriminate against wheelchair-bound firefighter applicants, but not if they are applying for office jobs. Unfortunately, many cases are not that easy, nor is the rule of reason relevant to such cases easy to state or apply.

[12] See, e.g., Jean-Jacques Laffont and Jean Tirole, The Politics of Government Decision Making: A Theory of Regulatory Capture, 106 Q.J. ECON. 1089 (1991).

[13] On the veil of ignorance, see JOHN RAWLS, A THEORY OF JUSTICE (1971).

The modern welfare state has raised havoc with those equal-protection principles, of course, for its countless programs distribute burdens and benefits unequally in endless ways, as the Michigan cases clearly show. First, public higher education in general is not for the benefit of all: as the demographics reveal, its dirty little secret is that it constitutes a massive wealth transfer from the lower to the upper classes of society. For although upper-income taxpayers tend to pay more in taxes, their children tend to use public higher education in far greater numbers than the children of lower-income taxpayers, who often never even go to college. The exceptions, which are invariably cited by proponents of public higher education, simply prove the rule.[14] Second, that wealth transfer is especially true of elite institutions like the University of Michigan Law School; the vast taxpaying public of Michigan is underwriting the education of a tiny group of people who, as a result of that education, will in most cases then join the highest income earners in the nation. But it's even worse than that in Michigan because, third, as Justice Clarence Thomas noted in his dissent in *Grutter*, "the Law School trains few Michigan residents and overwhelmingly serves students who, as lawyers, leave the State of Michigan."[15] One wonders why the citizens of Michigan allow themselves to be so fleeced, assuming they know the facts. Be that as it may, we have here a textbook example from public-choice economics of a skilled and well-placed minority (those with a direct interest in the Law School) having captured the political process for their own benefit.

---

[14] Milton and Rose Friedman stated the matter succinctly:

> We know of no government program that seems to us so inequitable in its effects, so clear an example of Director's Law, as the financing of higher education. In this area those of us who are in the middle- and upper-income classes have conned the poor into subsidizing us on the grand scale—yet we not only have no decent shame, we boast to the treetops of our selflessness and public-spiritedness.

MILTON FRIEDMAN & ROSE FRIEDMAN, FREE TO CHOOSE: A PERSONAL STATEMENT 183 (1979). *See, e.g.,* Jenny B. Wahl, *A Bigger Bang for the Public Buck: Achieving Efficiency and Equity in Higher Education,* Jan. 14, 2002, *at* http://www.aicup.org/resources/Higher_Ed_Paper.pdf (last visited Aug. 22, 2003); Lee Hansen and B. A. Weisbrod (1969), *The Distribution of the Costs and Benefits of Public Higher Education: The Case of California,* 4 J. HUM. RESOURCES 176 (1969).

[15] *Grutter,* 123 S. Ct. at 2355. As Thomas notes, only 27 percent of the Law School's 2002 entering class are from Michigan, and less than 16 percent of the Law School's graduating class elects to stay in Michigan after law school. *Id.*

Those are the most searching equal-protection concerns in the Michigan cases, but they were not the concerns directly before the Court. Rather, they arose only obliquely, largely in the Thomas dissent in connection with the more immediate question of whether having a racially diverse student body is a compelling state interest, as the school argued. Thomas answered that Michigan had no compelling interest even in having a public law school (not all states do), much less an elite law school, still less a marginally better law school because of racial discrimination, as Michigan contended.[16]

Although those more searching concerns were not before the Court, they are central to true equal protection, and they bring out how far we have strayed from that ideal. But in other ways too our anti-discrimination law today—federal, state, and local—is often far removed from the first principles just outlined. Private discrimination, for example, has been outlawed in a vast and bewildering array of contexts, with forced association effectively replacing free association.[17] And in the public sector, discrimination is not simply permitted but required for "remedial" purposes, although the burdens and benefits of such remedies rarely fall on those who did wrong or were wronged.[18] With *Gratz* and *Grutter*, however, nonremedial public-sector discrimination is now permitted as well. Let's see how the Court justified that.

Gratz and *Grutter*

When an act is presumed to be wrong, we justify doing it by giving reasons that are sufficient to overcome the presumption. Because it seeks to be objective, law looks for sufficient reasons in principles, for the most part, not in subjective values. Thus, unequal treatment by the government can be justified for remedial purposes if it remedies a prior wrong, matching wrongdoers with wronged, thereby restoring the status quo of equality the prior wrong disturbed. Unequal treatment is justified, that is, because it remedies prior unequal treatment that, left unremedied, constitutes a continuing

[16] *Id.* at 2353–54.

[17] *See, e.g.,* Uniform Guidelines on Employee Selection Procedures, 28 C.F.R. § 50.14 (1978); *see also* Griggs v. Duke Power Co., 401 U.S. 424, 433 n.9 (1971) (quoting text of EEOC guidelines on Employment Testing Procedures).

[18] *See generally,* SAMUEL LEITER AND WILLIAM M. LEITER, AFFIRMATIVE ACTION IN ANTIDISCRIMINATION LAW AND POLICY (2002).

wrong. The backward-looking aim is to restore the status quo of equality—unequal treatment to rectify unequal treatment that itself disturbed equality. Looked at in that fundamental way, public-sector discrimination for remedial purposes, if it matches wrongdoers with those wronged, is grounded in ordinary tort principles.

But the methods of the modern Court are often not that analytical, objective, or deductive. Rather than look for a benchmark of equality as a starting point, then apply backward-looking principles of natural right to the facts of the case, the post-*Carolene Products* Court allows government to treat people unequally—to do what would otherwise be wrong, constitutionally—if the government has a good reason.[19] And the characteristics of a good reason—quite apart from what constitutes a good reason—vary by the character of the government wrong. If the wrong is racial discrimination, for example, the Court employs "strict strictly," which means that the government must have a "compelling interest" (or reason) to do the wrong, and the means it employs must be "narrowly tailored" to serve that interest.[20] But if the wrong is gender discrimination, the Court relaxes its scrutiny, demanding only that the government have an "important" interest and that the means be "substantially related" to it—although recently the Court said that the justification in gender discrimination cases must be "exceedingly persuasive."[21]

Plainly, that methodology is replete with subjective value judgments nowhere to be found in the Constitution. The difference between a "compelling" and an "important" governmental interest is a matter of degree, not kind, as is the difference between means that are "narrowly tailored" and those that are "substantially related" to an interest. As a practical matter, the Court's methodology has immersed its members in endless disputes over those judgments,

[19]Famous footnote four of United States v. Carolene Products Co., 304 U.S. 144 (1938), was the great watershed in American constitutional law, completing the New Deal constitutional revolution and introducing modern "scrutiny theory." Professor Owen M. Fiss has called it "[t]he great and modern charter for ordering the relations between judges and other agencies of government." Owen M. Fiss, *The Supreme Court: 1978 Term—Forward: The Forms of Justice*, 93 HARV. L. REV. 1, 6 (1979). For a fuller, critical discussion, *see* Randy Barnett, *Justice Kennedy's Libertarian Revolution: Lawrence v. Texas*, 2002–2003 CATO SUPREME COURT REVIEW 21.

[20]City of Richmond v. J.A. Croson Co., 488 U.S. 469 (1989).

[21]United States v. Va. Military Acad., 518 U.S. 515, 531–34 (1996).

to no one's surprise. As a matter of principle, however, there is no constitutional basis whatever for different levels of judicial scrutiny. If the Constitution restricts government from discriminating, then every governmental action brought before the Court that ignores that restriction should be strictly scrutinized. In the parlance of the modern practice, all classes are "suspect."[22]

Interestingly, three days after the Michigan cases were handed down, the Court gave us its decision in *Lawrence v. Texas*.[23] There it seemed to abandon its post-*Carolene Products* methodology, as discussed elsewhere in this volume.[24] Without ever saying it was engaged in "strict scrutiny," or searching for some "compelling state interest," the Court simply insisted that Texas justify its restriction of Lawrence's liberty. The state failed to offer the kind of reason that would overcome the presumption of liberty, and that was the end of it. To be sure, *Lawrence* was not an equal-protection case, but that should matter not at all. It was a case about the government's doing something it was presumptively forbidden to do, just as in *Gratz* and *Grutter*.

The problem in the Michigan cases, however, is rather less with the Court's invocation than with its application of strict scrutiny. There are two aspects to that. First, not only did the Court fail to give us a rigorous, constitutional standard for discerning "compelling interests," but its abject deference to the university's account of its interests amounts to abandoning the very scrutiny the Court invokes. Second, in *Grutter* even if the Law School did have a compelling interest in discriminating on the basis of race, the means it employed were not narrowly tailored to overcome the presumption against doing so. Let's take those two points in order, starting with *Grutter*, which is where the Court discusses the "compelling state interest" prong of strict scrutiny, concluding that the Law School has satisfied it.

---

[22]I discuss scrutiny theory more fully in Roger Pilon, *A Modest Proposal on "Must-Carry," the 1992 Cable Act, and Regulation Generally: Go Back to Basics*, 17 HASTINGS COMM. & ENT. L.J. 41 (1994).

[23]123 S. Ct. at 2472.

[24]*See* Barnett, *supra* note 19.

"Compelling State Interest"

The very idea of "compelling-interest" analysis is problematic within the theory of legitimacy that underpins American governments, federal and state. That theory begins with individuals and their rights. As individuals, we come together to form governments, delegating *powers* to them, not "interests." Delegated powers are thus "authorized" and hence legitimate, as are powers entailed by the delegated powers—means that, under the federal Constitution, must be "necessary and proper" toward achieving the purposes or ends enumerated in the Constitution. The execution of federal and state powers must also respect retained rights, of course, both enumerated and unenumerated. As thus conceived, therefore, the theory is deductive, with legitimacy following from whether a power does or does not conform to that chain of reasoning. A legitimate power is thus exercised by right. An unauthorized power or a power that violates rights is ultra vires.[25]

To say that a government has "interests," however, is not the same as saying it has powers. Nor is the word used here as it is used when we say, for example, that someone has an "interest" in a property. Rather, the term connotes something we'd like to see done or brought about. We all have interests: some are pursued by right, others not. So too with governments. With governments, however, one of two things is true. Either an interest is entailed by one of its powers as necessary and proper for realizing the end for which the power was authorized, or it is not, in which case pursuing that interest takes the government beyond its authority. Regrettably, the latter is what much of modern interest analysis amounts to, with "interest" having about it the ring of a policy sought, not a principle followed. One imagines a government in the Progressive Era or New Deal mold, pursuing policies that reflect interests that have been distilled in the legislative caldron unrestrained by any charter of authorized and hence limited purposes. Today, of course, that pretty much describes government in America, imbued as it is with all but plenary power to address all manner of public and private problems, constitutional limits notwithstanding.

---

[25]I have discussed those issues more fully in Roger Pilon, *On the First Principles of Constitutionalism: Liberty. Then Democracy*, 8 AM. U. J. INT'L L. & POL'Y 531 (1992–93).

Yet as just noted, government that pursues interests beyond its authorized powers or contrary to retained rights is to that extent illegitimate. In the early stages of his searing dissent in *Grutter*, we see Thomas struggling with that issue. He begins where the majority did not, with a look at the Court's prior treatment of "compelling state interest" in the equal-protection, racial-classifications context. A majority of the Court, he says, "has validated only two circumstances where 'pressing public necessity' or a 'compelling state interest' can possibly justify racial discrimination by state actors:"[26] ensuring national security (*Korematsu v. United States*[27]); and remedying past discrimination by the state (*Richmond v. J.A. Croson Co.*[28]). He also cites Justice Hugo Black, concurring in *Lee v. Washington*,[29] who suggested that protecting prisoners from violence might justify narrowly tailored racial discrimination. And in the same vein he quotes Justice Scalia, concurring in the judgment in *Croson*: "At least where state or local action is at issue, only a social emergency rising to the level of imminent danger to life and limb ... can justify [racial discrimination]."[30]

Notice that in each of those cases the "pressing public necessity" or "compelling state interest" is not a separate policy concern but rather an integral component of a basic power authorized to the government. The justification for overriding the presumption against racial discrimination is thus entailed, given the facts, in the underlying power to protect life and limb or rectify wrongs. The departure from principle, that is, is itself principled—indeed, it is a departure grounded in the same principle. In fact, were the government to refrain from thus departing, it would be charged, rightly, with denying the equal protection of the laws.

Thomas does not bring that point out explicitly, but it is implicit in his sampling of rationales for racial discrimination that have failed. Thus, he cites *Wygant v. Jackson Bd. of Ed.*[31] in which the Court threw out a discriminatory collective-bargaining agreement the school

---

[26] *Grutter*, 123 S. Ct. at 2351.

[27] 323 U.S. 214 (1944).

[28] 488 U.S. 469, 504 (1989).

[29] 390 U.S. 333, 334 (1968) (*per curiam*) (Black, J., concurring).

[30] *Croson*, 488 U.S. at 521 (Scalia, J., concurring in judgment).

[31] 476 U.S. 267 (1986).

board had defended on policy grounds: minority teachers provided role models for minority students; and a racially "diverse" faculty would improve the education of all students. The Court deemed both asserted interests "insufficiently compelling," Thomas notes.[32] Unfortunately, that reduces the Court's rationale to a value judgment, no better in principle, or worse, than the school board's value judgment. A more principled rationale would hold the board's policy interests as not necessarily entailed by its power to run a school: the board could perform its functions perfectly well without discriminating, that is—or claiming, by implication, that its ends justified those means. Equally important, a principled rationale would hold that the board's policies violated rather than secured rights of equal protection, unlike in the previous examples. Two other examples Thomas cites of failed rationales exhibit similar problems. Thus, in child custody determinations, the state's concern for the best interests of a child does not constitute a compelling state interest that justifies racial discrimination. Nor, more broadly, can remedying general societal discrimination, presumably by private parties, justify racial discrimination by the state.[33] In both cases, governmental discrimination would not secure equal protection of the law but would violate it—in the name of policies about which reasonable people may reasonably disagree.

As we will now see, Justice Sandra Day O'Connor's arguments for the Court in *Grutter* are similar in all respects to the failed rationales cited by Thomas. From the start, they are policy arguments, not arguments from principle. And the Law School's policy interests are served by denying the equal protection of the law. In fact, we should be clear at the outset that there is no ambiguity about what the Court upheld. For the Court itself acknowledges that it is sanctioning "a race-conscious admissions program"[34] and "racial preferences,"[35] even though "there are serious problems of justice connected with the idea of preference itself."[36] The only questions, therefore, are whether the racial discrimination serves a compelling state

---

[32]Grutter v. Bollinger, 123 S. Ct. 2325, 2351 (2003). As Thomas notes, "The [*Grutter*] Court's refusal to address *Wygant*'s rejection of a state interest virtually indistinguishable from that presented by the Law School is perplexing." *Id.* at n.2.

[33]*Id.* at 2351–52.

[34]*Id.* at 2345.

[35]*Id.* at 2347.

[36]*Id.* at 2345 (citing *Bakke*, 438 U.S. at 298) (opinion of Powell, J.).

interest, understood as a matter of principle, and whether it is narrowly tailored to do so.

As noted earlier, the Court gives us no account of the concept "compelling state interest." Instead, it dives straightaway into the question of whether, in the context of higher education, racial "diversity" among students is such an interest, as the Law School contended. The last time the Court addressed the use of race in public higher education admissions policies, 25 years ago in *Bakke*, it split 4–4, with Justice Lewis Powell casting the deciding vote against California's set-aside program, which reserved a fixed number of seats in the medical school class for members of certain minority groups. Writing for himself in dicta, however, Powell concluded, after rejecting several other rationales, that "the attainment of a diverse student body"[37] would be a compelling governmental interest justifying racial discrimination. O'Connor points out that Powell "grounded his analysis in the academic freedom that 'long has been viewed as a special concern of the First Amendment,'"[38] noting how he emphasized that the nation's future depended on leaders exposed to a wide variety of views.

When she herself takes up the argument left by Powell, O'Connor continues in that same policy vein. From the start, however, she is less than clear about just what the state's interest is, as she conflates two "compelling interests." The Law School, she says, asserts "only one justification for [its] use of race in the admissions process: obtaining 'the educational benefits that flow from a diverse student body.' . . . In other words, the Law School asks us to recognize . . . a compelling state interest in student body diversity."[39] That implies, Thomas says, "that both 'diversity' and 'educational benefits' are components of the Law School's compelling state interest."[40] In fact, the Court speaks of both, he notes, as "compelling interests."[41] Yet the reason the Law School cannot realize those interests without discriminating, he continues, is because it refuses to change its admissions standards and status, which indicates that its real interest is broader. In his

[37] *Id.* at 2336 (citing *Bakke*, 438 U.S. at 311) (opinion of Powell, J.).

[38] *Id.* (citing *Bakke*, 438 U.S. at 312, 314).

[39] *Id.* at 2338 (citing Respondents' Brief at i).

[40] *Id.* at 2352.

[41] *Id.* at 2353.

separate dissent, joined by Thomas, Scalia succinctly states what he takes that broader interest to be: "maintaining a 'prestige' law school whose normal admissions standards disproportionately exclude blacks and other minorities."[42] Given the clear constitutional prohibition on racial discrimination, Thomas concludes that "the Law School should be forced to choose between its classroom aesthetic and its exclusionary admissions system—it cannot have it both ways."[43]

One way to read O'Connor's contention is this: the Law School has a compelling interest in achieving student diversity; its reason or justification is to secure the educational benefits that purportedly follow; but it can achieve that diversity, and hence those benefits, only by discriminating on the basis of race; therefore it has a compelling interest in discriminating. If that indeed is a correct construction of O'Connor's point, the Thomas-Scalia rejoinders still stand. Here's why.

"Context matters when reviewing race-based governmental action under the Equal Protection Clause,"[44] O'Connor says. Then let's look at the context. Like several other states, Michigan has a public higher education system composed of many units, each with its own admissions standards. The "flagship" Law School at the Ann Arbor campus has very high standards—reflecting, presumably, the wishes or interests of the citizens of Michigan in having such a school. But if the function of the school is to train the "best and brightest," as is evidenced by those standards, then certain other interests are not simply not entailed by that function but are outright excluded by it. Achieving student diversity is one such inconsistent interest, for it would require either lowering admissions standards or employing a discriminatory, race-conscious admissions plan. In fact, as the Law School's own expert testified, "a race-blind admissions system would have a 'very dramatic,' negative effect on underrepresented minority admissions."[45] But the Law School does not want to lower its admissions standards. It's only option, therefore, is to employ a two-tiered admissions system—to discriminate on the basis of race.

[42] *Id.* at 2349.
[43] *Id.* at 2356.
[44] *Id.* at 2338.
[45] *Id.* at 2334.

Thus, Thomas is right: the school cannot have both diversity and an exclusionary admissions system without engaging in constitutionally prohibited discrimination.

The "compelling interest" that purports here to justify racial discrimination is thus nothing like the interests discussed previously that the Court has validated. It is not entailed of necessity in a state power. Nor is it grounded in principle, much less required to secure a principle. In fact, its pursuit violates principle—the principle of equal protection. There may indeed be educational benefits from diversity, ranging from promoting "cross-racial understanding" to "breaking down racial stereotypes" to "better prepar[ing] students for an increasingly diverse workforce and society,"[46] concerning which the Court defers unreservedly to the Law School's educational judgment. Those policy interests may be rational, or important, or even "compelling"—depending on one's values. But the policy arguments the Court invokes are just that—arguments from policy, appropriate for the legislative arena, if constitutionally authorized, not the judiciary. However "compelling" they may be from some evaluative perspective, they cannot be pursued by the state in violation of a citizen's constitutional rights. For once you allow that, you soon find that there is no end to "good reasons" for violating rights, and every reason starts to look "compelling." At that point, interests trump rights, policy trumps principle, and that is the end of principle. Nor does the First Amendment save the Law School, for it hardly authorizes a public university to do what the Fourteenth Amendment forbids. In effect, the Court has allowed narrow, special-interest politics, the politics of the Law School, to trump law. Thomas sums it up perfectly: "the Court holds . . . that the Law School has a compelling state interest in doing what it wants to do."[47]

"Narrow Tailoring"

Assume, however, that the Court got it right, that diversity is a compelling state interest that justifies racial discrimination. The university would still have to satisfy the narrow-tailoring prong of strict scrutiny: the means it employs to secure a diverse student body, that is, would have to be "narrowly tailored" to that end. In

[46] *Id.* at 2339–40.
[47] *Id.* at 2356.

Gratz, the University of Michigan's College of Literature, Science, and the Arts (LSA) failed that test. There the Court simply incorporated the diversity-as-compelling-state-interest argument from *Grutter* and proceeded to examine whether the LSA's means were narrowly tailored. The Court held they were not. Let's look first at those arguments, then return to *Grutter*, where the means the Law School employed did pass the test.

We should start, however, by asking what "narrow tailoring" means, because the idea is hardly intuitive. Once it has a compelling interest to do so, we know the university can discriminate on the basis of race, provided its means are narrowly tailored to serve that interest. It doesn't help, of course, that the *Grutter* majority was unclear about just what the compelling interest is. Set that problem aside, however, assume that diversity is that interest, and focus on the essence of the matter. To secure a diverse student body, the university can do what would otherwise be wrong—discriminate on the basis of race. But its discrimination must be narrowly tailored. Why? The answer is not obvious. Perhaps it is so that no more damage or wrong than is necessary be done. The university may discriminate—bad enough. It just has to do it carefully so as not to make things worse.

As with "compelling state interest," one struggles to make sense of this idea of "narrow tailoring." Take the validated examples Thomas cites, as discussed previously. In those, ensuring national security and remedying past discrimination by the state were compelling interests that justified racial discrimination. The government's compelling interest was inherent in its power, not a policy standing apart from it, and the government violated equal protection as a means of securing equal protection. If national security is the compelling interest, presumably narrow tailoring means that one wants to impinge on all and only those rights of all and only those people as may be necessary to secure that interest. Likewise, if equal protection is denied for remedial reasons, narrow tailoring means one wants to burden all and only those who benefited from wrongful prior discrimination and benefit all and only those who were previously burdened.

But how does that understanding of "narrow tailoring" operate in the cases at hand? How do we do little damage beyond the damage racial discrimination is already doing? Why, for example, do the racial set-asides in *Bakke*, or the point system in *Gratz*, which looks to race to award 20 of the 100 points needed for admission, do more damage than the approach of *Grutter*, which seeks a "critical mass" (10 to 17 percent of the class) of "underrepresented minorities"? Could the answer be as simple as this: the first two means bring the discrimination closer to the surface, making it obvious for all to see, whereas the means the Law School uses are more subtle, disguising what is going on? Is that what "narrow tailoring" is all about? Let's see.

Chief Justice William Rehnquist, who dissented forcefully in *Grutter*, wrote for the Court in *Gratz*, finding that the admissions policy the LSA employed was not narrowly tailored because it "automatically distributes 20 points, or one-fifth of the points needed to guarantee admission, to every single 'underrepresented minority' applicant solely because of race."[48] In *Bakke*, Rehnquist notes, Powell thought "it would be permissible for a university to employ an admissions program in which 'race or ethnic background may be deemed a "plus" in a particular applicant's file.'"[49] A system that looked at each applicant individually "might allow for '[t]he file of a particular black applicant [to] be examined for his potential contribution to diversity without the factor of race being decisive'"[50] in comparison with other applicants. Such a system would be "flexible enough to consider all pertinent elements of diversity in light of the particular qualifications of each applicant,"[51] unlike the LSA's policy, which "has the effect of making 'the factor of race . . . decisive' for virtually every minimally qualified underrepresented minority applicant."[52]

It would seem, in brief, that a narrowly tailored policy must be individualized, flexible, and not automatic in the sense of assuring admission on the basis of race. The LSA policy failed on those counts. But surely those "weaknesses" are strengths insofar as they assure diversity, for which they are the means. They get the job done, so to speak, which an outright quota would do too. What is it that

---

[48] *Gratz*, 123 S. Ct. at 2427.
[49] *Id.* at 2428 (citing *Bakke*, 438 U.S. at 317) (opinion of Powell, J.).
[50] *Id.*
[51] *Id.*
[52] *Id.*

makes those straightforward, above-board policies impermissible, whereas "narrow tailoring" succeeds? What is the virtue that narrow tailoring secures? Let's see if we can find it in *Grutter*, which does exhibit narrow tailoring, the Court says.

Not surprisingly, the same narrow-tailoring terms arise in *Grutter* as did in *Gratz*, but here the terms are satisfied. Writing for the Court, O'Connor makes it clear that "a race-conscious admissions program cannot use a quota system—it cannot 'insulat[e] each category of applicants with certain desired qualifications from competition with other applicants,'"[53] as happened in *Bakke*. Again, race may be considered only as a "plus" factor in an applicant's file. There must be an "individualized" consideration that is "flexible" and "nonmechanical." The Law School's program meets those requirements, the Court holds. It "engages in a highly individualized, holistic review of each applicant's file, giving serious consideration to all the ways an applicant might contribute to a diverse educational environment."[54] Its goal of attaining a "critical mass" of minority students does not transform the program into a quota in which "a certain fixed number or proportion of opportunities" are reserved for minorities.[55]

In his incisive dissent, Rehnquist takes particular aim at the Law School's goal of attaining a "critical mass" of *each* underrepresented minority—justified because only so will there be a sufficient number of each group to ensure against isolation, to provide opportunities for interaction, and so forth. Yet the school's actual program, Rehnquist says, "bears little or no relation to its asserted goal," because the admissions practices with respect to the different groups differ dramatically.[56] If a critical mass of each group is needed, how can one explain that Hispanics are admitted at only one-half the rate of blacks, and Native Americans at only one-sixth the rate of blacks? As Rehnquist concludes, "the Law School's disparate admissions practices with respect to these minority groups demonstrate that its alleged goal of 'critical mass' is simply a sham."[57] Indeed, "the

[53] *Grutter*, 123 S. Ct. at 2342 (citing *Bakke*, 438 U.S. at 315) (opinion of Powell, J.).
[54] *Id.* at 2343.
[55] *Id.* at 2342.
[56] *Id.* at 2366.
[57] *Id.* at 2367.

ostensibly flexible nature of the Law School's admissions program that the Court finds appealing appears to be, in practice, a carefully managed program designed to ensure proportionate representation of applicants from selected minority groups."[58]

Still, how is any of this "narrow tailoring"? And how does it in any way reduce or minimize the harm done by the underlying racial discrimination? The Law School is not discriminating any less than the LSA; it's just doing it more subtly—but affecting, proportionally, just as many people. The Court tells us that narrow tailoring requires that a race-conscious admissions program must not "unduly burden individuals who are not members of the favored racial or ethnic groups."[59] What does "unduly burden" mean in this context? Surely, those individuals whose applications are rejected because they "are not members of the favored racial or ethnic groups" are duly burdened. And on that, how do the two programs at issue here differ in the least?

In her concurring opinion in *Gratz*, Justice Ruth Bader Ginsburg put it well: "If honesty is the best policy, surely Michigan's accurately described, fully disclosed College affirmative action program is preferable to achieving similar numbers through winks, nods, and disguises."[60] But that needs to be tempered by Rehnquist's observation on the narrow tailoring of *Grutter*: "Stripped of its 'critical mass' veil, the Law School's program is revealed as a naked effort to achieve racial balancing."[61]

Conclusion

It is noteworthy, at least, that toward the end of its opinion in *Grutter*, the Court returns to the first principles of the matter: " '[a] core purpose of the Fourteenth Amendment was to do away with all governmentally imposed discrimination based on race.' Accordingly, race-conscious admissions policies must be limited in time."[62] That is a non sequitur. The Fourteenth Amendment was no more

---

[58] *Id.* at 2369.

[59] *Id.* at 2345 (citing Metro Broad., Inc. v. FCC, 497 U.S. 547, 630 (1990)) (O'Connor, J., dissenting).

[60] *Gratz*, 123 S. Ct. at 2446.

[61] *Grutter*, 123 S. Ct. at 2365.

[62] *Id.* at 2346 (citing Palmore v. Sidoti, 466 U.S. 429, 434 (1984)).

written to "do away" with governmental discrimination over time than the Thirteenth Amendment was written to do away with slavery over time. They were both written to end the respective evils they addressed immediately. The Court concludes its reflections on duration by saying, "We expect that 25 years from now, the use of racial preferences will no longer be necessary to further the interest approved today."[63] Whether that is an expectation or just a hope, it rings hollow. For if diversity is indeed such a compelling state interest, then discrimination to achieve it should be legitimate for as long as it is needed. One imagines that the Court broached this issue of duration because it senses, deep down, that there is something fundamentally wrong in its opinion, something wrong in denigrating principle for mere policy.

But as a consequential matter, even more is wrong with these decisions. For not only do they encourage further denigration of principle when we think we have "good reasons," but they shield us from having to face the real issues. The underlying problem, of course, is that too many minorities cannot gain admission to higher education on neutral admissions standards, which tells us that the roots of the problem are far broader and much deeper. Regrettably, as Thomas points out, the Court's decisions in these cases will only postpone the day when we face that hard truth. They buy a small gain for a few today at the cost of a huge gain for many tomorrow.

[63] *Id.* at 2347.

Nike v. Kasky and the Definition of "Commercial Speech"

Thomas C. Goldstein

A Term highlighted by constitutional rulings of lasting significance also produced one monumental disappointment—a dud—in
the Supreme Court's failure to resolve the continuing uncertainty
about the definition of "commercial speech" in First Amendment
jurisprudence. The Court had agreed to review the California
Supreme Court's holding in *Nike v. Kasky* that essentially any public
discussion by businesses of their operations is commercial speech,
subject to strict government regulation, even if not included in advertising or product labels. [1] But in the U.S. Supreme Court's last order
issued on the last day of the Term, the justices dismissed the writ
of certiorari,[2] issuing an "unexpected 'never mind'" to a case that
"attracted some three dozen briefs and became the focus of an
intense debate, on the Internet, in the Court, and elsewhere over the
role of multinational corporations, the effects of globalization, and
the constitutional contours of commercial speech. "[3]

The dismissal of the *Kasky* case immediately generated loud criticism from the dissenting justices,[4] newspaper editorial boards,[5] and

[1] Kasky v. Nike, 27 Cal. 4th 939 (2002), *cert. granted*, 123 S. Ct. 817, *and cert. dismissed*,
123 S. Ct. 2254 (2003).

[2] 123 S. Ct. 2554 (2003).

[3] Linda Greenhouse, *Nike Free Speech Case Is Unexpectedly Returned To California*,
N.Y. TIMES, June 26, 2003, at A1.

[4] 123 S. Ct. at 2560 (Breyer, J. , dissenting, joined by O'Connor, J.) ("In my view,
. . . the questions presented directly concern the freedom of Americans to speak about
public matters in public debate, no jurisdictional rule prevents us from deciding
those questions now, and delay itself may inhibit the exercise of constitutionally
protected rights of free speech without making the issue significantly easier to decide
later on.").

[5] *E.g.*, *Nike Left Speechless*, CHI. TRIB., July 6, 2003, at C-8; *Nike Has the Right to Engage
in Debate*, DETROIT NEWS, June 28, 2003, at 8D; *Court Disappoints on Nike Ruling*, ROCKY
MTN. NEWS, June 30, 2003, at 34A; *Court Drops the Ball*, ST. PETERSBURG TIMES, June 28,
2003, at 18A.

commentators,[6] all rightly concerned that it was essential for the Court to address the meaning of the commercial speech doctrine and to overturn the lower court's decision, which presented a genuine threat to speech by businesses on the important social and political issues of our day. With the case now returned to the lower courts, speakers are left to wonder whether to limit their speech in light of the California Supreme Court's ruling. That is a genuine concern because a plaintiff can successfully assert jurisdiction in that state's courts based on any communication on the Internet or in a substantial publication, almost all of which are received in California.[7] Indeed, immediately on the heels of the dismissal of certiorari in *Kasky*, People for the Ethical Treatment of Animals sued Kentucky Fried Chicken under the same statutory scheme regarding statements on KFC's Web site about its treatment of chickens.[8]

In this article, I argue that the California Supreme Court's decision is seriously misguided as a matter of First Amendment law and that it will inevitably be overturned by the U.S. Supreme Court. That fact may not give much solace to corporate speakers now facing the prospect of burdensome suits under the *Kasky* regime. But it should

[6] *E.g.*, Caroline Marshall, *Commercially Speaking, Speech Is Not Always Free*, LONDON DAILY TELEGRAPH, July 8, 2003, at 27; Robert J. Samuelson, *A Tax on Free Speech*, WASH. POST, July 9, 2003, at A27; Jim Wooten, *A Non-Ruling on Nike Puts Biz in a Bind*, ATL. J. & CONST., July 1, 2003, at 13A.

[7] Furthermore, because plaintiffs in these cases disavow any personal injury and right to recovery, the suit will almost certainly not be removable to a federal court that would not be bound by the California Supreme Court's ruling. *See, e.g.*, Mortera v. N. Am. Mortgage, 172 F. Supp. 2d 1240 (N.D. Cal. 2001); Toxic Injuries Corp. v. Safety-Kleen Corp., 57 F. Supp. 2d 947 (C.D. Cal. 1999); Mangini v. R.J. Reynolds Tob., 793 F. Supp. 925 (N.D. Cal 1992).

[8] *See* Elizabeth Becker, *Animal Rights Group to Sue Fast-Food Chain*, N.Y. TIMES, July 7, 2003, at A11; Valerie Elliott, *KFC in Court Over Chicken Warfare*, LONDON TIMES, July 8, 2003, at 4; Patrick Howington, *Animal-Rights Group Sues KFC*, LOUISVILLE COURIER-J., July 8, 2003, at 1F. PETA dropped the suit after KFC agreed to change the statements on its web-site and its responses to consumers' questions. *See Rights Group for Animals Drops Lawsuit Against KFC*, N.Y. TIMES, Sept. 2, 2003 at A19. But suits characterizing businesses' discussion of matters of public importance as "commercial speech" entitled to lesser First Amendment protection are not uniformly brought by individuals or public interest groups against corporations. Monsanto, for example, has recently sued a small dairy over its statements regarding the use of hormones in milk. *E.g.*, David Barboza, *Monsanto Sues Dairy in Maine Over Label's Remarks on Hormones*, N.Y. TIMES, July 12, 2003, at C1; J.M. Lawrence, *Monsanto Sour on Milk Marketers' Hormones Claim*, BOSTON HERALD, July 4, 2003, at 10.

provide some reassurance to companies reviewing their communications policies in light of the decision.

I. Background of the *Kasky* Case

Nike v. Kasky arose out of the passionate worldwide debate over globalization. Nike, the world's leading athletic, footwear, and apparel manufacturer, has for years been at the center of moral and political disagreements about the impact and regulation of multinational investment in the developing world because of its 900 factories in 51 countries with more than 600,000 employees. Beginning in 1995, Nike was the target of allegations that it maintained dangerously unsafe factories and mistreated and underpaid workers in its Southeast Asian factories, frequently accompanied by demands for legislative action and calls for boycotts of Nike products.

Nike responded by commissioning former United Nations Ambassador Andrew Young to conduct an independent review of its operations. When Ambassador Young concluded that the charges against Nike were largely false, Nike publicized the results, purchasing "editorial advertisements," issuing press releases, and writing letters to newspapers around the country and to officers of national universities. These various statements conveyed the view that Nike does act morally because its investments produce substantial economic and political benefits for workers and because it puts its best effort toward ensuring that employees at its contract facilities are paid fairly and treated well. None of the statements at issue appeared in advertisements of Nike's products or urged consumers to buy those products.

In 1998, Marc Kasky, a resident of California, sued Nike under California's Unfair Competition Law (UCL)[9] and False Advertising Law (FAL)[10] on behalf of the general public of the State of California. Kasky alleged that Nike responded to the public allegations against it by making misstatements about working conditions at the Southeast Asian factories that manufacture certain Nike products. In particular, Kasky identified six classes of allegedly false or misleading statements:

---

[9] CAL. BUS. & PROF. CODE § 17200 *et seq.* (West 2002).

[10] *Id.* § 17500 *et seq.* (West 2002).

65

- Claims that workers who make Nike products are protected from and not subjected to corporal punishment and/or sexual abuse
- Claims that Nike products are made in accordance with applicable governmental laws and regulations governing wages and hours
- Claims that Nike products are made in accordance with applicable laws and regulations governing health and safety conditions
- Claims that Nike pays average line-workers double the minimum wage in Southeast Asia
- Claims that workers who produce Nike products receive free meals and health care
- Claims that the Andrew Young report proves that Nike is doing a good job and operating morally.

Equally notable is what Kasky did not allege. Kasky did not claim that he or any other California citizen had suffered harm or damages by purchasing products in reliance upon Nike's statements. Nor did Kasky claim that Nike made a false or misleading statement in a label or advertisement. Finally, Kasky did not claim that Nike was anything more than negligent in making the challenged statements, that is, he did not claim that Nike misspoke knowingly or with reckless disregard of the truth. Kasky sought an injunction requiring Nike to disgorge all monies it acquired from selling its products in California in violation of the UCL and FAL and to undertake a court-approved public information campaign to correct any statement deemed false or misleading, and barring Nike from misrepresenting the working conditions under which Nike products are made. Kasky also sought attorneys' fees and costs.

Nike filed a demurrer to the complaint, contending that Kasky's suit was barred by the First Amendment.[11] The California Superior Court agreed with Nike and dismissed the complaint. Kasky appealed, and the California Court of Appeal affirmed, holding that Nike's statements "form[ed] part of a public dialogue on a matter of public concern within the core area of expression protected by the First Amendment."[12]

---

[11] Nike also contended that the suit was barred by the California Constitution. *See* CAL. CONST. art. I, § 2(a). The California Supreme Court held that the federal and state constitutions are co-extensive on this question. 27 Cal. 4th 939, 958–59 (2002).

[12] Kasky v. Nike, Inc., 79 Cal. App. 4th 165, 178 (Cal. Ct. App. 2000).

The California Supreme Court reversed, four to three, and remanded the case for further proceedings.[13] The court held that Nike's statements constituted "commercial speech" under a three-part test the majority found "consistent with, and implicit in" the Supreme Court's "commercial speech decisions."[14] The court explained that "categorizing a particular statement as commercial or non-commercial speech requires consideration of three elements: the speaker, the intended audience, and the content of the message."[15]

First, the court found that Nike is a commercial speaker because the company manufactures, distributes, and sells athletic shoes and apparel worldwide.[16]

Second, the court reasoned that Nike's statements were made to a commercial audience. The court explained that the "intended audience [of commercial speech] is likely to be actual or potential buyers or customers of the speaker's goods or services, or persons acting for actual or potential buyers or customers, or persons (such as reporters or reviewers) likely to repeat the message to or otherwise influence actual or potential buyers or customers."[17] Even if the speaker "has a secondary purpose to influence lenders, investors, or lawmakers," the speech is nevertheless commercial so long as it is "primarily intended to reach consumers and to influence them to buy the speaker's products."[18] Because Nike sent letters "directly to actual and potential purchasers," namely, university presidents and directors of athletic departments," and because Nike's press releases were "intended to reach and influence actual and potential purchasers of Nike products,"[19] the second prong of the commercial speech test was satisfied.

Third, the court concluded that in "describing its own labor policies, and the practices and working conditions in factories where its products are made, Nike was making factual representations about

[13] 27 Cal. 4th 939 (2002).
[14] *Id.* at 960.
[15] *Id.*
[16] *Id.* at 963.
[17] *Id.* at 960.
[18] *Id.* at 968.
[19] *Id.* at 963.

its own business operations."[20] The court reasoned that statements "made for the purpose of promoting sales" could include "statements about the manner in which . . . products are manufactured, distributed or sold, about repair or warranty services that the seller provides to purchasers of the product, or about the identity or qualifications of persons who manufacture, distribute, sell, service or endorse the product," as well as "statements about the education, experience, and qualifications of the persons providing or endorsing the service."[21]

The court was unconcerned with the potential chilling effect its ruling would have on speech by corporations like Nike: "To the extent that application of these laws may make Nike more cautious, and cause it to make greater efforts to verify the truth of its statements, these laws will serve the purpose of commercial speech protection by 'insuring that the stream of commercial information flow[s] cleanly as well as freely.' "[22]

Three justices dissented. They concluded that Nike's statements were fully protected as speech on an important public issue. "Nike's labor practices and policies, and in turn, its products, *were* the public issue."[23] As Justice Janice Rogers Brown explained:

> Nike faced a sophisticated media campaign attacking its overseas labor practices. As a result, its labor practices were discussed on television news programs and in numerous newspapers and magazines. These discussions have even entered the political arena as various governments, government officials and organizations have proposed and passed resolutions condemning Nike's labor practices. Given these facts, Nike's overseas labor practices were undoubtedly a matter of public concern, and its speech on this issue was therefore "entitled to special protection."[24]

[20] *Id.*

[21] *Id.* at 961.

[22] *Id.* at 963–64 (quoting Va. State Bd. of Pharmacy v. Va. Citizens Consumer Council, Inc., 425 U.S. 748, 772 (1976)).

[23] *Id.* at 975 (Chin, J., dissenting).

[24] *Id.* at 990 (Brown, J., dissenting) (quoting Connick v. Myers, 461 U.S. 138, 145 (1983)).

In these circumstances, "Nike could hardly engage in a general discussion on overseas labor exploitation and economic globalization without discussing its own labor practices."[25]

The majority's legal regime, the dissenters explained, chills speech on this important issue. "[T]he corporation [can] never be sure whether its truthful statements may deceive or confuse the public and would likely incur significant burden and expense in litigating the issue."[26] Further, the majority's ruling distorts the marketplace of ideas by discriminating against a particular viewpoint. "Under the majority's test, only speakers engaged in commerce are strictly liable for their false or misleading representations. . . . Meanwhile, other speakers who make the same representations may face no such liability, regardless of the context of their statements."[27] "Handicapping one side in this important worldwide debate," the dissenters concluded, "is both ill considered and unconstitutional."[28]

After the California Supreme Court denied Nike's petition for rehearing, the U.S. Supreme Court granted certiorari.[29] Nike's argument for reversal was supported not only by the media and the business community but also by the United States (which enforces the Federal Trade Commission Act) and organized labor (which had generated much of the vituperative allegations regarding Nike's labor practices).[30]

After briefing and argument, the Court dismissed the case.[31] Of note, however, a *majority* of the Court rejected the California

[25] *Id.* at 980 (Chin, J., dissenting).

[26] *Id.* at 985 (Brown, J., dissenting).

[27] *Id.* (Brown, J., dissenting).

[28] *Id.* at 971 (Chin, J., dissenting).

[29] 123 S. Ct. 817 (2003).

[30] *See* Brief for U.S. at 7, *Nike v. Kasky, supra* (No. 02-575) ("Respondent seeks judicial relief for allegedly false statements that have concededly caused respondent no harm whatsoever. The First Amendment does not countenance that novel form of private action in light of its severe threat to freedom of speech."); Brief for AFL-CIO as *Amicus Curiae* at 3, *Nike v. Kasky, supra* (No. 02-575) ("From all that appears in the complaint, then, the AFL-CIO stands on the same side of the debate over Nike's labor practices as the plaintiff in this case. Where we part company with the plaintiff, however, is that we are certain that this debate is, and in the interest of the disputants and the public should be, an open free speech debate under the First Amendment and not one subject to legal regulation under the commercial speech doctrine.").

[31] 123 S. Ct. 2554 (2003) (per curiam). Three Justices—O'Connor, Kennedy, and Breyer—openly dissented from the dismissal, suggesting that the vote was six to three.

Supreme Court's holding that Nike's statements were pure commercial speech. The three justices who wrote in support of the dismissal on the ground that further factual development was required—Stevens, Souter, and Ginsburg—agreed that "the speech at issue represents a blending of commercial speech, noncommercial speech and debate on an issue of public importance."[32] Justices Breyer and O'Connor similarly concluded that "the communications at issue are not purely commercial in nature," but rather "are better characterized as involving a mixture of commercial and noncommercial (public issue-oriented) elements."[33]

II. The California Supreme Court's Definition of Commercial Speech Is Insupportable

Nike v. Kasky gave the U.S. Supreme Court the perfect opportunity to clarify the definition of commercial speech. Since 1980, the Court has articulated three inconsistent tests for identifying "commercial speech," generating substantial uncertainty and confusion regarding the boundaries of commercial speech. For its part, the California Supreme Court in *Nike* defined "commercial speech" to cover everything said by anyone "engaged in commerce," to an "intended audience" of "potential . . . customers" or "persons (such as reporters . . .)" likely to influence actual or potential customers that conveys factual information about itself "likely to influence consumers in

---

[32]*Id.* at 2558 (Stevens, J., concurring); *see also id.* at 2559 ("On the other hand, the communications were part of an ongoing discussion and debate about important public issues that was concerned not only with Nike's labor practices, but with similar practices used by other multinational corporations. *See* Brief for AFL-CIO as *Amicus Curiae* at 2. Knowledgeable persons should be free to participate in such debate without fear of unfair reprisal. The interest in protecting such participants from the chilling effect of the prospect of expensive litigation is therefore also a matter of great importance. *See e.g.* , Brief for ExxonMobil *et al.* as *Amici Curiae* at 2, *Nike v. Kasky, supra* (No. 02-575); Brief for Pfizer, Inc., as *Amicus Curiae* at 11-12, *Nike v. Kasky, supra* (No. 02-575). That is why we have provided such broad protection for misstatements about public figures that are not animated by malice. *See also* New York Times Co. v. Sullivan, 376 U.S. 254, 11 L. Ed. 2d 686, 84 S. Ct. 710 (1964).").

[33]123 S. Ct. at 2565 (Breyer, J., dissenting); *see also id.* at 2566 ("These three sets of circumstances taken together—circumstances of format, content, and regulatory context—warrant treating the regulations of speech at issue differently from regulations of purer forms of commercial speech, such as simple product advertisements, that we have reviewed in the past. And, where all three are present, I believe the First Amendment demands heightened scrutiny.").

their commercial decisions."[34] This novel definition, which gives Nike's statements in the *New York Times* about labor conditions in its Southeast Asian factories no more protection under the First Amendment than a supermarket flyer advertising Nike shoes, cannot be reconciled with any of the U.S. Supreme Court's tests. Thus, by reversing the California court's decision, the Supreme Court could have clarified the ambiguities and conflicting signals in its own precedents.

The first of the Supreme Court's tests was articulated in *Central Hudson Gas & Electric Co. v. Public Service Commission*, in which the Court defined "commercial speech" as "expression related solely to the economic interests of the speaker and its audience."[35] Under the "*Central Hudson* definition," Nike's speech was clearly not commercial, for it principally targeted consumers who purchase (or boycott) goods for *non*economic reasons. And Nike's motivation for speaking was principally the prospect of government action restricting foreign investment or condemning the company and increasing company morale,[36] concerns that can be considered "solely" economic only in the sense that virtually *everything* a company does is ultimately intended to improve its financial bottom line.

The Supreme Court articulated a second test for identifying commercial speech three years after *Central Hudson* in *Bolger v. Youngs*

---

[34]Kasky v. Nike, 27 Cal. 4th 939, 960 (2002).

[35]Central Hudson Gas & Elec. Co. v. Public Serv. Comm'n, 447 U.S. 557, 561 (1980)

[36]*E.g., March Down Fifth Avenue in New York City Protesting the Use of Child Labor Abroad to Make Products Which American Consumers Buy Relatively Cheap* (Nat'l Pub. Radio broadcast, Dec. 11, 1998) (linking proclamation by President Clinton urging "an end to sweatshop conditions both in the United States and abroad" to protests against Nike); Bernie Sanders, *Webwire—Nike Corporate Practices Come Under Attack,* Congressional Press Release, Oct. 24, 1997 (reporting on letter from 53 U.S. congressional representatives seeking meeting with Nike to address overseas labor issues and asserting that "Nike believes that workers in the United States are good enough to purchase [its] shoe products, but are no longer worthy enough to manufacture them"); Paula L. Green, *Nike, Jordan Challenged on Conditions Indonesian Worker in Court Battle,* J. Com., July 25, 1996, at 3A (describing efforts to pressure Nike by, *e.g.,* an AFL-CIO youth group and Rev. Jesse Jackson, as well as attempts to link issue to "crusade" by U.S. Department of Labor to eliminate domestic sweatshops); Robin Bulman, *Nike's Tainted Cash?,* J. Com., July 23, 1996, at 7A (reporting on resolution of Portland Metropolitan Human Rights Commission urging local school board to decline Nike donation of $500,000 to cover budget shortfall on the basis of "alleged human rights abuses by the company's overseas suppliers").

Drug Products Corp.[37] Bolger concluded that a pamphlet advertising condoms was commercial speech based on three factors in "combination": (1) advertising format, (2) explicit reference to a product, and (3) economic motivation.[38] The California Supreme Court's decision in *Nike* fared no better under this revised standard, however, for two reasons. The California Supreme Court's conclusion that the format and the forum of a statement are irrelevant to the commercial speech inquiry is plainly inconsistent with *Bolger*'s reasoning that an advertisement has less communicative value than a statement with the same message contained in a newspaper editorial that plays a role in broader public discussion. In effect, the California Supreme Court would have collapsed the *Bolger* inquiry into a single prong: economic motivation.[39]

Just as important, Kasky never asserted that Nike had made a false or misleading statement about its *products*, and indeed none of the statements at issue even referred to characteristics (such as price, availability, or suitability) of Nike's products. But in an Orwellian ipse dixit, the California Supreme Court held that "product references" require *no* reference to *any* product, instead encompassing every factual statement a business makes about its operations or the conditions in which employees supplying its firms work.[40]

Finally, the California Supreme Court's decision is inconsistent with the third (and most often-repeated) definition of commercial speech offered by the U.S. Supreme Court: "speech that does no more than propose a commercial transaction."[41] The California court omitted any requirement that the speech make a commercial proposal at all, much less that it do so exclusively. Kasky argued that Nike's speech met this definition because it sought to induce a sales transaction and therefore "propose[d] a commercial transaction."But that argument, if correct, would have eliminated the requirement of a "proposal" entirely from the definition of commercial speech

---

[37] 463 U.S. 60 (1983).

[38] Bolger v. Youngs Drug Prods. Corp., 463 U.S. 60, 66–67 & n.13 (1983).

[39] *Contra* Hustler v. Falwell, 435 U.S. 46, 53 (1988) (constitutional protection of public discourse does not depend on the motivation for expression); New York Times v. Sullivan, 376 U.S. 254, 265 (1964) (same).

[40] 27 Cal. 4th at 961.

[41] United States v. United Foods, Inc., 533 U.S. 405, 409 (2001); *see also* Edenfield v. Fane, 507 U.S. 761, 767 (1993); Bd. of Trustees v. Fox, 492 U.S. 469, 473–74 (1989).

because virtually everything a business says or does is intended to increase its sales in some ultimate sense.

Thus, although the California Supreme Court characterized its result as "consistent with" and "implicit in" the Supreme Court's decisions,[42] in fact the definition it proposed went well beyond the Court's definitions of commercial speech. By declining to decide the case, the U.S. Supreme Court also left in place a definition of commercial speech that runs afoul of three core First Amendment values.

First, the California court's definition of commercial speech restricted speech on public issues that have traditionally been entitled to full First Amendment protection. Though it has substantial value for listeners, commercial speech does not receive full First Amendment protection because it has been thought to lack the communicative value of fully protected speech to the speaker and to society generally and in that sense has been said to make less of a "direct contribution to the interchange of ideas."[43] By contrast, "speech on public issues occupies the highest rung of the hierarchy of First Amendment values, and is entitled to special protection."[44] Through fully protected speech, individuals participate in the polity,

---

[42] 27 Cal. 4th at 960.

[43] Va. State Bd. of Pharmacy v. Va. Citizens Consumer Council, 425 U.S. 748, 780 (1976). That argument has been subjected to heavy criticism from Justice Thomas and from commentators who would abandon the commercial versus non-commercial speech distinction. *See, e.g.,* 44 Liquormart v. Rhode Island, 517 U.S. 484, 522–23 (1996) (Thomas, J., concurring in part and concurring in the judgment): "I do not see a philosophical or historical basis for asserting that 'commercial' speech is of 'lower value' than 'noncommercial' speech. Indeed, some historical materials suggest to the contrary."); Lorillard Tobacco Co. v. Reilly, 533 U.S. 525, 572 (2001) (Thomas, J., concurring in part and concurring in the judgment) ("I continue to believe that when the government seeks to restrict truthful speech in order to suppress the ideas it conveys, strict scrutiny is appropriate, whether or not the speech in question may be characterized as 'commercial.' "); Alex Kozinski & Stuart Banner, *Who's Afraid of Commercial Speech?*, 76 VA. L. REV. 627 (1990); Barbara M. Mack, *Commercial Speech: A Historical Overview of Its First Amendment Protections and an Analysis of Its Future Constitutional Safeguards*, 38 DRAKE L. REV. 59 (1988); Martin H. Redish & Howard M. Wasserman, *What's Good for General Motors: Corporate Speech and the Theory of Free Expression*, 66 GEO. WASH. L. REV. 235 (1998); Steven Shiffrin, *The First Amendment and Economic Regulation: Away from a General Theory of the First Amendment*, 78 NW. U.L. REV. 1212, 1223 (1983); Rodney A. Smolla, *Information, Imagery, and the First Amendment: A Case for Expansive Protection of Commercial Speech*, 71 TEX. L. REV. 777 (1993).

[44] Connick v. Myers, 461 U.S. 138, 145 (1983) (citation omitted).

73

expressing views and engaging in debate that collectively makes up the nation's social and political consciousness, triggering our "profound national commitment to the principle that debate on public issues should be uninhibited, robust, and wide-open."[45]

The California court's decision in *Nike* is irreconcilable with this distinction between commercial speech and fully protected "speech on public issues." The court concluded that statements on matters of public importance are nevertheless "commercial speech" for purposes of the First Amendment whenever they involve the company's business practices. That theory cuts the heart out of the First Amendment's protections for statements by commercial entities on nearly *every* public issue—from a company's diversity policy to its community relations efforts to its political activities—all of which can be said to "matter in making consumer choices."[46] The California court's decision thus swallows up public discussion of *all* "matter[s] of political, social, or other concern to the community," as distinguished from the narrow categories of "matters only of personal interest"[47] and of "speech solely in the individual interest of the speaker and its specific business audience."[48]

Consider the facts of *Nike*. Unlike a traditional false advertising complainant, Kasky did not claim that petitioner misled consumers

[45] New York Times v. Sullivan, 376 U.S. 254, 270 (1964).

[46] 27 Cal. 4th at 969. To be sure, advertising does not receive the full protections of the First Amendment when it merely uses the *artifice* of "link[ing]" a product to a current public debate." *Cent. Hudson Gas & Elec. Co.*, 447 U.S. at 563 n.5. *See also, e.g.,* Zauderer v. Office of Disciplinary Counsel of Ohio Supreme Court, 471 U.S. 626, 637 n.7 (1985). But, as the Court recognized in *Bolger*, the state's augmented power to regulate commercial speech coexists with the principle that speech on matters of public importance (including that by corporations) loses none of its protection by virtue of the fact that it may alter consumer behavior. 463 U.S. at 86. Indeed, it is precisely *because* "[a] company has *the full panoply of constitutional protections* available to its *direct comments on public issues*, [that] there is no reason for providing similar constitutional protection when such comments are made in the context of commercial transactions."*Id.* at 68 (emphasis added). Thus, when a corporation's statements on public issues do not appear in "commercial speech"—which petitioner's statements plainly do not under any of the three tests announced by the Court—they are fully protected by the First Amendment.

[47] *Connick*, 461 U.S. at 146–47.

[48] Dun & Bradstreet, Inc. v. Greenmoss Builders, Inc., 472 U.S. 749, 762 (1985 (plurality). For a discussion of "ethical purchase behavior," which posits that some consumers purchase products based not just on price and quality but also on their "moral judgment" about the seller, *see* N. CRAIG SMITH, MORALITY AND THE MARKET 177 (1990).

into believing that Nike offers them a "better deal," that its products are better made, or even that they are "cooler" than the competition's. Rather, he claimed that petitioner's labor practices in Southeast Asia raise so important a social issue that citizens make moral judgments on that basis about Nike, and that those judgments, in turn, influence their purchasing decisions.

But that simply shows why Nike's statements belong at the very core of the First Amendment's protections: It presents a classic dispute between business and labor of the precise sort that the Court has located squarely "within that area of free discussion that is guaranteed by the Constitution,"[49] reasoning that "labor relations are not matters of mere local or private concern," and that "[f]ree discussion concerning the conditions in industry and the causes of labor disputes [is] indispensable to the effective and intelligent use of the processes of popular government to shape the destiny of modern industrial society."[50] Thus, although both Nike's statements and traditional advertising may address matters of public importance, only the former are integrally related to public *dialogue*, dealing with public issues in a different and deeper sense than mere advertising.[51]

Second, the California court's definition applied to public statements unrelated to any state regulatory scheme governing advertisements and representations of product qualities.[52] Another reason

---

[49] Thornhill v. Alabama, 310 U.S. 88, 103 (1940).

[50] *Id.; see also* Linn v. United Plant Guard Workers, 383 U.S. 53, 58 (1966) (characterizing labor disputes as inevitably producing "bitter and extreme charges, countercharges, unfounded rumors, vituperations, personal accusations, misrepresentations, and distortions." For examples of fully protected speech by the other side in the Nike labor debate, *see e.g., Big Labor Rips Nike at Big PR's Annual Outing,* O'DWYER'S PR SERVICES REPORT, July 1998, at 1; Bob Herbert, *In America; Nike's Bad Neighborhood,* N.Y. TIMES, June 14, 1996, at A29.

[51] *See* Bob Herbert, *Let Nike Stay in the Game,* N.Y. TIMES, May 6, 2002, at A21 ("Whatever one thinks of Nike, it is a crucial participant in this continuing debate.").

[52] It bears emphasizing that Kasky did not allege that he or any other California resident in fact relied on any false statement by Nike in purchasing its products, and therefore the case raised no issue regarding the power of government to prosecute those who use deliberate deception to extract money from the public, *see* Cantwell v. Connecticut, 310 U.S. 296, 306 (1940), to enjoin swindling schemes, *see* Donaldson v. Read Magazine, 333 U.S. 178, 191 (1948), or to provide a remedy for consumers who were otherwise fraudulently induced to purchase a product.

commercial speech receives less than full First Amendment protection is that, because advertising does not ordinarily generate the intense media scrutiny and public discussion and reflection typically associated with editorials and other speech on social, political, and moral matters of public moment, direct government regulation may be the only mechanism to ensure that consumers receive accurate information about the products and services they might wish to purchase.[53]

This defining linkage between commercial *speech* and commercial *activity*[54] is completely absent from the California Supreme Court's "commercial speech" test. The speech by Nike targeted for regulation by the court's ruling is not tethered to the state's authority to regulate commercial transactions—although Nike sells products in California, no resident of that state need have purchased any product manufactured by Nike in Southeast Asia for *Kasky* liability to attach.

Thus, under the California court's ruling, the state may regulate all statements of "fact" by a commercial entity about its operations that are "likely to influence consumers in their commercial decisions."[55] But the protection afforded to discussion of matters of public importance certainly extends to such statements of "fact." Facts are the bedrock on which judgments about public issues are reached. "Freedom of discussion, if it would fulfill its historic function in this nation, must embrace all issues 'about which information is needed or appropriate to enable the members of society to cope with the exigencies of their period.'"[56] A contrary rule would produce "innocuous and abstract discussions" and, because the line between fact and opinion is so hazy, would "so becloud even this with doubt, uncertainty and the risk of penalty" that "freedom of speech . . . [would] be at an end."[57]

---

[53] *See Edenfield*, 507 U.S. at 767; *Bolger*, 463 U.S. at 69.

[54] Friedman v. Rogers, 440 U.S. 1, 10 n.9 (1979) ("By definition, commercial speech is linked inextricably to commercial activity.").

[55] 27 Cal. 4th at 969.

[56] First Nat'l Bank v. Bellotti, 435 U.S. 765, 776 (1978) (quoting Thornhill v. Alabama, 310 U.S. 88, 101–02 (1940)).

[57] Thomas v. Collins, 323 U.S. 516, 536–37 (1945). The California Supreme Court expressly declined to follow *Thomas* and *Thornhill* on the ground that they had been superseded by "the modern commercial speech doctrine." 27 Cal. 4th at 965. But the U.S. Supreme Court has cited *Thornhill* and *Thomas* favorably more than 125 times, often in leading free speech precedents. In particular, those decisions undergird the recognition of the First Amendment right to speak on matters of public importance,

The California Supreme Court seemed principally motivated by a desire "to adequately categorize statements made in the context of a modern, sophisticated public relations campaign intended to increase sales and profits by enhancing the image of a product or of its manufacturer or seller."[58] But the commercial speech doctrine needs no expansion to accommodate government's legitimate interest in regulating "image campaigns." Many "image *advertisements*" are commercial speech in the classic sense. Nor may an advertiser circumvent the commercial speech doctrine through the nicety of "link[ing] a product to a current public debate."[59] And the fact that some "image campaigns" fall outside of the "commercial speech" category does not render them altogether immune either from regulation or from the marketplace consequences of whatever misstatements are uncovered.

Nor has a new and more expansive view of government's regulatory authority been shown necessary to protect consumers, given how readily matters of public importance that concern consumers draw media attention. The media and the Internet provide innumerable outlets through which the Kaskys of the world may voice their accusations—accusations to which corporations already feel pressure to respond. And those responses do not go unexamined. When they are revealed in the press to be false or misleading, those responsible are likely to suffer not just embarrassment but substantial losses in sales. That prospect, in turn, gives companies a powerful incentive to ensure that they speak accurately. The proper operations of the marketplace of ideas and the marketplace of goods are thus mutually reinforcing.

Kasky argued that Nike's statements should receive reduced First Amendment protection because Nike knew that some consumers would be influenced by its statements in their purchasing choices. This rationale, however, is both overinclusive, because the California

---

including the right to engage in social protest. *E.g.*, Meyer v. Grant, 486 U.S. 414, 421 (1988); Pac. Gas & Elec. Co. v. Pub. Utils. Comm'n, 475 U.S. 1, 8 9 (1986); FCC v. League of Women Voters, 468 U.S. 364, 381–82 (1984); Consol. Edison Co. v. Pub. Serv. Comm'n, 447 U.S. 530, 534–35 (1980); *Bellotti*, 435 U.S. at 783; Branzburg v. Hayes, 408 U.S. 665, 705 n.40 (1972); Time, Inc. v. Hill, 385 U.S. 374, 388 (1967).

[58] 27 Cal. 4th at 962.

[59] Central Hudson Gas & Elec. Co. v. Public Serv. Comm'n, 447 U.S. 557, 563 n.5 (1980).

law imposes liability even without reliance, and underinclusive, because it excludes a manufacturer's statements of opinion and political views, which may also influence consumer choices. In short, California's determination to police speech affecting consumers' ethical conclusions is unrelated to the traditional state power to regulate commercial dealings.

Finally, the California Supreme Court's definition of commercial speech amounted to viewpoint discrimination. Traditional governmental regulation of commercial advertising applies neutrally to the class of statements on which consumers directly rely in making purchasing decisions. By contrast, the California statutes apply to commercial sellers but *not* to persons and entities that launch accusations against those sellers—despite the fact that the accusations appear in the identical fora and have an indistinguishable effect on consumer behavior. The government's power "to regulate price advertising in one industry but not in others, because the risk of fraud . . . is in its view greater there" does *not* imply the power to engage in "viewpoint discrimination."[60] To the contrary, "discrimination between commercial and noncommercial speech" is forbidden as a form of viewpoint-based censorship when "the distinction bears no relationship *whatsoever* to the particular interests that the [government] has asserted."[61] That rule respects the basic First Amendment principle that "[t]here is an 'equality of status in the field of ideas,' and government must afford all points of view an equal opportunity to be heard."[62]

Under such a legal regime, the discovery of truth is the loser. For the "best test of truth is the power of the thought to get itself accepted in the competition of the market. . . ."[63] That is why a core purpose of the First Amendment is to foreclose public authority from attempting to control the public mind through regulating speech.[64] In the classic words of Judge Learned Hand, the First Amendment "presupposes that right conclusions are more likely to be gathered out

[60] R.A.V. v. St. Paul, 505 U.S. 377, 388–89 (1992).

[61] City of Cincinnati v. Discovery Network, 507 U.S. 410, 424 & n.20 (1993).

[62] Police Dep't of Chicago v. Mosley, 408 U.S. 92, 96 (1972).

[63] Consol. Edison Co. v. Public Serv. Comm'n, 447 U.S. 530, 534 (1980) (quoting Whitney v. California, 274 U.S. 357, 375 (1927) (Brandeis, J., concurring)); *Abrams v. United States*, 250 U.S. 616, 630 (1919) (Holmes, J., dissenting).

[64] *See* Riley v. Nat'l Fed'n of the Blind, 487 U.S. 781, 791 (1988).

of a multitude of tongues, than through any kind of authoritative selection. To many this is, and always will be, folly; but we have staked upon it our all."[65]

III. Conclusion

It is deeply unfortunate that the U.S. Supreme Court did not seize the opportunity presented by *Nike v. Kasky* to bring greater coherence to the commercial speech doctrine. But until the justices return to the issue, the lower courts should recognize that the California Supreme Court's decision in the case is unpersuasive and destined ultimately to be rejected.

[65]United States v. Associated Press, 52 F. Supp. 362, 372 (S.D.N.Y. 1943).

Unholy Fire: Cross Burning, Symbolic Speech, and the First Amendment
Virginia v. Black

James L. Swanson

Americans love to speak not only through their words, but through expressive conduct, often called symbolic speech. In the twentieth century, people have expressed themselves by displaying the red flag as a symbol of international revolution,[1] by incorporating the Confederate stars and bars battle flag into the official flags of several southern states to symbolize opposition to desegregation,[2] by pledging allegiance to the national flag of the United States—or by refusing to,[3] by defacing the national flag,[4] by wearing clothing[5] and armbands[6] to protest the Vietnam War, by sit-ins, marches, and even by sleeping in Lafayette Park in sight of the White House.[7] Indeed, one can hardly think of the civil rights or anti-Vietnam War movements without visualizing the memorable acts that symbolized them.

Of all mediums of symbolic expression, Americans have displayed an especial affection for fire. Throughout our history we have burned things to communicate a message. Hanging and burning in effigy one's enemies was a traditional, albeit alarming, form of American political protest, particularly in the eighteenth and nineteenth centuries. In 1794, when John Jay returned to the United States after

---

[1]Stromberg v. California, 283 U.S. 359 (1931).

[2]For a discussion of the revival of the Confederate flag, *see* GEORGE SCHEDLER, RACIST SYMBOLS AND REPARATIONS (1998).

[3]West Virginia State Board of Education v. Barnette, 319 U.S. 624 (1943).

[4]Spence v. Washington, 418 U.S. 405 (1974) (per curiam); Smith v. Goguen, 415 U.S. 566 (1974).

[5]Schact v. United States, 398 U.S. 58 (1970).

[6]Tinker v. Des Moines School District, 393 U.S. 503 (1969).

[7]Clark v. Community for Creative Non-Violence, 468 U.S. 288 (1984).

negotiating the unpopular treaty that bears his name, he was so vilified that he said that he could find his way home in the dark from the number of burning effigies that illuminated the roads. In the nineteenth century John Brown, William Lloyd Garrison, and Abraham Lincoln were hanged or burned in effigy as hated enemies of slavery. In the presidential campaign of 1860, clubs of young men called "Wide-Awakes" marched at night carrying blazing torches atop tall poles in support of their candidate Abraham Lincoln. Five years later Washington, D.C. celebrated victory in the Civil War with a "grand illuminination" of the city created by thousands of torches, flares, and explosions.[8] More recently Americans protested another war by burning draft cards[9] and flags,[10] and feminists demonstrated for equal rights by burning bras. After President Kennedy's assassination his grave was marked by fire—an eternal flame. Americans have used fire to communicate a multitude of ideas: political support or protest, military victory, remembrance, shared ideology, dissent, patriotism, joy, inspiration—and hate. Of all the fiery symbols in American history, one stands out as the most notorious and the most feared—the burning cross.

For the past eighty-eight years, ever since the first recorded cross burning in the United States in 1915, that flaming object has been the trademark of one group—the Ku Klux Klan.[11] To the members of the Klan, that symbol represents an ideology of white supremacy and racial solidarity. To African Americans, the burning cross symbolizes a sinister history of toxic racism reaching back to the Civil War.[12] To this audience, a cross aflame also symbolizes danger: threats, arson, violence, robed night riders, lynchings, and murder.[13]

---

[8] JAMES L. SWANSON & DANIEL R. WEINBERG, LINCOLN'S ASSASSINS: THEIR TRIAL AND EXECUTION (2001).

[9] United States v. O'Brien, 391 U.S. 367 (1968).

[10] See, e.g., State v. Royal, 113 N.H. 224 (1973); State v. Waterman, 190 N.W. 2d 809 (1971); State v. Mitchell, 32 Ohio App. 2d 16 (1972). For a flag burning to protest the murder of civil rights figure James Meredith, see Street v. New York, 394 U.S. 576 (1969).

[11] American cross burning has a fictional origin. Thomas Dixon's 1905 novel, THE CLANSMAN: AN HISTORICAL ROMANCE, fantasized a cross burning Ku Klux Klan. The 1915 film "Birth of a Nation," which was based on the novel, depicted a fictional cross burning, and that imagery inspired the real Klan to adopt the ritual.

[12] Although the Klan did not burn its first cross until 1915, fifty years after the Civil War ended, the symbol became so powerful that it came to represent in the popular mind a reign of terror that began shortly after the end of the war.

[13] For a history of these crimes, see STETSON KENNEDY, SOUTHERN EXPOSURE (1946); RICHARD KLUGER, SIMPLE JUSTICE (1975); WYN CRAIG WADE, THE FIERY CROSS: THE KU KLUX KLAN IN AMERICA (1988); NANCY K. MACLEAN, BEHIND THE MASK OF CHIVALRY: THE MAKING OF THE SECOND KU KLUX KLAN (1994).

From the outset, the image of rampaging, cross burning Klansmen was considered potentially explosive. D. W. Griffith's 1915 motion picture *Birth of a Nation*, an adaptation of Thomas Dixon's 1905 novel, *The Clansman*, provoked several jurisdictions to censor the film, fearing that screenings would incite race riots.[14] In time a number of states banned cross burnings, including Virginia, which passed a statute against it.[15]

In 2003, the Supreme Court of the United States ruled on the constitutionality of that statute. In *Virginia v. Black*,[16] the Court struggled with how much one can suppress conduct without banning expression. We have a long history of protecting speech that we hate, even when that speech comes close to causing real harm. There is no question that a burning cross is a combination of speech and conduct, and that the symbol can convey ideas and intimidation. In *Virginia v. Black* the Court found burning a cross to be sufficiently different to allow restrictions that would otherwise be prohibited by the First Amendment. In so doing, the Court applied an unsatisfactory ad hoc test that might lead to the suppression of not only intimidation, but ideas. It was a hard question to balance, and the best answer might be to ban not just cross burning, but *all* intimidation. That solution will serve the interests of the First Amendment best.

Background

Virginia v. Black arose from two separate incidents that resulted in convictions under Virginia's cross burning statute, which provides

---

[14] *See* EDWARD DE GRAZIA & ROGER K. NEWMAN, BANNED FILMS: MOVIES CENSORS AND THE FIRST AMENDMENT 3–6, 180–183 (1982). Fearing that the film would be suppressed, Dixon screened the film at the White House for his old friend, President Woodrow Wilson, and members of the Cabinet. "It is like history written with lightning," said Wilson. The next day Dixon prevailed upon Chief Justice Edward Douglass White, a former Klan member, to view the film that night at the Raleigh Hotel in Washington. White, the justices, and members of Congress attended the screening.

[15] Brief of Amici Curiae of the States New Jersey, Arizona, Connecticut, Iowa, Maryland, Massachusetts, Michigan, Nebraska, Nevada, North Carolina, Oklahoma, Oregon, Utah, and Vermont, Virginia v. Black, 123 S. Ct. 1536 (2003) (No. 01-1107).

[16] Virginia v. Black, 123 S. Ct. 1536 (2003).

> It shall be unlawful for any person or persons, with the intent of intimidating any person or group of persons, to burn, or cause to be burned, a cross on the property of another, a highway or other public place. Any person who shall violate any provision of this section shall be guilty of a Class 6 felony.
>
> Any such burning of a cross shall be prima facie evidence of an intent to intimidate a person or group of persons.[17]

In the first incident, on the night of May 2, 1998, Richard Elliott, Jonathan O'Mara and David Targee attempted to burn a small, hastily constructed cross in the front yard of Elliott's neighbor, James Jubilee, an African American. Elliott wanted to "get back" at Jubilee for complaining to Elliott's mother about gunshots being fired in the Elliott backyard target range. The cross burning trio entered Jubilee's property, erected the cross, splashed it with lighter fluid and set it ablaze. Jubilee did not witness the burning cross, but the next morning he noticed a partially burned cross about 20 feet from his house. Jubilee seized the cross, secured it in his garage, and summoned the police. Elliott and O'Mara were arrested and charged with cross burning and conspiracy to commit cross burning. Although they were not connected to the Ku Klux Klan, Elliott and O'Mara did, prior to the cross burning, refer to Jubilee's race. O'Mara pleaded guilty to both counts but reserved the right to challenge the constitutionality of the statute. He was sentenced to 90 days in jail (of which 45 were suspended) and fined $2,500.00 (which was reduced to $1,500.00). Elliott was tried, convicted and sentenced to 90 days in jail and a $2,500.00 fine. The Court of Appeals of Virginia affirmed both convictions.[18]

In the second incident, which occurred on August 22, 1998, the fact pattern was quite different than in the first. Barry Black led a Ku Klux Klan rally not in a targeted victim's yard, but on private property with the permission—indeed the participation—of the owner. That property was a semi-secluded open field near a state highway, with eight to ten houses in the area. Twenty-five to thirty people participated in the rally, which included Klan members speaking to each other about their beliefs, about their dislike of

---

[17] *Id.* at 1541, 1542 (O'Connor, J.).
[18] *Id.* at 1543.

blacks and Mexicans, about Bill and Hillary Clinton, and about how their tax money goes to black people.[19]

At the rally's climax the Klan members formed a circle around a 25-to 30-foot-tall cross, set it on fire, and played a recording of *Amazing Grace*. At that point the local sheriff, who had observed the cross burning from the state highway 300 to 350 yards away, entered the property. Black was charged under the Virginia statute with burning a cross to intimidate a person or group of persons. At trial the jury was instructed that "intent to intimidate means the motivation to intentionally put a person or group of people in bodily fear of harm," and also that "the burning of a cross by itself" is sufficient evidence to infer the required intent.[20] Black was found guilty, fined $2,500.00, and his conviction was confirmed by the state Court of Appeals.

On appeal the Supreme Court of Virginia consolidated the cases and held that the cross burning statute was "facially unconstitutional because it prohibits otherwise permitted speech solely on the basis of its content, and the statute is overbroad."[21] The Virginia Supreme Court reasoned that the statute was "analytically indistinguishable" from the ordinance that the Supreme Court of the United States found unconstitutional several years earlier in another cross burning case, *R.A.V. v. St. Paul*[22]; that the statute engaged in improper content-and-viewpoint based discrimination because it "selectively chooses only cross burning because of its distinctive message"[23]; and because the statute's prima facie evidence provision condemns it as overbroad because "the enhanced probability of prosecution under the statute chills the expression of protected speech."[24]

The U.S. Supreme Court granted certiorari and heard oral argument on December 11, 2002.

Oral Argument

As soon as the U.S. Supreme Court granted certiorari, *Virginia v. Black* became one of the most eagerly anticipated cases of October

[19] *Id.* at 1542.
[20] *Id.*
[21] Black v. Commonwealth, 262 Va. 764, 768 (2001) (Lemons, J.).
[22] R.A.V. v. City of St. Paul, 505 U.S. 377 (1992).
[23] *Virginia v. Black*, 123 S. Ct. at 1543 (citations omitted).
[24] *Id.* (citations omitted).

Term 2002.[25] Although the Court hears several First Amendment cases each term, seldom does the subject matter of any case command as much widespread public attention as *Virginia v. Black*.[26] Court watchers expected a classic duel pitting the right to engage in unpopular speech against the desire to suppress it, and many assumed the Court would extend the principles of *Texas v. Johnson*[27] and *R.A.V. v. St. Paul*[28] and hold that the Virginia cross burning statute, like the regulations in the aforementioned cases, was impermissible, content-based discrimination against unpopular speech, and unconstitutional.

In one of the most unusual oral arguments of the term (for both what was said and how the press reported it) the justices surprised Court watchers by telegraphing that *Virginia v. Black* might not be an easy win for the First Amendment.[29] Given the recent precedents of *Texas v. Johnson* and *R.A.V. v. St. Paul*, plus a core collection of historic free speech cases, it was assumed by many that the Court would simply affirm the principle that the First Amendment requires us to tolerate even the speech that we hate, in order to safeguard

[25] *See, e.g.*, Linda Greenhouse, *Supreme Court Roundup: Free Speech or Hate Speech? Court Weighs Cross Burning*, N.Y. TIMES, May 29, 2002, at A18.

[26] It is easier for the public to grasp the idea of a burning cross than the more abstract ideas of library internet filtering in *United States v. American Library Association*, 123 S. Ct. 2297 (2003), or the political speech of non-profit organizations in *Federal Election Commission v. Beaumont*, 123 S. Ct. 2200 (2003), two other significant First Amendment cases in October Term 2002.

[27] Texas v. Johnson, 491 U.S. 397 (1989).

[28] R.A.V. v. City of St. Paul, 505 U.S. 377 (1992).

[29] *See e.g.*, Linda Greenhouse, *An Intense Attack by Justice Thomas on Cross Burning*, N.Y. TIMES, December 12, 2002, at A1; Charles Lane, *High Court Hears Thomas on KKK Rite; Justice Weighs in on Virginia Cross-Burning Ban*, WASH. POST, December 12, 2002; Joan Biskupic, *Cross-Burning Case Agitates Thomas*, USA TODAY, December 12, 2002, at 3A; Jan Crawford Greenburg, *Emotional Court Weighs Cross Burning: Thomas Speaks Against "Terror,"* CHICAGO TRIBUNE, December 12, 2002, at 10; David G. Savage, *Thomas Assails Cross Burning as Terror Tactic*, L.A. TIMES, December 12, 2002, at 41; Lyle Denniston, *Thomas Breaks Silence to Denounce Klan: Court Weighs Cross Burning*, BOSTON GLOBE, December 12, 2002, at A2; Dahlia Lithwick, *Personal Truths and Legal Fictions*, N.Y. TIMES, December 17, 2002, at A35. The fact that Justice Thomas spoke during oral argument so transfixed some commentators that they lost sight of the case. In a bizarre, and false, account Dahlia Lithwick asserted that in a "stunning" episode of "emotional outburst," Justice Thomas indulged in a "personal narrative" that she claimed might be "unforgivable." In fact there was no outburst. Instead Justice Thomas spoke quietly and courteously. Furthermore he related no personal narrative or experience.

the speech that we love. But several justices, led by Clarence Thomas, suggested through their questioning that the message of a burning cross was uniquely threatening, and might therefore qualify for unique treatment by the Court.

Justice Thomas, in an exchange with Michael Drebeen, deputy solicitor general arguing on behalf of the United States, as amicus curiae supporting the State of Virginia, suggested that Drebeen could make an even stronger case in support of the statute. "[M]y fear is . . . that you're actually understating the symbolism of . . . the burning cross."[30] Recalling nearly a century of lynchings Thomas argued that "this was a reign of terror and the cross was a symbol of that reign of terror," then asked, "isn't that significantly greater than intimidation or a threat?"[31] The burning cross, concluded Thomas, "is unlike any other symbol in our society,"[32] and it was used "to terrorize a population."[33]

Justice O'Connor asked Rodney Smolla, arguing on behalf of the respondents, "why isn't this just a regulation of a particularly virulent form of intimidation? And why can't the State regulate such things?"[34] Smolla responded that cross burning is not a particularly virulent form of intimidation. That prompted an instantaneous rejoinder from O'Connor: "Well, it *is* for the very reasons we've explored this morning. What if I think it is?"[35]

Justice Scalia suggested that a burning cross was more intimidating than a loaded gun. "If you were a black man at night, you'd rather see a man with a rifle than see a burning cross on your front lawn."[36]

Of course it is always perilous—and potentially embarrassing—to read the tea leaves of a Supreme Court oral argument. Justices often play the devil's advocate, and can appear by their questions to be hostile to their true position in the case. But the oral argument

---

[30] In the Supreme Court of the United States, Virginia v. Black, No. 01-1107, transcript of oral argument, Dec. 11, 2002, at 23. (Hereinafter cited as "Transcript.")

[31] *Id.*

[32] *Id.*

[33] *Id.* at 24.

[34] *Id.* at 31.

[35] *Id.*

[36] *Id.* at 30.

in *Virginia v. Black* proved, in retrospect, to be remarkably accurate by suggesting that the case could go either way; by revealing that some members of the Court questioned not only whether cross burning was protected speech, but whether it was speech at all; and by hinting that the Court found hate speech and threatening speech to be a troublesome area in which it had reached no consensus or general theory.

The Opinion

Reflecting the diversity of views that they expressed at oral argument, 5 justices wrote separately in *Virginia v. Black* and decided discreet issues in the case by votes of 6 to 3, 7 to 2, and 8 to 1. In the main holding, the Court held 6 to 3, with Justice O'Connor writing for the majority, and Chief Justice Rehnquist and Justices Scalia, Breyer, Stevens, and Thomas in agreement, that cross burning was "a particularly virulent form of expression" that could be singled out by the state for regulation.[37] Three justices, Souter, Ginsburg, and Kennedy dissented. At the same time, 7 justices—O'Connor, Rehnquist, Breyer, Stevens, Souter, Ginsburg and Kennedy—agreed that the Virginia cross burning statute was unconstitutional. The first four justices so holding because its prima facie evidence provision failed to exempt those circumstances when cross burning was done *not* to intimidate and *could* qualify as protected speech, and the last three justices so holding because the statute was unconstitutional anyway, even without taking the prima facie provision into account. Justices Scalia and Thomas disagreed with the majority on this issue and concluded that the statutory inference of intent was constitutional. Eight justices agreed that, regardless of whether cross burning was symbolic speech protected by the First Amendment, there was no doubt that at least it was speech, and that any attempt to regulate it triggered First Amendment scrutiny of some kind. Only Justice Thomas disagreed: "[T]hose who hate cannot terrorize and intimidate to make their point. In light of my conclusion that the statute here addresses only conduct, there is no need to analyze it under any of our First Amendment tests."[38]

---

[37] Virginia v. Black, 123 S. Ct. 1536, 1549 (2003).
[38] *Id.* at 1566.

The multiple writings, shifting coalitions, and partial dissents that comprised the opinion were confusing enough to prompt seasoned *New York Times* Supreme Court correspondent Linda Greenhouse to observe that *Virginia v. Black* "produced a range of opinions more amenable to a chart than to a verbal description."[39]

Justice O'Connor's opinion has three central themes. First, cross burning does not enjoy a per se First Amendment immunity from state regulation. Second, although cross burning can be regulated, not all cross burning can be prohibited. Third, although cross burning enjoys some First Amendment protection, there is something unique about cross burning that justifies treating it as a true threat, different from any other form of speech.

Justice O'Connor wrote that not all cross burnings are the same, and she catalogued three types with three different purposes: to communicate a shared "group identity and ideology"[40] among members of the Klan; to anger other people; or to serve as a "message of intimidation, designed to inspire in the victim a fear of bodily harm."[41]

Regarding the first type, O'Connor characterized cross burning as, for members of the Klan, "a sign of celebration and ceremony . . . a symbol of Klan ideology and Klan unity."[42] She stated that "a burning cross is not always intended to intimidate. Rather, sometimes the cross burning is a statement of ideology, a symbol of group solidarity. It is a ritual used at Klan gatherings, and it is used to represent the Klan itself."[43] In support of her position that this type of cross burning can qualify as core political speech, she quoted Justice White's comment in *R.A.V. v. St. Paul* that "burning a cross at a political rally would almost certainly be protected expression."[44]

Regarding the second type of cross burning, one that angers others, Justice O'Connor wrote, "It may be true that a cross burning, even at a political rally, arouses a sense of anger or hatred among the

[39] Linda Greenhouse, *Justices Allow Bans on Cross Burnings Intended as Threats*, N.Y. TIMES, April 8, 2003, at A1.

[40] *Virginia v. Black*, 123 S. Ct. at 1546.

[41] *Id.*

[42] *Id.*

[43] *Id.* at 1551.

[44] *Id.*

vast majority of citizens who see a burning cross. But this sense of anger or hatred is not sufficient to ban all cross burnings."[45] True, concedes Justice O'Connor, there remains the so-called "fighting words" doctrine from the vintage case *Chaplinsky v. New Hampshire*,[46] which purports that speech likely to provoke a violent response may be proscribed under the First Amendment. But later precedents diluted the authority of *Chaplinsky* and, while the Court has never overruled it, *Chaplinsky* has certainly been marginalized and might be viewed today as an ill-advised endorsement of the "heckler's veto."[47]

It is the third type of cross burning, done to intimidate others, that troubles Justice O'Connor. In a concise history of the practice, she recounts the violence of the Klan and how cross burning became intimately associated with "bombings, beatings, shootings, stabbings, and mutilations."[48] The cross is a symbol of hate, "designed to inspire in the victim a fear of bodily harm . . . the history of violence associated with the Klan shows that the possibility of injury or death is not just hypothetical . . . often the cross burner intends that the recipients of the message fear for their lives."[49] Indeed, concludes Justice O'Connor, "when a cross burning is used to intimidate, few if any messages are more powerful."[50]

Given this history, Justice O'Connor concluded that "the First Amendment permits Virginia to outlaw cross burnings with the intent to intimidate because burning a cross is a particularly virulent form of intimidation."[51] The Constitution does not require Virginia to choose between prohibiting all intimidating messages or none at all. Instead, "a state may choose to prohibit only those forms of intimidation that are likely to inspire fear of bodily harm."[52] Therefore, "Virginia may choose to regulate this subset of intimidating

---

[45] *Id.*

[46] Chaplinsky v. New Hampshire, 315 U.S. 568 (1942).

[47] *Chaplinsky* has since been narrowed by several important cases, including *Cohen v. California*, 403 U.S. 15 (1971).

[48] *Virginia v. Black*, 123 S. Ct. at 1545.

[49] *Id.* at 1546, 1547.

[50] *Id.* at 1547.

[51] *Id.* at 1549.

[52] *Id.* at 1549, 1550.

messages in light of cross burning's long and pernicious history as a signal of impending violence."[53]

But Virginia went too far by including in the statute a "prima facie evidence" provision that permits a jury to convict in every cross burning case, "based solely on the fact of cross burning itself."[54] The prima facie clause made cross burning into a kind of strict liability crime that made the statute unconstitutional on its face. As Justice O'Connor stated

> The prima facie provision makes no effort to distinguish among these different types of cross burnings. It does not distinguish between a cross burning done with the purpose of threatening or intimidating a victim. It does not distinguish between a cross burning at a public rally or a cross burning on a neighbor's lawn. It does not treat the cross burning directed at an individual differently from the cross burning directed at a group of like-minded believers... The prima facie evidence provision in this case ignores all of the contextual factors that are necessary to decide whether a particular cross burning is intended to intimidate. The First Amendment does not permit such a shortcut.[55]

As a result, the U.S. Supreme Court affirmed the judgment of the Supreme Court of Virginia that the cross burning statute was unconstitutional.

The Dissents

Justice Thomas—The First Amendment Need Not Apply

Although Justice Thomas agreed with the majority that it is constitutional to ban cross burning with the intent to intimidate, he argued that the majority failed to go far enough. He would have upheld the statute and, beyond that, would have allowed Virginia to ban all cross burning, with or without intent. "[T]he majority errs in imparting an expressive component to the activity in question....

---

[53] *Id.* at 1549.
[54] *Id.* at 1551.
[55] *Id.*

In my view, whatever expressive value cross burning has, the legislature simple wrote it out by banning only intimidating conduct undertaken by a particular means."[56]

Thomas argued that the Ku Klux Klan is a "terrorist organization," that there exists a "connection between cross burning and violence," and that a burning cross is "now widely viewed as a signal of impending terror and lawlessness."[57] He concluded that the Virginia statute prohibited merely conduct, not constitutionally protected expression, and reasoned that "just as one cannot burn down someone's house to make a political point and then seek refuge in the First Amendment, those who hate cannot terrorize and intimidate to make their point. In light of my conclusion that the statute here addresses only conduct, there is no need to analyze it under any of our First Amendment tests."[58]

Thomas was untroubled by the prima facie evidence provision, which he and Justice Scalia treated as a mere presumption, rebuttable at trial. Still, Thomas admonished the plurality for "lament[ing] the fate of an innocent cross burner, who burns a cross, but does so without an intent to intimidate."[59] He noted that the Virginia General Assembly had already resolved that issue. "The legislature finds the behavior so reprehensible that the intent is satisfied by the mere act committed by a perpetrator. Considering the horrific effect cross burning has on its victims, it is also reasonable to presume intent to intimidate from the act itself."[60]

Thomas suggests that the Court could have easily upheld the Virginia statute by analyzing cross burning as a case of "unwanted communication" of the sort that the Court dealt with in the abortion clinic case *Hill v. Colorado*.[61] There the Court upheld as narrowly tailored a restriction that protected patients in "vulnerable physical and emotional conditions" from "unwanted advice" and "unwanted communication"[62] from anti-abortion protestors.

---

[56] *Virginia v. Black*, 123 S. Ct. at 1563 (Thomas, J., dissenting).

[57] *Id.* at 1563, 1564.

[58] *Id.* at 1566.

[59] *Id.* at 1568.

[60] *Id.*

[61] Hill v. Colorado, 530 U.S. 703 (2000).

[62] *Virginia v. Black*, 123 S. Ct. at 1568, 1569.

Thomas concludes his dissent with a paradox. "That cross burning subjects its targets, and, sometimes, an unintended audience . . . to extreme emotional distress, and is virtually never viewed merely as 'unwanted communication,' but rather as a physical threat, is of no concern to the plurality. Henceforth, under the plurality's view, physical safety will be valued less than the right to be free from unwanted communications."[63]

Justice Scalia—The First Amendment, to a Degree

Justice Scalia agreed with the Court that, under *R.A.V. v. St. Paul,* a state may prohibit cross burning carried out with the intent to intimidate. But he disagreed that Virginia's statute was facially invalid and, in a partial dissent, argued that "the prima facie evidence provision in Virginia's cross burning statute is constitutionally unproblematic."[64] Scalia criticizes the court for engaging in "unprecedented" overbreadth analysis. "We have never held that the mere threat that individuals who engage in protected conduct will be subject to arrest and prosecution suffices to render a statute overbroad. Rather, our jurisprudence has consistently focused on whether the *prohibitory terms* of a particular statute extend to protected conduct."[65] Scalia concedes that the plurality is correct that cross burning done without the intent to intimidate can be protected speech, but that, under the statute, such a cross burner might nonetheless be arrested, prosecuted, and convicted. "[S]ome individuals who engage in protected speech, may, because of the prima-facie-evidence provision, be subject to conviction."[66] But the appropriate response, says Scalia, is not for the Supreme Court to declare the statute facially invalid. Rather, "[s]uch convictions, assuming they are unconstitutional, could be challenged on a case-by-case basis."[67]

Justice Souter—The First Amendment, Unabashed

Justice Souter, joined by justices Kennedy and Ginsburg, agreed with the judgment of the Court that the Virginia statute was unconstitutional, but went beyond Justice O'Connor's opinion and said

[63] *Id.* at 1569.
[64] *Id.* at 1558 (Scalia, J.).
[65] *Id.* at 1554.
[66] *Id.*
[67] *Id.*

that the statute was unconstitutional even without the prima facie evidence provision. Souter, Kennedy, and Ginsburg dissented from the majority's view that cross burning with the intent to intimidate could be banned. Instead, the dissenters argued that cross burning is protected speech, that the statute engaged in content-based discrimination that failed to qualify for an exception under *R.A.V.*, and that no "exception should save Virginia's law from unconstitutionality under the holding of *R.A.V.* or any acceptable variation of it."[68] According to Justice Souter, "the specific prohibition of cross burning with intent to intimidate selects a symbol with particular content from the field of all possible expression meant to intimidate."[69] Although Souter concedes that content can include an intimidating message of possible physical harm, and he acknowledges the historical association of cross burning with arson, beating, and lynching, he insists that cross burning also contains an ideological message from which it cannot be divorced. "But even when the symbolic act is meant to terrify, a burning cross may carry a further ideological message of white Protestant supremacy."[70]

Souter applies an *R.A.V.* analysis to test whether the statute falls under *R.A.V.*'s "general condemnation of limited content-based proscription within a broader category of expression proscribable generally."[71] *R.A.V.* recognizes that certain types of speech are not protected by the First Amendment and that even within those categories of speech a state may engage in content discrimination only so long as such discrimination "consists entirely of the very reason the entire class of speech at issue is proscribable."[72] According to Souter, *R.A.V.* recognizes as constitutional those content-based subclasses of proscribable expression when the prohibition by subcategory "is made 'entirely' on the 'basis' of 'the very reason' that 'the entire class of speech at issue is proscribable' at all."[73]

According to Justice Souter, when Virginia rejected "a general prohibition of intimidation . . . in favor of a distinct proscription of

---

[68] *Virginia v. Black*, 123 S. Ct. at 1559 (Souter, J.).

[69] *Id.*

[70] *Id.*

[71] *Id.*

[72] *Id.*

[73] *Id.* at 1560.

intimidation by cross burning," that indicated discrimination on the basis of the message conveyed.[74] "The cross may have been selected because of its special power to threaten, but it may also have been singled out because of disapproval of its message of white supremacy, either because a legislature thought white supremacy was a pernicious doctrine or because it found that dramatic, public espousal of it was a civic embarrassment."[75]

Discussion

To summarize, in *Virginia v. Black* a divided Court overturned a state statute that outlawed cross burning. The Court concluded that sometimes the First Amendment protects cross burning, but when done to intimidate others, cross burning is a "particularly virulent" form of indimidation that can be banned. The Court was right to affirm that the First Amendment protects symbolic speech, cross burning is a type of such speech, and the Virginia statute that banned it was unconstitutional. But in holding that cross burning with the intent to intimidate can be proscribed, the Court failed to draw a sufficiently clear line between protected and unprotected speech. Moreover, the Court condoned content-based discrimination and chilled protected expression.

The opinion was a confusing combination of majority and plurality votes, concurrences in the judgment, partial and full dissents, and arguments about whether cross burning was speech in the first place. The justices achieved consensus on but one issue: that the burning of a cross merits unique treatment by the Court. That view might restrain the Court from proscribing other forms of offensive or threatening speech. But even if thus limited, *Virginia v. Black* raises profound questions about the very purpose of the First Amendment and the circumstances under which individuals can be protected from offensive or threatening expression.

The Legitimacy of Symbolic Speech

The idea that expressive conduct can qualify as speech, once a novel concept in American law, is today so well accepted that Justice O'Connor did not feel it necessary in her opinion to argue in support

[74] *Id.*
[75] *Id.*

•

of the concept. And no justice questioned the doctrine at oral argument or in the opinions. As Justice Brennan stated in *Texas v. Johnson*, "[t]he First Amendment literally forbids the abridgement only of 'speech,' but we have long recognized that its protection does not end at the spoken or written word."[76] Before determining whether a type of conduct merits First Amendment protection, the Court will, according to Brennan, apply a threshold test. "We have asked whether '[a]n intent to convey a particularized message was present, and [whether] the likelihood was great that the message would be understood by those who viewed it.'"[77] Under this test the Court has recognized a number of acts as symbolic speech, including "the expressive nature of students wearing black armbands to protest American military involvement in Vietnam . . . of a sit-in by blacks in a 'whites only' area to protest segregation . . . of the wearing of American military uniforms in a dramatic presentation criticizing American involvement in Vietnam . . . of picketing about a wide variety of causes . . . [of] attaching a peace sign to the flag . . . refusing to salute the flag . . . and displaying a red flag."[78]

Cross burning easily satisfies both prongs of the test set forth by Brennan and is, therefore, expressive conduct. Indeed, the argument of those who seek to ban the practice is that at least part of the message is understood all too well by those who view it.

Expressive Conduct Not Necessarily Protected Expression

Just because conduct can be expressive does not mean, of course, that all forms of symbolic speech are immunized by the First Amendment. Otherwise, as Judge Posner pointed out, a political assassin like John Wilkes Booth could claim that murdering Abraham Lincoln was protected "speech."[79] Similarly, as Justice Stevens argued, vandals could deface the Lincoln Memorial or Washington Monument, or extinguish the eternal flame at John F. Kennedy's grave, and claim that their crimes were acts of protected political speech.[80]

---

[76] *Texas v. Johnson*, 491 U.S. at 404 (Brennan, J.).

[77] *Id.*, quoting Spence v. Washington, 418 U.S. 405, at 410–411.

[78] *Texas v. Johnson* at 404 (Brennan, J.) (citations omitted).

[79] United States v. Soderna, 82 F. 3d 1370, 1375 (7th Cir. 1996) ("[K]illing a political opponent invades a right of personal liberty at the same time that it makes a political statement, as in the case of John Wilkes Booth's killing of Abraham Lincoln. The distinction is engraved in the case law interpreting the First Amendment.").

[80] *Texas v. Johnson*, 491 U.S. at 437–439 (Stevens, J., dissenting).

In the draft card burning case, *United States v. O'Brien*,[81] Chief Justice Earl Warren wrote that "we cannot accept the view that an apparently limitless variety of conduct can be labeled 'speech' whenever the person engaging in the conduct intends thereby to express an idea."[82] To evaluate conduct that combines "speech" and "nonspeech" elements, and to decide when "a sufficiently important governmental interest in regulating the nonspeech element can justify incidental limitations on First Amendment freedoms,"[83] the Court announced what became known as the "O'Brien test." The Court held that a government regulation is sufficiently justified

> [I]f it is within the constitutional power of the Government; if it furthers an important or substantial governmental interest; if the governmental interest is unrelated to the suppression of free expression; and if the incidental restriction on alleged First Amendment freedoms is no greater than is essential to the furtherance of that interest.[84]

Because the O'Brien test could, if applied improperly, suppress protected expression, the Court noted in *Texas v. Johnson* that "we have limited the applicability of *O'Brien*'s relatively lenient standard to those cases in which 'the governmental interest is unrelated to the suppression of free expression.'"[85] Therefore, in order to decide whether the *O'Brien* test should apply to cross burning, it becomes necessary to know whether a ban on cross burning is unrelated to the suppression of expression. If the interest in banning cross burning is related to expression, then we are outside of the *O'Brien* test and "under a more demanding standard."[86] The Court was right in *Virginia v. Black* to conclude that the statute was inextricably involved in suppressing expression and was correct, therefore, to refrain from invoking the O'Brien test to uphold the statute. Virginia had not banned cross burning for a nonspeech purpose of preventing forest fires, fighting global warming, or conserving scarce wood and fuel.

---

[81] United States v. O'Brien, 391 U.S. 367 (1968).

[82] *Id.* at 376 (Warren, C.J.).

[83] *Id.*

[84] *Id.* at 377.

[85] *Texas v. Johnson*, 491 U.S. at 397.

[86] *Id.* at 403.

On the contrary, Virginia sought to suppress the powerful message that cross burning expressed.

An Unconstitutional Statute

The Court was right to declare the Virginia statute unconstitutional. Indeed, it had to. The statute had announced that *only* cross burnings done with the intent to intimidate others were felonies. But then the statute declared that *all* cross burnings were prima facie evidence of that intent. The language of the statute implied the existence of a larger universe of cross burnings in which those carried out with the intent to intimidate were but one subcategory. Nevertheless, the statute went on to say that all categories of cross burning could be prosecuted. Once Justice O'Connor divided the universe of cross burnings into three categories 1) those that expressed ideology and group solidarity, 2) those that offended or angered people, and 3) those that put people in fear of bodily harm, and once she announced that the first two categories were protected by the First Amendment, it was obvious that the statute punished protected expression and was, thus, overbroad. At that point the Court had no choice but to, under its own well established precedents, declare the statute unconstitutional. That result is unremarkable. What is remarkable, however, is what the Court did next.

A Limited Holding

The Court was quick to limit its holding. Just because this particular statute was unconstitutional did not mean that it was open season for cross burners to pursue their hobby. Once Justice O'Connor's opinion overturned the statute, it announced a second holding: cross burning can still be banned. "The First Amendment permits Virginia to outlaw cross burnings with the intent to intimidate because burning a cross is a virulent form of intimidation."[87] But what exactly did "intimidate" mean?

The Court had the option of turning to at least three doctrines—fighting words, incitement, and true threats—to support that holding. Justice O'Connor gave short shrift to the first two. Having already despatched the *O'Brien* test, she did the same to the *Chaplinsky*[88] fighting words test and the *Brandenburg*[89] incitement test by

[87] *Virginia v. Black*, 123 S. Ct. at 1549 (O'Connor, J.).

[88] Chaplinsky v. New Hampshire, 315 U.S. 568 (1942).

[89] Brandenburg v. Ohio, 395 U.S. 444 (1968).

citing them and moving on. Under *Chaplinsky*, speech directed at a particular individual with the intention to "incite an immediate breach of the peace" can be proscribed as fighting words.[90] This doctrine does not apply to cross burning. The intent of cross burners might be to awe their victims into submission and fear, but it is certainly not to provoke them to come out and fight. And certainly the intent of the Virginia Assembly when it passed the cross burning statute was not to prevent breaches of the peace by viewers of the cross. Moreover, "words and symbols do not become fighting words merely because the speaker deeply offends the listeners."[91]

Under *Brandenburg*, expression cannot be proscribed unless the speaker incites imminent lawless action, which explains why the Court reversed the conviction of a Ku Klux Klan leader who advocated possible violence at some future time.[92] In an incitement case, the imminence element is strict, and speech cannot be suppressed unless it threatens to incite violence at that moment, or almost immediately. A cross burning alone, without the existence of additional factors (such as a cross burner screaming to a mob of his followers "let's get them now!") does not rise to this level of incitement. Indeed, at oral argument counsel for Virginia conceded the distance between *Brandenburg* and cross burning by stating that a long period of time might elapse between a cross burning and violence.[93]

So, after moving past fighting words and incitement, Justice O'Connor rested her holding on the last of the three doctrines, "true threat." As she stated in her opinion, "'True threats' encompass those statements where the speaker means to communicate a serious expression of an intent to commit an act of unlawful violence to a particular individual or group of individuals."[94] More precisely, Justice O'Connor explained

---

[90]*Chaplinsky*, 315 U.S. at 572.

[91]Ronald D. Rotunda, *A Brief Comment on Politically Incorrect Speech in the Wake of R.A.V.*, 47 SMU Law Review 9, 15 (1993).

[92]In *Brandenburg*, a Klan leader invited a television station to film a Klan rally at a farm. In a speech that was filmed and shown later, the speaker said "[w]e're not a revengent organization, but if our President, our Congress, our Supreme Court, continues to suppress the white, Caucasian race, it's possible that there might have to be some revengence taken." 395 U.S. at 446.

[93]Transcript at 10.

[94]*Virginia v. Black*, 123 S. Ct. at 1548 (O'Connor, J.).

> Intimidation in the constitutionally proscribable sense of the word is a type of true threat, where a speaker directs a threat to a person or a group of persons with the intent of placing the victim in fear of bodily harm or death. Respondents do not contest that some cross burnings fit within this meaning of intimidating speech, and rightly so . . . the history of cross burning in this country shows that cross burning is often intimidating, intended to create a pervasive fear in victims that they are a target of violence.[95]

An Imprecise Rule?

The result in *Virginia v. Black* is the product of one of Justice O'Connor's trademark methods of constitutional analysis, which is to focus on the particular facts and circumstances of each case, much in the manner of a common law judge. Rather than seeking opportunities to make sweeping pronouncements, she prefers to approach issues on a case by case basis, scrutinizing the facts and context. Thus, one must not ignore "all of the contextual factors that are necessary to decide whether a particular cross burning is intended to intimidate."[96] She used that as a limiting principle to proscribe as little cross burning as necessary to protect people from fear of injury or death.

But the "true threat" rule is susceptible to expansive interpretation that might chill protected expression. What evidence shall be deemed sufficient proof of an intent to intimidate? Cross burners are unlikely to furnish self-incriminating testimony about their hateful plans. Absent that, is intent proved whenever any witness to a cross burning testifies that he or she was afraid? Or, should we presume intent if a "reasonable man" would have known that a cross burning was likely to intimidate people? Does burning a cross in any place that African Americans can see it demonstrate intent to intimidate? The Virginia statute suggested so. Recall that the statute covered cross burnings "on the property of another, a highway or other public place." At oral argument, counsel for Virginia explained that "public place" meant any place from which a burning cross could be seen, including the private property of the cross burner. After *Virginia v. Black*, a careful cross burner who seeks to express an ideology but not

---

[95] *Id.*
[96] *Id.* at 1551.

to intimidate others, and who wishes to avoid prosecution, would be wise to burn a cross in a remote and secret place far from any accidental witnesses. One effect of *Virginia v. Black* might be to chill expression by driving all cross burning underground and out of the public square. That may be good social policy, but it is not good constitutional law.

If the Court's holding does not provide all the answers, neither does First Amendment extremism that would advocate the right to unfettered cross burning any time and any place and would pervert the "freedom of speech" into a weapon of true intimidation. But no one can agree that the Constitution allows members of the Ku Klux Klan to trespass upon an African American family's property, stand in front of their home, and ignite a cross in their front yard.

And what of Justice Thomas, in lone dissent arguing that cross burning is not expression and should not, therefore, be analyzed under any First Amendment test? Much of his dissent rings true. It *was* a reign of terror, even more hateful, violent, and monstrous than his dissent, Justice O'Connor's opinion, the briefs of the parties, or the oral argument suggested.[97] The robe, the noose, and the flaming cross will remain eternal symbols of the century-long journey from slavery to freedom that began at the end of the Civil War. Thomas is right that there is no more explosive symbol in America today, and he is right to conclude that racial supremacists must not be allowed to with impunity burn crosses that place people in fear of life and limb. But denying that the burning cross has symbolic, expressive meaning is mistaken, and not necessary to protect people from intimidation and true threats. Recognizing that cross burning is expressive conduct does not mean that it will *always* be protected, but likewise it means that it will not *never* be protected.

When, as in *Virginia v. Black*, so many justices write in a case, and speak in multiple voices concurring in the judgment, or in only part of the opinion, or dissenting in part, or in full, along with all other

---

[97] For the most shocking history of the reign of terror ever published, see JAMES ALLEN (Ed.), WITHOUT SANCTUARY: LYNCHING PHOTOGRAPHY IN AMERICA (2000). White mobs often burned African Americans alive, then distributed their bones among men, women, and even children as souvenirs of the festive occasion. Several thousand lynchings are known to have taken place, not counting many of which there is no record.

variants thereof, it often reflects that the Court is struggling to understand the core issues of the case, or cannot even agree on basic premises.

If that is true in *Virginia v. Black*, it is so because the Court, by singling out the cross for special treatment and proscription, engaged in content-based discrimination. In *R.A.V.* the Court overturned a cross burning ordinance that, in contrast to Virginia's statute, did "not single out for opprobrium only that speech directed toward 'one of the specified disfavored topics.'"[98] In other words, the inference of an intent to intimidate did not depend on the victim's race, gender, religion, political affiliation, union membership, homosexuality, or anything else. In other words, Virginia's statute passes constitutional muster because it is regarded as content-neutral. But therein lies the fatal logical trap. The history of cross burning proves that it served two predominant purposes: to express racial supremacy, and to terrorize African Americans.[99] *That* is why we single out cross burning as unique; that is what a cross aflame conjures up in the mind; and that is why Virginia banned it. But the content discrimination is not in *who* you hate, but the *fact* of your hatred, and by which symbol you use to express it.

By banning some types of cross burning, *Virginia v. Black* might serve as incentive to those who seek to ban other hated symbols and offensive words. The Supreme Court has singled out from the universe of all hated symbols one symbol, the burning cross, for unique treatment because it is a "particularly virulent" form of intimidation. Establishing one exception to the First Amendment sets the stage for the next. Isn't the Nazi swastika equally or even more virulent than the Klan's cross? The swastika remains a symbol of death to all Jews, and a totalitarian abomination to everyone else. It is hard to argue that the swastika is any less virulent a form of intimidation than the burning cross. How would the Supreme Court

---

[98] *Virginia v. Black*, 123 S. Ct. at 1549 (O'Connor, J.) (citation omitted).

[99] Although Justice O'Connor is correct that not all cross burnings have been directed at African Americans (Virginia v. Black 123 S. Ct. at 1549 (O'Connor, J.)), and that targets have included Jews, union leaders, lawyers, and others, history indicates that cross burning was created to target African Americans, and that they comprised the vast majority of victims.

decide today the notorious case of the Nazis in Skokie?[100] Is the swastika the next "particularly virulent" form of intimidation that should be banned? Although it is true that the "slippery slope" argument has become almost a cliché, one must be watchful for attempts to sanitize the public square from hateful symbols, words, and thoughts. Or will the Court's repeated emphasis on the uniqueness of the burning cross restrain the Court from proscribing other expression? Perhaps *Virginia v. Black* is a sui generis case of one.[101]

The most elegant solution is to recognize the burning cross for what it is: as a symbol that can never be divorced from its expressive conduct. Do not ban cross burning. Do not ban the burning of any object with the intent to intimidate, because the cross is still the real target of such a ban. Instead, ban *all* intimidating speech that threatens people with bodily harm or death. That rule will certainly proscribe some cross burnings, but not *because* they are cross burnings. That rule will cut through the Gordian knot that has tied up the Court, legislatures, and First Amendment theorists ever since *R.A.V.* Moreover, such a plan has ample support in the common law, and even in tort law. One could not argue that the common law of threats of bodily harm, or the private action of intentional infliction of emotional distress, violates the First Amendment. It is possible that a proscription against all intimidating speech might incidentally burden in total more speech than a proscription against cross burning alone. But it is the better choice to incidentally burden a greater volume of speech under a content-neutral law than to intentionally suppress less speech from content discrimination.

Oliver Wendell Holmes Jr. once wrote, "Great cases like hard cases make bad law. For great cases are called great, not because of their real importance in shaping the law of the future, but because of some accident or immediate overwhelming interest which appeals

---

[100]National Socialist Party of America v. Skokie, 432 U.S. 43 (1977) (per curiam). *See* DONALD DOWNS, NAZIS IN SKOKIE: FREEDOM, COMMUNITY AND THE FIRST AMENDMENT (1985); DAVID HAMLIN, THE NAZI/SKOKIE CONFLICT: A CIVIL LIBERTIES BATTLE (1980); ARYEH NEIER, DEFENDING MY ENEMY: AMERICAN NAZIS, THE SKOKIE CASE, AND THE RISKS OF FREEDOM (1979).

[101]The Supreme Court declined to review the so called "Nuremberg Files" case, involving a virulent anti-abortion website and alleged threats. In a 6–5 split, the 9th Circuit upheld a verdict against anti-abortion activists. Planned Parenthood of the Columbia/Willamette, Inc. v. American Coalition of Life Scientists, 290 F. 3d 1058 (9th Cir. 2003) (en banc).

to the feelings and distorts the judgment."[102] *Virginia v. Black* was an emotional case that resurrected memories of an infamous, racist era in America's not so distant past. Although the Court did not make "bad law," and made some good law, it could have made better law by treating cross burning in a content-neutral manner and not singling it out for unique treatment.

---

[102] Northern Securities Co. v. United States, 193 U.S. 197 (1904).

United States v. American Library Association: A Missed Opportunity for the Supreme Court to Clarify Application of First Amendment Law to Publicly Funded Expressive Institutions

Robert Corn-Revere

In *United States v. American Library Association* the Supreme Court rejected a First Amendment challenge to federal funding conditions set forth in the Children's Internet Protection Act (CIPA) that require the use of content filters to block pornographic images on Internet access terminals in public libraries.[1] The case confronted the difficult issues arising from public Internet access in libraries. While this phenomenon has obliterated the limitations of shelf space by making available to library patrons the virtually limitless information resources of the Internet and the World Wide Web, it also has provided access to information that, in a traditional collection policy, would rarely be selected by a librarian for inclusion in the stacks. This applies to much of the information on the Web, and not just pornography, since the medium is anything but selective. Accordingly, the case presented the question whether federal filtering requirements should be viewed as nothing more than an updated form of a typical book selection policy, or whether mandating the use of third-party software designed solely to exclude information from a vast medium is more akin to censorship. A majority of Justices viewed the filtering mandate as analogous to book selection, and in the process presented starkly different views about the nature and purpose of public libraries.

The decision in *American Library Association* resolved the immediate dispute as to the facial validity of CIPA, but the ruling may have

[1]United States v. American Library Association, 123 S. Ct. 2297 (2003).

105

raised more questions than it answered. The practical effect on the day-to-day administration of Internet access is speculative, since a majority of justices appeared to agree that the law may require libraries to disable filters for adults upon request—a conclusion that could permit libraries to continue to provide unfiltered Internet access for most adult patrons. For libraries that adopt more restrictive approaches, the decision raises the possibility of further challenges to the statute as applied. In doctrinal terms, the various opinions highlight the poor fit of the First Amendment doctrines of the "public forum" and "unconstitutional conditions" when applied to restrictions on public institutions created for the purpose of disseminating speech. The public forum doctrine, which originated as a way to preserve a "First Amendment easement" for private speakers on public streets and sidewalks, is not well-suited to the task of analyzing restrictions imposed on public institutions that are designed for the purpose of disseminating information. Likewise, the doctrine of unconstitutional conditions, which prohibits the government from accomplishing forbidden results indirectly, such as through incentives rather than prohibitions, may be of little use where there remains some doubt about how far the government may go in restricting information in public libraries. As a consequence, the precedential value of the *American Library Association* decision is questionable, and the case represents a missed opportunity for the Court to clarify constitutional doctrine.

Background

A growing debate over Internet content filtering emerged after the Supreme Court struck down key portions of the Communications Decency Act (CDA) in *Reno v. ACLU*. That law was designed to shield children from access to indecent and pornographic speech on the Internet. Holding that the CDA unduly restricted online speech, the Court noted that "[s]ystems have been developed to help parents control the material that may be available on a home computer with Internet access."[2] The *Reno* Court was not considering the question of government-mandated content filtering but instead was commenting only on the voluntary private use of filters in the home. Almost immediately thereafter, however, the debate over Internet

---

[2] *Reno v. ACLU*, 521 U.S. 821, 854–855 (1997).

filtering software centered on whether such filters should be required at the principal public institutions that provide Internet access—public libraries and schools.

Confrontations over filtering requirements tracked the rapid growth of public Internet access in schools and libraries. By 1999, more than 96 percent of public libraries provided public access to the Internet, according to a survey prepared for the American Library Association.[3] This represented a significant increase in public Internet access from what the same researchers found in 1998, when 73 percent of the nation's public libraries offered basic Internet access to their patrons.[4] A 1996 survey had found that only 28 percent of libraries offered Internet access. At the same time a growing number of schools began to provide Internet access. This increase in Internet access was promoted in part by Section 254(h) of the Telecommunications Act of 1996, which established the "e-rate" program to subsidize telecommunications services and computer networking equipment for schools and libraries. A primary goal of the e-rate program is to provide affordable Internet connections to all public schools.[5] Subsidies were also provided through the Elementary and Secondary Education Act (ESEA) and the Library Services and Technology Act (LSTA).

The rapid growth of Internet use brought with it access to information rarely, if ever, seen in the library setting. This access included personal Web pages, online gaming sites, and fringe political sites to name but a few examples. It also included access to the 2 percent of the Web that includes pornographic sites. This development prompted libraries to adopt a wide variety of measures, such as acceptable use policies, to cope with the challenges presented by this new medium. Some libraries also began to use filtering software. By 1999, 16.8 percent of the libraries that offered public Internet access reported the use of filters on some or all access terminals,

[3] JOHN CARLO BERTOT AND CHARLES R. MCCLURE, SURVEY OF INTERNET ACCESS MANAGEMENT IN PUBLIC LIBRARIES (Library Research Center, Univ. of Illinois, June 2000) ("Library Survey 2000").

[4] JOHN CARLO BERTOT AND CHARLES R. MCCLURE, THE 1998 NATIONAL SURVEY OF U.S. PUBLIC LIBRARY OUTLET INTERNET CONNECTIVITY (ALA, Office of Information Technology Policy, Oct. 1998).

[5] *See* FEDERAL-STATE JOINT BOARD ON UNIVERSAL SERVICE, REPORT AND ORDER, 12 FCC Rcd. 8776 (1997).

while 83.2 percent did not use filters.[6] The 1998 survey had found that more than 85 percent of public libraries with Internet access did not use content filters. Of the libraries that used filters to restrict Internet content, most—approximately 60 percent—provided patrons with access to terminals without filters as well.[7] However, some libraries adopted more restrictive policies, thus spawning litigation over the issue.

Early cases held that public libraries could not adopt filtering policies that unduly restricted Internet access and that libraries were not compelled to use filtering to protect children. In *Mainstream Loudoun v. Board of Trustees*, the U.S. District Court for the Eastern District of Virginia held that the Internet access policy for the public library in Loudoun County, Virginia, was unconstitutional.[8] The court held that the policy, which required the use of blocking software at all times for all users, violated the First and Fourteenth Amendments to the United States Constitution. It concluded that the mandatory filtering policy was not necessary to further a compelling government interest in that no problem of accessing pornography had been demonstrated in the Loudoun County system. The court also found that the policy restricted adult library patrons to accessing only information suitable for minors, that it lacked adequate standards for restricting speech, and that it had inadequate procedural safeguards. In an earlier ruling denying the library board's motion to dismiss the case, the court found that the First Amendment governs library policies regarding Internet access, thereby rejecting the county's comparison of its policy with a book acquisition or interlibrary loan system.[9]

With regard to an obligation to protect children, the California Court of Appeals rejected a claim that the public library is required to install Internet content filters. In *Kathleen R. v. City of Livermore*, a parent filed suit to compel the use of filters after her son reportedly downloaded sexually oriented images using the library computer terminal. The trial court dismissed the claim under Section 230(c) of the Telecommunications Act of 1996 which provides that "[n]o

---

[6] BERTOT AND MCCLURE, *supra* note 3, at 7.

[7] *Id.* at 8.

[8] Mainstream Loudoun v. Board of Trustees, 24 F. Supp.2d 552 (E.D. Va. 1998).

[9] *Id.* at 783.

provider or user of an interactive computer service shall be treated as the publisher or speaker of any information provided by another information content provider" and that "[n]o cause of action may be brought and no liability may be imposed under any State or local law that is inconsistent with this section."[10] The California Court of Appeals affirmed the judgment of dismissal pursuant to Section 230.[11]

The Children's Internet Protection Act

The Children's Internet Protection Act added a provision conditioning federal subsidies on the use of Internet content filters as an amendment to the 2001 Labor, Health and Human Services Appropriations Bill, H.R. 4577.[12] Among other things, CIPA added the filtering mandate to e-rate subsidies administered by the Federal Communications Commission (FCC), funding via the Elementary and Secondary Education Act, and funding through the Library Services and Technology Act, programs that affected Internet access in public schools and libraries. The amendment combined earlier proposals submitted in both the 105th and 106th Congresses.

The law requires recipients of federal funds under the specified programs to develop "Internet safety policies" that meet a number of specific requirements. As part of this requirement all libraries and schools that receive e-rate funding for Internet access, Internet service, or internal connections must install and use blocking and filtering technology to preclude access to "visual depictions" that are obscene, constitute child pornography, or are harmful to minors.[13] Filters are required for all users on all access terminals regardless of the number of computers with Internet access that a school or library provides. However, when adults are using Internet terminals CIPA allows filters to be configured (theoretically, at least) so as not to block images that merely are "harmful to minors" but not obscene.

The various subsidy programs include provisions that allow blocked sites to be restored or filters to be turned off under certain

---

[10]47 U.S.C. § 230(c)(1), (3)(1996).
[11]Kathleen R. v. City of Livermore, 87 Cal. App. 4th 684 (Cal. App. 2001).
[12]Pub. L. No. 106-554, 114 Stat. 2763A-335.
[13]20 U.S.C. §§ 9134(f)(1)(A)(i) and (B)(i); 47 U.S.C. §§ 254(h)(6)(B)(i) and (C)(i).

conditions. The e-rate program permits recipients of funds to "disable the technology protection measure . . . during use by an adult, to enable access for bona fide research or other lawful purpose."[14] The LSTA funding restrictions also permit institutions to "disable a technology protection measure . . . to enable access for bona fide research or other lawful purposes."[15] Institutions that receive subsidies through multiple programs must adhere to the more restrictive e-rate provision that permits disabling filters only for adult access.

Judicial Challenge to CIPA

Two challenges were filed against the CIPA.[16] The complaints focused on the funding conditions that related to public libraries, rather than schools, and did not challenge the general requirement that recipients of funds create "Internet safety policies." The cases were filed under the expedited judicial review provisions of CIPA, which provide that any facial constitutional challenge be heard by a three-judge district court, with a right of direct appeal to the Supreme Court if the law is found to be invalid.

The two cases were consolidated and in May 2002 the U.S. District Court for the Eastern District of Pennsylvania held in *American Library Association v. United States* that the CIPA filtering requirements for public libraries were unconstitutional. As a threshold matter, the district court found that Internet access in public libraries was a designated public forum and that filtering requirements were an effort to exclude certain speech selectively from the forum. Thus, the court reasoned that "where the state designates a forum for expressive activity and opens the forum for speech by the public at large on a wide range of topics, strict scrutiny applies to restrictions that single out for exclusion from the forum particular speech whose content is disfavored."[17] Such exclusions "risk fundamentally distorting the unique marketplace of ideas that public libraries create when they open their collections, via the Internet, to the speech of

[14] 47 U.S.C. §§ 254(h)(6)(D).

[15] 20 U.S.C. § 9134(f)(3).

[16] American Library Ass'n. v. United States, No. 01-CV-1303 (E.D. Pa. filed March 20, 2001); Multnomah County Public Library v. United States, No. 01-CV-1322 (E.D. Pa. filed March 20, 2001).

[17] American Library Association v. United States, 201 F. Supp. 2d 401, 460–461 (E.D. Pa. 2002).

millions of individuals around the world on a virtually limitless number of subjects."[18]

In applying strict scrutiny, the court agreed that the government has a compelling interest in limiting the distribution of obscenity and child pornography, but rejected the claim of a compelling interest in preventing unlawful or inappropriate conduct in libraries. It reasoned that the appropriate response to improper behavior in the library was to impose sanctions on the conduct, not to limit access to speech.[19] Ultimately, after an exhaustive review of available technology, the court found that the use of filters resulted in substantial overblocking (restricting nonpornographic information) as well as underblocking (failing to block pornographic information). Consequently, it concluded that CIPA was not narrowly tailored and could not survive First Amendment scrutiny. While the First Amendment "does not demand perfection when the government restricts speech in order to advance a compelling interest," the court noted, "the substantial amounts of erroneous blocking inherent in the technology protection measures mandated by CIPA are more than simply *de minimis* instances of human error."[20] CIPA's filtering requirements were also found to be constitutionally infirm because acceptable use policies and other measures represented a less restrictive alternative means of serving the government's asserted interest.[21]

The Supreme Court Decision

In *United States v. American Library Association* the Supreme Court reversed the district court in a fractured decision that garnered no clear majority position and generated five separate opinions.[22] Led by Chief Justice Rehnquist's plurality opinion, the Court rejected claims that CIPA exceeded Congress's spending power to impose conditions on federal programs. A majority of the Justices agreed that the government did not create a designated public forum by

[18] *Id.* at 464.
[19] *Id.* at 475.
[20] *Id.* at 479.
[21] *Id.* at 480.
[22] *American Library Ass'n.*, 123 S. Ct. at 2297 (2003).

providing Internet access in public libraries, and, based on a questionable reading of the law regarding the disabling of filters, concluded that the restrictions on speech were modest. Justices Stevens, Souter, and Ginsburg dissented.

The plurality reasoned that Congress has wide latitude to attach conditions on the receipt of federal assistance to further its policy objectives, although it may not "induce" the recipient of funds to engage in unconstitutional activities.[23] In this regard, the inquiry focused on whether the condition Congress attached would be unconstitutional if it was performed by the library itself. Chief Justice Rehnquist concluded that the use of Internet filters was not unconstitutional, because libraries normally exercise great discretion in selecting books for their collections and do not traditionally include pornography in their stacks.[24] The principal thrust of the plurality opinion was to characterize the federal funding conditions as reinforcing the traditional mission of libraries.

The plurality minimized the First Amendment significance of the case by classifying a library's decision to use filtering software as "a collection decision, not a restraint on private speech."[25] The goal of libraries has never been to provide "universal coverage," according to the Chief Justice, but to provide materials "that would be of the greatest direct benefit or interest to the community." Describing the Internet as "no more than a technological extension of the book stack,"[26] the plurality maintained that a library's need to exercise judgment in making collection decisions is based on its traditional role of identifying suitable and worthwhile material and that "it is no less entitled to play that role when it collects material from the Internet than when it collects material from any other source."[27]

The plurality rejected the district court's finding that providing Internet access in the public library created a designated public forum. Chief Justice Rehnquist was quite clear on this point:

---

[23] 123 S. Ct. at 2303 (plurality opinion) (citing *South Dakota v. Dole*, 483 U.S. 203, 206 (1987).

[24] *Id.* at 2303–04.

[25] *Id.* at 2307 n.4.

[26] *Id.* at 2305 (quoting S. Rep. 141, 106th Cong., 1st Sess. at 7 (1999)).

[27] *Id.* at 2306.

> A public library does not acquire Internet terminals in order
> to create a public forum for Web publishers to express them-
> selves, any more than it collects books in order to provide
> a public forum for the authors of books to speak. It provides
> Internet access, not to "encourage a diversity of views from
> private speakers" . . . but for the same reasons it offers other
> library resources: to facilitate research, learning, and recre-
> ational pursuits by furnishing materials of requisite and
> appropriate quality.

Accordingly, he concluded that Internet access in public libraries is
neither a "traditional" nor a "designated" public forum.[28] This point
was bolstered by reference to *Arkansas Educ. Television Comm'n v.
Forbes*, 523 U.S. 666 (1998), where the Court held that public broadcast
stations could exercise editorial discretion in presenting debates by
political candidates, and *National Endowment for the Arts v. Finley*, 524
U.S. 569 (1998), where it upheld the use of "standards of decency" as
one factor in making arts grants. On the basis of these analogous
decisions, the plurality concluded that "the government has broad
discretion to make content-based judgments in deciding what private speech to make available to the public."[29]

The plurality also discounted the significance of CIPA's burden
on speech in the library setting. Responding to the district court's
conclusion that filters erroneously block access to constitutionally
protected speech, it noted that any constitutional concerns are dis-
pelled by the "ease with which patrons may have the filtering software disabled." Individual cases of improper blocking may be
brought to the attention of the librarian or the filtering company
and the problem can be corrected. Or, under the law, filters may be
disabled upon request "to enable access for bona fide research or
other lawful purposes."[30] The plurality opinion relied heavily on the
Solicitor General's characterization of this provision, quoting his
statement during oral argument that a librarian can unblock the
filtering mechanism upon request, and that the patron "would not
have to explain . . . why he was asking a site to be unblocked or

---

[28] *Id.* at 2305.
[29] *Id.* at 2304.
[30] *Id.* at 2306.

the filtering to be disabled.' "[31] It discounted the district court's concern that requiring patrons to make such a request would be stigmatizing, noting that "the Constitution does not guarantee the right to acquire information at a public library without any risk of embarrassment."[32]

The plurality opinion also rejected the alternative grounds cited by the district court that CIPA imposed an unconstitutional condition on the use of federal funds. In doing so, the plurality bypassed the government's broader argument that government entities do not have First Amendment rights, but instead reaffirmed the holding in *Rust v. Sullivan*, 500 U.S. 173 (1991), that the government has a right to insist that public funds be used for the purpose for which they were authorized. In this case, it noted that the e-rate and LSTA programs "were intended to help public libraries fulfill their traditional role of obtaining material of requisite and appropriate quality for educational and informational purposes."[33] Chief Justice Rehnquist distinguished *Legal Services Corp. v. Velazquez*, 531 U.S. 533 (2000), where the Court invalidated funding conditions imposed on legal aid lawyers. In that case, the Court found that the restrictions distorted the usual functioning of the legal profession by precluding zealous advocacy against the government on behalf of indigent clients. In *American Library Association*, the plurality opined that there is no comparable assumption that public libraries "must be free of conditions that their benefactors might attach to the use of donated funds or other assistance."[34]

Justice Kennedy based his brief concurring opinion on the lack of evidence that adult access to material on the Internet had been burdened in a significant way. Although he acknowledged a statement in the district court's opinion that unblocking might take days or may be unavailable in some libraries, he said that the statement "does not appear to be a specific finding." Accordingly, Justice Kennedy suggested that "there is little to this case" if, "on the request of an adult user, a librarian will unblock filtered material or disable

[31] *Id.* at 2306–07 (quoting Argument Tr. at 4).
[32] *Id.* at 2307.
[33] *Id.* at 2308.
[34] *Id.* at 2309.

the Internet software without significant delay."[35] But while he rejected the facial challenge to the CIPA conditions, Justice Kennedy noted that as-applied challenges might be brought if particular libraries lack the capacity to unblock specific Web sites, to disable the filter, or if they impose other burdens on adult users' access to constitutionally protected information.[36]

Justice Breyer agreed with the plurality opinion that public libraries do not create a public forum when they make Internet access available to the public and that the CIPA conditions are facially valid. However, he rejected the plurality's assumption that CIPA is valid if it is supported only by a rational basis, and he disputed the government's suggestion that the Court should presume CIPA is constitutional. Thus, unlike the plurality Justice Breyer applied "a form of heightened scrutiny" because "[t]he Act directly restricts the public's receipt of information."[37] This did not rise to the level of strict scrutiny, he explained, because such a rigorous test "would unreasonably interfere with the discretion necessary to create, maintain, or select a library's 'collection' (broadly defined to include all the information the library makes available)." Justice Breyer compared the level of constitutional scrutiny that should be applied in this case with the intermediate scrutiny appropriate to the regulation of commercial speech or broadcast content, or that which applies to content-neutral rules for cable television.[38]

Applying this level of review, Justice Breyer concluded that CIPA satisfied constitutional demands. Like the other Justices, he found the government's interest to be legitimate and often compelling, and he found that software filters " 'provide a relatively cheap and effective' means of furthering [its] goals."[39] He also agreed that filters tended to both overblock and underblock the speech targeted by

[35] *Id.* (Kennedy, J., concurring).

[36] *Id.* at 2310.

[37] *Id.* (Breyer, J., concurring).

[38] *Id.* at 2311 (citing Board of Trustees v. Fox, 492 U.S. 469 (1989) (commercial speech); Denver Area Educ. Telecomm. Consortium, Inc. v. FCC, 518 U.S. 727 (1996) (cable television leased access rules); Turner Broadcasting System v. FCC, 520 U.S. 180 (1997) (mandatory carriage rules for cable television); Red Lion Broadcasting Co. v. FCC, 395 U.S. 367 (1969) (broadcast content regulations)).

[39] *American Library Ass'n.*, 123 S. Ct. at 2312 (Breyer, J., concurring) (quoting *American Library Ass'n.*, 201 F. Supp. 2d at 448).

CIPA, but noted that "no one has presented any clearly superior or better fitting alternatives." Justice Breyer pointed to the provisions that allow libraries to unblock disputed Web sites or disable filters altogether, and concluded that the burden on patrons of having to make such requests is no more onerous than traditional library practices associated with requesting access to closed stacks for certain restricted materials or interlibrary loan practices.[40] He left open the possibility that local library policies may be more restrictive when allowing access to overblocked material or disabling filters, but explained that the Court was considering only a facial challenge to CIPA's overall mandate.

The Dissents

The dissenters were far less sanguine about the minimal extent to which the CIPA conditions restricted protected speech. However, they argued that the CIPA requirements were unconstitutional without reference to the public forum doctrine that had been the centerpiece of the district court decision and was a major focus of the plurality opinion. Instead, they addressed the effect of filtering as a prior restraint and on the CIPA requirements as unconstitutional conditions.

Justice Stevens pointed out that only 7 percent of libraries had chosen to require filters on all Internet terminals, so that CIPA necessarily required the remaining 93 percent of the libraries to do likewise (to the extent they accepted federal funds). He described CIPA as "a blunt nationwide restraint on adult access to 'an enormous amount of valuable information' that individual librarians cannot possibly review."[41] Citing the district court's findings regarding the imprecision of filtering technology, Justice Stevens described the effect of overblocking as "the functional equivalent of a host of individual decisions excluding hundreds of thousands of individual constitutionally protected messages from Internet terminals located in public libraries throughout the Nation."[42] He pointed to various less restrictive alternatives cited by the court below (including optional filtering policies, parental consent requirements, acceptable

[40] Id.
[41] Id. at 2313 (Stevens, J., dissenting).
[42] Id. at 2313–14.

use policies, privacy screens, etc.) and suggested that the choice of alternatives should be left to local decisionmakers and not mandated by the federal government.

Justice Stevens was less impressed than the plurality with the Solicitor General's assurance that filters could be disabled at a library patron's request, noting that a person would be unlikely to know which information was being excluded in advance, and therefore could not know whether making an unblocking request would be worthwhile. He compared it with a library keeping a substantial portion of its resources in unmarked locked rooms or cabinets. In such a scenario "[s]ome curious readers would in time obtain access to the hidden materials, but many would not."[43] But in Justice Stevens's view the most significant problem was not the empirical question of how many patrons would be intimidated from seeking unfiltered access but the fact that CIPA requires them to make the request in the first place. He described it as a "significant prior restraint" because a law that "prohibits reading without official consent" is like a law "that prohibits speaking without consent." Both, in his view, constitute "a dramatic departure from our national heritage and constitutional tradition."[44]

Justice Stevens concluded that the CIPA requirements imposed an unconstitutional condition on protected expression. Building on the plurality's discussion of a library's need for discretion to make collection decisions, he compared the need with a university's interest in freedom "to determine for itself on academic grounds who may teach, what may be taught, how it shall be taught, and who may be admitted to study."[45] He also cited unconstitutional conditions cases relating to employment, as well as *Velazquez*, and concluded that the CIPA conditions distort the usual functioning of libraries. Justice Stevens distinguished these cases from *Rust v. Sullivan*, cited by the plurality, noting that *Rust* had been limited to cases in which the government was sponsoring its own speech.[46] Here,

[43] *Id.* at 2315.

[44] *Id.* (quoting Watchtower Bible & Tract Soc. of N.Y., Inc. v. Village of Stratton, 536 U.S. 150, 166 (2002)).

[45] *Id.* (quoting Sweezy v. New Hampshire, 354 U.S. 234, 263 (1957) (Frankfurter, J., concurring in the result)).

[46] *Id.* at 2316–17.

however, he noted that the LSTA and e-rate programs were designed to foster Internet access and to make a vast amount of information available to library patrons, not to promote any particular governmental message.

Justice Stevens pointed to ways in which the CIPA conditions limit the discretion of libraries. For example, CIPA requires a library to install filters on all computers if it receives any discount from the e-rate program or any funds from the LSTA program. As a consequence, a library that seeks to provide Internet service for even a single computer through the federal subsidy programs is obligated to filter all of its computers for both patron and staff use.[47] Nevertheless, he would have approved the mandatory use of filters if the library adopted the policy on its own and not in compliance with a federally imposed condition. Justice Stevens, on the one hand, agreed with the plurality that the 7 percent of libraries that required use of filtering software on all of their Internet terminals "did not act unlawfully."[48]

Justice Souter, on the other hand, joined by Justice Ginsburg, wrote that requiring Internet content filters, at least as to adult access, violated the First Amendment whether imposed by the federal government or by local library policies. He disputed the plurality's conclusions about the nature and function of libraries as well as its comparison of filters with book selection policies. In an extended discussion of the history and development of library practices, Justice Souter noted that the traditional function of libraries was to make information freely available, not to censor it. He wrote that the "[i]nstitutional history of public libraries in America discloses an evolution toward a general rule, now firmly rooted, that any adult entitled to use the library has access to any of its holdings."[49]

Justice Souter disparaged the plurality's conception of libraries as collecting only materials deemed to have "requisite and appropriate quality" as effectively claiming that "the traditional responsibility of public libraries has called for denying adult access to certain books, or bowdlerizing the content of what libraries let adults see."[50]

---

[47] *Id.* at 2318.
[48] *Id.* at 2313.
[49] *Id.* at 2322 (Souter, J., dissenting).
[50] *Id.* at 2322.

He observed, for example, that the plurality's notion of librarianship could not justify denying an interlibrary loan request on grounds that the patron's purpose in seeking the information was "unacceptable," but that CIPA's unblocking procedure operated in just that way. Tracing the history of librarians' opposition to organized censorship during the latter half of the 20th century, including their reactions to what Justice Souter described as the "assaults" of McCarthyism, he concluded it was "out of the question for a library to refuse a book in its collection to a requesting adult patron, or to presume to evaluate the basis of a particular request."[51]

Justice Souter argued that the use of filtering technology "defies comparison to the process of acquisition." In the traditional setting, he explained, a library must affirmatively decide to expend funds to obtain a new resource and must make room on its limited shelf space. In the Internet context, by contrast, the library must expend extra funds for software to restrict access to information that the Internet already has made available. He concluded that "[t]he proper analogy therefore is not to passing up a book that might have been bought; it is either to buying a book and then keeping it from adults lacking an acceptable 'purpose,' or to buying an encyclopedia and then cutting out pages with anything thought to be unsuitable for all adults."[52]

Like Justice Kennedy, Justice Souter agreed that it would "tak[e] the curse off the statute for all practical purposes" if adult patrons could obtain an unblocked Internet terminal "simply for the asking." But he disagreed that CIPA could be read to require such an outcome, even where such a reading would permit the Court to avoid ruling on a difficult constitutional question. Not only had the FCC declined to set forth criteria governing unblocking requests, but also the statute said only that libraries "may" unblock Internet terminals for "lawful purposes" and "bona fide research." The vague statutory criteria provided additional reason for constitutional doubt, according to Souter's dissent, because it would vest unlimited discretion among library staffs about permitting or denying requests for unfiltered Internet access.[53]

[51] *Id.* at 2322–24.
[52] *Id.* at 2321–22.
[53] *Id.* at 2319–20.

The Failure of Doctrine

The *American Library Association* decision resolved the immediate question of CIPA's facial validity, but it is not clear how any future as-applied challenges may fare or whether the case will be influential beyond its specific context. An important reason for this uncertainty, which also explains the splintered opinions and the ambiguous direction of the Court, is that the case was a poor fit under the established First Amendment doctrines of the public forum and unconstitutional conditions. The more precise problem this case presents is the need to determine which kind of First Amendment rules apply to public institutions that are created for the purpose of spreading information and engaging in expressive activities. Various decisions have touched on this issue but no well-defined doctrinal approach has yet emerged. In this regard, *American Library Association* may be considered a missed opportunity to clarify an ambiguous area of constitutional law.

Whither the Public Forum Doctrine?

The plurality confronted the district court's decision to analyze the case under the public forum rubric, which asks whether permitting Internet access in public libraries creates a forum for private speakers. By deciding that such access does not create a forum, the plurality concluded that the CIPA filtering conditions did not trigger any type of heightened First Amendment scrutiny.[54] Justice Breyer agreed that no forum had been created, although he subjected CIPA to intermediate scrutiny because "[t]he Act directly restricts the public's receipt of information."[55] The remaining four Justices declined to discuss the forum question at all, which suggests that the issue was unnecessary to the Court's ultimate decision. This point was underscored by Justice Breyer's concurrence, for if it is possible to conclude that some form of heightened constitutional scrutiny should be applied without finding that libraries have created a public forum, then conducting a forum analysis may unnecessarily confuse the issues.

The public forum doctrine emerged from Supreme Court cases to become the primary analytic tool for applying the First Amendment

---

[54] *Id.* at 2304–05.

[55] *Id.* at 2310 (Breyer, J., concurring).

to government property dedicated for expressive purposes. Although the doctrine originated with cases involving various forms of speech and parades on public thoroughfares,[56] it evolved over the years to encompass any form of government property that can be used as a "channel of communication." Courts have devised three categories in which public property may be considered public fora: (1) the traditional public forum, such as streets, sidewalks and public parks, in which members of the public generally have a right to engage in speech activities; (2) the designated public forum, such as university meeting rooms, which have been intentionally opened for expressive purposes for identified groups (*e.g.*, student organizations); and (3) the nonpublic forum, such as an intra-school mail system, which has not been generally opened to the public for communicative purposes.[57] The Supreme Court has identified a variety of factors that reflect the government's intention to create a designated forum, including its practice or policy of allowing or disallowing unrestricted speech in the forum, the characteristics of the property, and the government's stated purpose.[58]

Given its emergence from controversies involving picketing in the streets, the public forum doctrine generally asks the question whether private parties can access government-controlled property in order to speak. Whether the doctrine is applied to buses,[59] mailboxes,[60] billboards,[61] high school student newspapers,[62] charitable campaign drives in federal offices,[63] or internal school mail systems,[64] the primary inquiry is whether private individuals or groups may

---

[56]Hague v. CIO, 307 U.S. 496, 515 (1939); Jamison v. Texas, 318 U.S. 413 (1943). The term "public forum" was coined by Professor Harry Kalven, Jr. in the 1960s. *See* Harry Kalven, Jr., *The Concept of the Public Forum: Cox v. Louisiana*, 1965 SUPREME COURT REVIEW 1.

[57]Perry Educ. Ass'n v. Perry Local Educators' Ass'n, 460 U.S. 37 (1983).

[58]Cornelius v. NAACP Legal Defense & Educ. Fund, Inc., 473 U.S. 788, 802–806 (1985).

[59]Lehman v. City of Shaker Heights, 418 U.S. 298, 301–302 (1974) (plurality opinion).

[60]United States Postal Serv. v. Council of Greenburgh Civic Ass'ns, 453 U.S. 114, 128–129 (1981).

[61]Lebron v. National R.R. Passenger Corp., 513 U.S. 374 (1995).

[62]Hazelwood Sch. Dist. v. Kuhlmeier, 484 U.S. 260, 267–270 (1988).

[63]*Cornelius*, 473 U.S. at 803.

[64]*Perry*, 460 U.S. at 49 n.9.

use the forum to convey a message. This certainly is the way the *American Library Association* plurality understood the issue. The four Justices observed that libraries do not acquire Internet terminals "in order to create a public forum for Web publishers to express themselves," and it cited other recent cases supporting the government's discretion to make content-based judgments in deciding "what private speech to make available to the public."[65]

But the question of restricting the resources available in a public library is somewhat different, and is not confined to asking whether publishers—on the Web or otherwise—have a constitutional right to place their materials on the physical or virtual shelves of the institution. Public libraries "are places of freewheeling and independent inquiry"[66] and "the quintessential locus of the receipt of information."[67] In this regard, the Supreme Court, in connection with restrictions on libraries, has emphasized that "the State may not, consistently with the spirit of the First Amendment, contract the spectrum of available knowledge."[68] In this spirit, Justice Souter's *American Library Association* dissent focused not on the rights of publishers but on "the First and Fourteenth Amendment rights of adult library patrons . . . to be free of paternalistic censorship."[69]

Government-Sponsored Speech Institutions and the First Amendment

Other public institutions created for expressive purposes illustrate the pitfalls of attempting to transform the public forum doctrine to fit a range of issues beyond mere access. Cases involving public broadcasting provide a good analogue to libraries because the licenses in many cases are held by government entities and the noncommercial broadcasting system is subsidized by public funds. The connection to government has spawned a number of cases in which viewers and program providers demanded various forms of

[65]*American Library Ass'n*, 123 S. Ct. at 2304–05 (plurality opinion).

[66]Board of Educ., Island Trees Union Free Sch. Dist. No. 26 v. Pico, 457 U.S. 853, 914 (1982) (Rehnquist, J., dissenting).

[67]Kreimer v. Bureau of Police, 958 F.2d 1242, 1255 (3d Cir. 1992).

[68]*Pico*, 457 U.S. at 866 (plurality op.) (quoting *Griswold v. Connecticut*, 381 U.S. 479, 482 (1965)).

[69]*American Library Ass'n*, 123 S. Ct. at 2324 n.8 (Souter, J., dissenting).

access to the medium, leading, in turn, to a series of decisions denying that noncommercial broadcasters are public fora.[70] In *Forbes*, the
Supreme Court held that public stations might create "a forum of
some type" when they sponsor debates between political candidates,
but it cautioned that "broad rights of access for outside speakers
would be antithetical, as a general rule, to the discretion that stations
and their editorial staff must exercise to fulfill their journalistic purpose and statutory obligations."[71]

The *American Library Association* plurality picked up on this notion
and concluded that a library must exercise judgment in making
collection decisions and it is "no less entitled to play that role when
it collects material from the Internet than when it collects material
from any other source."[72] Justice Rehnquist likewise cited *Finley*,
a case involving NEA grants, to reinforce the point that federal
grantmakers must have discretion. But the filtering mandates of
CIPA are not a good analogy because they do not expand librarians'
discretion. Libraries had the option before CIPA was enacted to use
filters to block Internet content and a number did so. As Justice
Stevens pointed out, CIPA effectively required most libraries to
change their Internet filtering policies and precluded any
experimentation.[73]

Rather than trying to extend the public forum analogy, the Court
might have gained greater insight from cases in which the government sought to use the spending power to restrict information that
public broadcasters may transmit. The Supreme Court addressed
this issue in *FCC v. League of Women Voters of California* and struck
down a ban on editorializing by noncommercial licensees on First
Amendment grounds.[74] Similarly, the U.S. Court of Appeals for the
District of Columbia Circuit invalidated a requirement that public
broadcast licensees make recordings of all broadcasts "in which any

[70]Knights of the Ku Klux Klan v. Curators of the University of Missouri, 203 F.3d
1085, 1093–94 (8th Cir.), *cert. denied*, 531 U.S. 814 (2000); Chandler v. Georgia Pub.
Telecomm. Comm'n, 917 F.2d 486 (11th Cir. 1990), *cert. denied*, 502 U.S. 816 (1991);
Muir v. Alabama Educ. Television Comm'n, 688 F.2d 1033, 1037 (5th Cir. 1982) (*en
banc*), *cert. denied*, 460 U.S. 1023 (1983).

[71]*Forbes*, 523 U.S. at 673.

[72]*American Library Ass'n*, 123 S. Ct. at 2306 (plurality opinion).

[73]*Id.* at 2313–14 (Stevens, J., dissenting).

[74]F.C.C. v. League of Women Voters of California, 468 U.S. 364 (1984).

issue of public importance is discussed" because it was designed to facilitate content control.[75] Whether or not noncommercial broadcast stations might be considered public fora was not a relevant question in these cases.

As the experience with the public broadcasting cases shows, the government's relationship with speech falls along a "complex spectrum, not a bipolar one." That is, when it comes to speech, the government often acts in various roles, including censor, regulator, manager, employer, policymaker, patron, speaker, or publisher.[76] In this regard, some public institutions "have a certain First Amendment aura." Examples include "the arts, libraries, universities, and the institutional press."[77] Similar to its pronouncements with respect to libraries, the Supreme Court has recognized universities as the quintessential "marketplace of ideas" with a "tradition of thought and experiment that is at the center of our intellectual and philosophic tradition."[78] Even when it upheld funding restrictions on abortion-related speech by doctors in *Rust v. Sullivan*, the Court emphasized that "the university is a traditional sphere of free expression so fundamental to the functioning of our society that the government's ability to control speech within that sphere by means of conditions attached to the expenditure of Government funds is restricted by the vagueness and overbreadth doctrines of the First Amendment."[79]

These cases suggest that the First Amendment imposes limits on the government's ability to restrict speech in some institutions in a way that is separate and apart from their possible status as public fora. The Supreme Court has not yet articulated a separate doctrine to

---

[75] Community-Service Broad. of Mid-America, Inc. v. FCC, 593 F.2d 1102, 1122–23 (D.C. Cir. 1978) (*en banc*).

[76] Randall P. Bezanson, *The Government Speech Forum: Forbes and Finley and Government Speech Selection Judgments*, 83 IOWA L. REV. 953, 964 (1997–98). *See also* Randall P. Bezanson and William G. Buss, *The Many Faces of Government Speech*, 86 IOWA L. REV. 1377, 1381 (2001); MARK YUDOF, WHEN GOVERNMENT SPEAKS 44 (1986).

[77] Frederick F. Schauer, *Principles, Institutions and the First Amendment*, 112 HARVARD L. REV. 84, 116 (1998).

[78] Rosenberger v. Rector & Visitors of the Univ. of Virginia, 515 U.S. 819, 835–836 (1995); Healy v. James, 408 U.S. 169, 180 (1972) ("vigilant protection of constitutional freedoms is nowhere more vital than in the community of American schools").

[79] *Rust*, 500 U.S. at 200.

explain the relationship of the First Amendment to such government-sponsored speech institutions, but recent cases suggest a possible approach that was overlooked in *American Library Association*. Such a threoretical approach could incorporate elements of the public forum doctrine, but would recognize that various institutions serve many different functions. Government-sponsored speech enterprises are distinguishable from the designated public forum in that the purpose of the institution is not to create an open platform for all speakers. Like a designated public forum, however, the speech enterprise would come into being only by deliberate action and could be eliminated at the government's option. A government-sponsored speech enterprise also is distinguishable from "government speech" in that the institution is created to promote free inquiry and expression, not to disseminate the state's message. No constitutional principle would require the government to create such an enterprise, but after having done so the government would be obligated to adhere to First Amendment principles.

The Supreme Court hinted at such an approach in *Legal Services Corp. v. Velazquez*, where the Court applied the First Amendment to invalidate funding restrictions that limited the speech of government-funded attorneys.[80] The Court analyzed prior cases involving government speech and the public forum and held that the government cannot constitutionally fund a particular speech activity and then impose conditions "which distort its usual functioning." The majority opinion suggested that the same principles apply to other speech enterprises, including universities and public broadcast stations. Thus, the government "could not elect to use a broadcasting network or a college publication structure in a regime that prohibits speech necessary to the proper functioning of those systems."[81] In a particularly relevant passage, the Court explained:

> Where the government uses or attempts to regulate a particular medium, we have been informed by its accepted usage in determining whether a particular restriction on speech is necessary for the program's purposes and limitations. In *FCC v. League of Women Voters of Cal.*, 468 U.S. 364, 104 S.Ct. 3106, 82 L.Ed.2d 278 (1984), the Court was instructed by its

[80] Legal Services Corp. v. Velazquez, 531 U.S. 533 (2000).
[81] *Id.* at 543.

> understanding of the dynamics of the broadcast industry
> in holding that prohibitions against editorializing by public
> radio networks were an impermissible restriction, even
> though the Government enacted the restriction to control
> the use of public funds. The First Amendment forbade the
> Government from using the forum in an unconventional way
> to suppress speech inherent in the nature of the medium.
> *See id.*, at 396–397, 104 S.Ct. 3106. In *Arkansas Ed. Television
> Comm'n v. Forbes*, 523 U.S. 666, 676, 118 S.Ct. 1633, 140 L.Ed.2d
> 875 (1998), the dynamics of the broadcasting system gave
> station programmers the right to use editorial judgment to
> exclude certain speech so that the broadcast message could
> be more effective.[82]

The *Velazquez* majority stressed that the public forum cases were not "controlling in a strict sense" but that they provided "some instruction" in how to apply the First Amendment to publicly funded institutions.[83] Finding cognizable First Amendment interests in cases of this type requires courts "to inquire much more deeply into the specific character of the institution, and the functions it serves" than they have in the past,[84] and the Court in *Velazquez* did just that. It examined the purposes for which the Legal Services Corporation was created (assisting indigent clients in litigation over welfare benefits), the traditional purposes of litigation ("the expression of theories and postulates on both, or multiple, sides of an issue"), and the primary mission of the judiciary ("[i]nterpretation of the law and the Constitution"), and concluded that the statute imposed a "serious and fundamental restriction on advocacy of attorneys and the functioning of the judiciary."[85]

A coherent theory for analyzing speech restrictions imposed on public institutions might have helped reduce confusion over the public forum doctrine in *American Library Association*. However, it is far from clear that better theoretical tools would have altered the outcome of the case because the plurality and the dissents expressed widely divergent views as to the nature and functions of libraries. Chief Justice Rehnquist took the narrow view that the traditional

[82] *Id.*

[83] *Id.* at 543–544.

[84] Schauer, *supra* note 77, at 116.

[85] *Velazquez*, 531 U.S. at 544–549.

mission of libraries is to provide material "of requisite and appropriate quality," while Justices Souter and Ginsburg traced a history of librarianship based on making information freely available without censorship.[86] In addition, the plurality opinion distinguished *Velazquez* on the theory that libraries do not oppose the government in the same way as legal aid lawyers, and, citing public forum cases, it suggested that there is no comparable assumption that libraries "must be free of any conditions that their benefactors might attach to the use of donated funds or other assistance."[87]

The plurality's attempt to distinguish *Velazquez*, however, does not hold up well when compared with the example on which it relied—public broadcasting. Chief Justice Rehnquist's statement that libraries, like public broadcast stations, are not public fora because they need discretion to make content-based choices cannot be extended to its logical conclusion. Applying this reasoning to the facts of *Forbes*, for example, the plurality would allow appropriations for public broadcast stations to be conditioned on prohibiting third parties from participating in candidate debates. After all, if noncommercial television stations are not public fora because they do not traditionally serve as platforms for private speech, then the government should be able to manipulate public funding so as to reinforce that traditional role. This, however, is not the law, as *League of Women Voters* attests. There, the Supreme Court held that federal appropriations could not be conditioned on banning editorials by public broadcasters. The one remaining distinction, that public libraries—unlike legal aid lawyers—do not have a tradition or function of opposing the government simply is beside the point. It is not the mission of a public broadcasting station to oppose the government either, yet funding conditions designed to restrict editorial choice and content have been ruled unconstitutional.

Given the doctrinal confusion arising from the overlay of the public forum doctrine in *American Library Association*, it is conceivable that a different theoretical framework might have assisted the Court in analyzing the problem presented by CIPA. Even if such a construct would not have affected the outcome, the case was a missed

---

[86] *American Library Ass'n*, 123 S. Ct. at 2306 (plurality opinion); *Id.* at 2321–24 (Souter, J., dissenting).

[87] *Id.* at 2309 & n.7 (plurality opinion).

opportunity for explaining the application of the First Amendment to publicly funded expressive institutions.

Government Speech and Unconstitutional Conditions

The same is true of the Court's discussion of the unconstitutional conditions doctrine. The plurality quickly dismissed the claim that CIPA imposed an unconstitutional condition because of the rule that the government is entitled to define the limits of the programs it creates.[88] Once again, however, the nature of the publicly funded institution was critical to the analysis. Chief Justice Rehnquist grounded his analysis of this issue on *Rust v. Sullivan*, where the Court upheld regulations prohibiting the use of funds under Title X of the Public Health Service Act from supporting counseling concerning the use of abortion as a method of family planning. In *Velazquez*, the Court described the program in *Rust* as an example of "government speech" where "the government is itself the speaker" and public officials "used private speakers to transmit information pertaining to its own program."[89]

Regardless of whether the mission of public libraries is construed narrowly as in the plurality opinion or broadly as in Justice Souter's dissent, it is at least clear that libraries should not be considered government speakers. That is, libraries as institutions are not comparable with traditional examples of government speech, such as publishing " 'journals, magazines, periodicals, and similar publications' that are 'necessary in the transaction of the public business.' "[90] Nor are libraries analogous to government-sponsored public service announcements "warning of the dangers of cigarette smoking or drug use, praising a career in the armed services, or offering methods for AIDS prevention."[91] Justice Stevens noted in his dissent that *Rust* does not apply to CIPA because the federal subsidy programs for libraries were not designed "to foster any particular governmental message."[92] Instead, as Chief Justice Rehnquist wrote in another

---

[88] *American Library Ass'n*, 123 S. Ct. at 2307–08 (plurality opinion).

[89] *Velazquez*, 531 U.S. at 541.

[90] *Muir*, 688 F.2d at 1050 (Rubin, J., concurring) (citation omitted).

[91] United States v. Frame, 885 F.2d 1119, 1131 (3d Cir. 1989), *cert. denied*, 493 U.S. 1094 (1990).

[92] *American Library Ass'n*, 123 S. Ct. at 2317 (Stevens, J., dissenting).

case, public libraries "are places of freewheeling and independent inquiry."[93]

Thus, in the end, *American Library Association* was a dispute about facts and not constitutional doctrine. There was no doubt but that CIPA imposed conditions on public libraries that restricted the information that may be provided to library patrons. The question that divided the Justices was whether the condition violated the First Amendment. This, in turn, was answered by each of the Justices' views on why libraries exist. For that reason, *American Library Association* provides little explanatory power for how the decision may be applied in other contexts. Once again, this problem might have been avoided if the Court had taken the opportunity to revise and clarify its approach to the public forum and unconstitutional conditions doctrines.

The Future and As-Applied Challenges

Not only is the doctrinal impact of *American Library Association* rather murky, but its practical implications are uncertain as well. A key factor in the plurality and concurring opinions was the Solicitor General's claim at oral argument that any adult patron could have the filters turned off without having to explain to the librarian "why he was asking to have a site unblocked or the filtering . . . disabled."[94] In fact, this reading of the statute could be considered necessary to sustain CIPA's constitutionality because the prevailing opinions suggested that libraries failing to unblock sites upon request or disable filters could be subject to as-applied challenges under the Act.[95] The FCC appears to have read the decision this way, for in its order implementing the e-rate program following *American Library Association* the Commission highlighted the Court's discussion of the "ease with which patrons may have the filtering software disabled" and it ruled that compliance with the statute's Internet filtering requirement requires libraries to "implement a procedure for unblocking the filter upon request by an adult."[96]

[93] *Pico*, 457 U.S. at 914 (Rehnquist, J., dissenting).

[94] Argument Tr. at 4.

[95] *American Library Ass'n*, 123 S. Ct. at 2306–07 (plurality opinion); *id.* at 2309–10 (Kennedy, J., concurring); *id.* at 2312 (Breyer, J., concurring). *Cf. id.* at 2319–20 & n.1 (Souter, J., dissenting).

[96] FEDERAL-STATE JOINT BOARD ON UNIVERSAL SERVICE, FCC 03-188 ¶¶ 9, 11 (Rel. July 24, 2003).

As a result, it is unlikely that *American Library Association* is the last word on the controversy surrounding Internet content filtering or about the First Amendment status of publicly funded speech institutions. When the next case comes, however, the first task will be to sort through the doctrinal confusion left by the Court's five opinions. The next opportunity to deal with the theoretical issues may not involve a library, but could arise instead from some controversy affecting another institution that has a "First Amendment aura" such as a university, museum, or public broadcast station. And when that decision comes, it may well have a more profound effect on libraries than *American Library Association* if it more coherently resolves the question of how the First Amendment applies to publicly funded institutions. It will not only affect how the as-applied challenges may be decided, but will also determine the limits of the government's ability to regulate expression through use of the purse strings.

A Page of Logic: *Eldred v. Ashcroft* and the Logic of a Written Constitution

Erik S. Jaffe

In the much-anticipated case of *Eldred v. Ashcroft*,[1] the Supreme Court upheld the 20-year extension of existing and future copyrights enacted in the Sonny Bono Copyright Term Extension Act of 1998 (CTEA).[2] The Court rejected constitutional challenges under both the Copyright Clause and the First Amendment. In doing so it placed considerable emphasis on Congress's unscrutinized historical practice of making copyright term extensions applicable to existing copyrights in addition to future copyrights. That heavy historical emphasis contrasted with the Court's light textual analysis of whether a retroactive extension of existing copyright terms could be squared with Congress's limited constitutional power "To promote the Progress of Science," through the narrow means of "securing for limited Times to Authors" the "exclusive Rights to their" writings.[3] The Court likewise avoided substantial analysis of the tension between congressional power under the Copyright Clause and the limits on congressional power established in the First Amendment.

Contrary to the Court's assertion that when seeking to "comprehend the scope of Congress's power under the Copyright Clause, 'a page of history is worth a volume of logic,' "[4] the *Eldred* opinion would have been better served by a smaller volume of largely irrelevant history and several more pages of logical analysis of the Constitution itself. In particular, a meaningful exposition of the content and limits of the terms of the Copyright Clause, and some articulation of

---

[1] 123 S. Ct. 769 (2003).

[2] Pub. L. No. 105–298, § 102(b) and (d), 112 Stat. 2827–2828 (amending 17 U.S.C. §§ 302, 304).

[3] U.S. Const. Art. I, § 8, cl. 8.

[4] 123 S. Ct. 778 (quoting *New York Trust Co. v. Eisner*, 256 U.S. 345, 349 (1921) (Holmes, J.)).

the First Amendment bounds on the copyright power would have been far more compelling and useful than a simple endorsement of historical congressional practice. Although such an approach would not necessarily have changed the outcome of the case, it would have provided a more cogent jurisprudence and valuable guidance for those concerned with both copyright and the First Amendment.

Background

In 1998, Congress extended by 20 years the term for most copyrights, including those already in existence under the prior law, so that they would run until 70 years after the death of the author.[5] For works published before 1978 and still under copyright, Congress extended the terms of those copyrights from 75 years to 95 years from publication.[6] Because numerous copyrighted works from the 1920s and beyond were nearing the end of their terms and were about to enter the public domain, the immediate effect of the CTEA was to prevent those works from becoming freely available to the public and to extend the monopoly on those works for another 20 years. Notable examples of works that soon would have entered the public domain, but which now will remain under copyright, include *The Prophet* by Kahlil Gibran, sheet music by Bartok, Ravel, and Strauss, and early poetry by Robert Frost.

The CTEA promptly was challenged by individuals and businesses that make use of public domain materials and that eagerly had been awaiting public access to tremendous volumes of early 20th-century music, literature, and film classics. The challengers sued in the U.S. District Court for the District of Columbia, claiming that the CTEA violated the Copyright Clause of the United States Constitution, which, along with the Patent Clause, reads:

> The Congress shall have Power . . . To promote the Progress
> of Science and useful Arts, by securing for limited Times to

---

[5]17 U.S.C. § 302(a). For works whose statutory "authors" were not identifiable natural persons—that is, works for hire, anonymous works, and pseudonymous works—the CTEA extended the copyright term alternatively from 75 years to 95 years from publication or from 100 years to 120 years from creation, whichever expires first. *Id.* § 302(c). As under the previous law, the new terms apply to all works not published by January 1, 1978. *Id.* §§ 302(a), 303(a).

[6]*Id.* § 304(a) & (b).

Authors and Inventors the exclusive Right to their respective Writings and Discoveries . . . [7]

Extending the previously fixed terms of existing copyrights, they argued, violated the "limited Times" requirement both because such extension could be repeated indefinitely and because, when interpreted in light of the initial language of the Copyright Clause, the extended term was not limited to that necessary to "promote the Progress of Science." The challengers also argued that the extension of both existing and future copyright terms abridged the freedom of speech of persons who would make use of copyrighted material that would otherwise more quickly enter the public domain. The district court rejected all of the challenges and upheld the CTEA.[8]

On appeal before the U.S. Court of Appeals for the D.C. Circuit, the challengers raised the same arguments and met a similar fate. Regarding the Copyright Clause challenge, a panel of the D.C. Circuit held 2 to 1 that the retroactive extension of existing copyright terms did not violate the Copyright Clause.[9] Judge Sentelle, dissenting in part, would have held that Congress's claimed authority to extend existing copyrights lacked any stopping point and neither promoted the progress of science nor secured exclusive rights for a limited time.[10] Regarding the First Amendment challenge, the panel unanimously held that copyrights are "categorically immune from challenges under the First Amendment."[11] The full D.C. Circuit subsequently denied rehearing *en banc* over the dissent of Judge Sentelle, this time joined by Judge Tatel.[12] The original panel majority simultaneously issued a supplemental opinion denying rehearing and rejecting arguments claiming that the retroactive extension of copyright terms failed to promote the progress of science.

The Supreme Court thereafter agreed to hear the case and, despite expressing considerable skepticism during oral argument as to the wisdom of the law, nonetheless reached the same result as the lower

[7]U.S. CONST. Art. I, § 8, cl. 8.

[8]Eldred v. Reno, 74 F. Supp.2d 1 (D.D.C. 1999).

[9]Eldred v. Reno, 239 F.3d 372, 377–80 (D.C. Cir. 2001).

[10]*Id.* at 380-84 (Sentelle, J., dissenting in part).

[11]239 F.3d at 375.

[12]Eldred v. Reno, 255 F.3d 849 (D.C. Cir. 2001).

courts and upheld the CTEA.[13] The decision was 7 to 2, with Justice Ginsburg writing the majority opinion and Justices Stevens and Breyer each writing individual dissents.

From the outset, the Court adopted a decidedly historical approach to the case, evaluating the constitutional challenges to the CTEA "against the backdrop of Congress' previous exercises of its authority under the Copyright Clause."[14] In particular, the Court looked to the nation's first copyright statute, enacted in 1790, which created the first federal copyrights and applied to future works and to certain existing works already protected by state copyrights.[15] The Court then looked to three subsequent copyright statutes from 1831, 1909, and 1976, each of which extended the terms of existing and future copyrights.[16] The Court also looked to early examples of Congress's extending various individual patents and copyrights and lower court decisions written by individual circuit justices upholding several patent extensions.[17] And while recognizing that it had not previously had "occasion to decide whether extending the duration of existing copyrights complies with the 'limited Times' prescription," the Court looked to its decision in the patent case of *McClurg v. Kingsland*,[18] which upheld the retroactive application of more lenient requirements for obtaining a patent, thus sustaining a patent that would otherwise have been invalid under the previous statute.[19]

Regarding the textual issue of whether retroactive extension of copyright terms violated the "limited Times" constraint in the Copyright Clause, the Court rejected the argument that a copyright term, "once set, becomes forever 'fixed' or 'inalterable,' " and held that

> [t]he word "limited," however, does not convey a meaning so constricted. At the time of the Framing, that word meant what it means today: "confine[d] within certain bounds,"

[13]Eldred v. Ashcroft, 123 S. Ct. 769 (2003).

[14]*Id.* at 775.

[15]*Id.* (citing Act of May 31, 1790, ch. 15, § 1, 1 Stat. 124 (1790 Act)).

[16]123 S. Ct. at 775 (citing Act of Feb. 3, 1831, ch. 16, §§ 1, 16, 4 Stat. 436, 439 (1831 Act); Act of Mar. 4, 1909, ch. 320, §§ 23–24, 35 Stat. 1080-1081 (1909 Act); Pub.L. 94–553, § 302(a), 90 Stat. 2572 (1976 Act)).

[17]123 S. Ct. at 779 (citing Acts from 1808, 1809, 1815, 1828, and 1830 and opinions by Chief Justice Marshall and Justice Story sitting as circuit justices).

[18]42 U.S. (1 How.) 202 (1843).

[19]123 S. Ct. at 779–80.

"restrain[ed]," or "circumscribe[d]." S. Johnson, A Dictionary of the English Language (7th ed. 1785); see T. Sheridan,
A Complete Dictionary of the English Language (6th ed.
1796) ("confine[d] within certain bounds"); Webster's Third
New International Dictionary 1312 (1976) ("confined within
limits"; "restricted in extent, number, or duration"). Thus
understood, a time span appropriately "limited" as applied
to future copyrights does not automatically cease to be "limited" when applied to existing copyrights.[20]

As for the related argument that repeated extensions vitiate the
limited times requirement, the Court responded that "a regime of
perpetual copyrights 'clearly is not the situation before us' " and
there was no reason to view the CTEA "as a congressional attempt
to evade or override the 'limited Times' constraint."[21] The Court
acknowledged the government's position that the average copyright
term under the CTEA "'resembles some other long-accepted dura-
tional practices in the law, such as 99-year leases of real property
and bequests within the rule against perpetuities,' " but went no
further, stating that "[w]hether such referents mark the outer boundary of 'limited Times' is not before us today."[22]

The Court also held that the CTEA was a rational exercise of
congressional authority and adequately promoted the progress of
science, noting that on such matters it "defer[s] substantially to
Congress."[23] Citing the life-plus-70 years copyright term adopted
by the European Union (EU), and the EU's denial of such an extended
term to works from countries without a similar copyright term, the
Court credited as rational Congress's desire "to ensure that American authors would receive the same copyright protection in Europe
as their European counterparts,[ ]" as well as Congress' potential
view that longer terms would provide a greater incentive for creation
and dissemination of works in the United States.[24] The Court also
accepted Congress's view that extending copyright terms "'provide[s] copyright owners generally with the incentive to restore

[20]*Id.* at 778.

[21]*Id.* at 783 (citation and footnote omitted).

[22]*Id.* at 784 n. 17 (citation omitted).

[23]*Id.* at 781; *id.* at 785 ("it is generally for Congress, not the courts, to decide how
best to pursue the Copyright Clause's objectives").

[24]*Id.* at 781 (footnote omitted).

older works and further disseminate them to the public,' " and that "as a result of increases in human longevity and in parents' average age when their children are born, the pre-CTEA term did not adequately secure 'the right to profit from licensing one's work during one's lifetime and to take pride and comfort in knowing that one's children—and perhaps their children—might also benefit from one's posthumous popularity.' "[25] Finally, the Court noted testimony from the Register of Copyrights that "extending the copyright for existing works 'could . . . provide additional income that would finance the production and distribution of new works.' "[26]

The Court rejected the argument that the so-called "preambular language" of the Copyright Clause, empowering Congress to "promote the Progress of Science," is incompatible with retroactive extensions of copyright terms "because it does not stimulate the creation of new works but merely adds value to works already created."[27] While acknowledging that the Copyright Clause is "'both a grant of power and a limitation,' " the Court observed that the "'constitutional command,' . . . is that Congress, to the extent it enacts copyright laws at all, create a 'system' that 'promote[s] the Progress of Science.' "[28] As to whether the congressional system promoted the progress of science, the Court again looked to history:

> Congress, from the start, has routinely applied new definitions or adjustments of the copyright term to both future works and existing works not yet in the public domain.[] Such consistent congressional practice is entitled to "very great weight, and when it is remembered that the rights thus established have not been disputed during a period of [over two] centur[ies], it is almost conclusive."[29]

The Court bolstered its reliance on historical congressional practice with the suggestion that the Framers themselves approved of retroactive copyright term extensions, noting that "'a contemporaneous legislative exposition of the Constitution when the founders of our

[25]*Id*. at 782 & n. 14 (citations omitted).

[26]*Id*. at 782 n. 15 (citations omitted).

[27]*Id*. at 784.

[28]*Id*. at 784–85 (quoting *Graham v. John Deere Co. of Kansas City*, 383 U.S. 1, 5, 6 (1966)).

[29]123 S. Ct. at 785 (footnote and citation omitted).

Government and framers of our Constitution were actively participating in public affairs, acquiesced in for a long term of years, fixes
the construction to be given [the Constitution's] provisions.' "[30] It
concluded that "Congress' unbroken practice since the founding
generation thus overwhelms petitioners' argument that the CTEA's
extension of existing copyrights fails *per se* to 'promote the Progress
of Science.' "[31]

After playing its historic-practice trump card, the Court wrapped
up by simply assuming, *arguendo*, that the Copyright Clause requires
a quid pro quo from an author in exchange for a grant of copyright,
"'to secure a bargain—this for that,' "[32] and held that "the legislative
evolution earlier recalled demonstrates what the bargain entails":

> Given the consistent placement of existing copyright holders
> in parity with future holders, the author of a work created
> in the last 170 years would reasonably comprehend, as the
> "this" offered her, a copyright not only for the time in place
> when protection is gained, but also for any renewal or exten-
> sion legislated during that time.[ ] Congress could rationally
> seek to "promote . . . Progress" by including in every copy-
> right statute an express guarantee that authors would receive
> the benefit of any later legislative extension of the copyright
> term. Nothing in the Copyright Clause bars Congress from
> creating the same incentive by adopting the same position
> as a matter of unbroken practice.[33]

The bargain having included an implied promise of future extensions, the CTEA's retroactive elements merely implemented the pre-
existing exchange that promoted creation of the earlier works and
did not offer something new for nothing.

Thus having disposed of the Copyright Clause challenge, the
Court proceeded to address the First Amendment challenge to the
CTEA. Although content-neutral regulations of speech are ordinarily
subject to heightened—though not strict—judicial scrutiny, the

---

[30]*Id.* (quoting *Myers v. United States*, 272 U.S. 52, 175 (1926)).

[31]123 S. Ct. at 785–86.

[32]*Id.* at 786 (citation omitted).

[33]*Id.* (citations and footnote omitted).

Court rejected the suggested "imposition of uncommonly strict scrutiny on a copyright scheme that incorporates its own speech-protective purposes and safeguards."[34] It began by observing that the "Copyright Clause and First Amendment were adopted close in time" and that such "proximity indicates that, in the Framers' view, copyright's limited monopolies are compatible with free speech principles."[35] Recalling its opinion in *Harper & Row, Publishers, Inc. v. Nation Enterprises*,[36] the Court reiterated that "'the Framers intended copyright itself to be the engine of free expression. By establishing a marketable right to the use of one's expression, copyright supplies the economic incentive to create and disseminate ideas.' "[37]

The Court then observed that "copyright law contains built-in First Amendment accommodations" such as the idea/expression dichotomy and the fair-use defense.[38] The idea/expression dichotomy reserves copyright protection only for expression and not for the ideas contained therein, thus striking "'a definitional balance between the First Amendment and the Copyright Act by permitting free communication of facts while still protecting an author's expression.' "[39] The fair use defense "allows the public to use not only facts and ideas contained in a copyrighted work, but also expression itself in certain circumstances."[40] And the CTEA slightly expands the scope of fair use "during the last 20 years of any term of copyright . . . for purposes of preservation, scholarship, or research" if the work is not already being exploited commercially and copies are unavailable at a reasonable price.[41]

Having recounted the speech-promoting and speech-protecting aspects of copyright law, the Court then distinguished its treatment

[34]*Id.* at 788.

[35]*Id.*

[36]471 U.S. 539, 558 (1985).

[37]123 S. Ct. at 788.

[38]*Id.*

[39]*Id.* at 788–89 (quoting *Harper & Row*, 471 U.S. at 556).

[40]123 S. Ct. at 789; 17 U.S.C. § 107 ("[T]he fair use of a copyrighted work, including such use by reproduction in copies . . ., for purposes such as criticism, comment, news reporting, teaching (including multiple copies for classroom use), scholarship, or research, is not an infringement of copyright.").

[41]17 U.S.C. § 108(h); *see also id.* § 110(5)(B) (limited exception from performance royalties for music).

of content-neutral cable television regulations at issue in *Turner Broadcasting System, Inc. v. FCC*[42] by observing that the CTEA "does not oblige anyone to reproduce another's speech against the carrier's will," but instead "protects authors' original expression from unrestricted exploitation."[43] It noted that the First Amendment "bears less heavily when speakers assert the right to make other people's speeches. To the extent such assertions raise First Amendment concerns, copyright's built-in free speech safeguards are generally adequate to address them."[44] While the Court recognized that "the D.C. Circuit spoke too broadly when it declared copyrights 'categorically immune from challenges under the First Amendment[,]' 239 F.3d, at 375," it concluded that "when, as in this case, Congress has not altered the traditional contours of copyright protection, further First Amendment scrutiny is unnecessary."[45]

Justice Stevens and Justice Breyer each wrote a dissenting opinion. Justice Stevens argued that just as Congress may not extend the scope of a patent monopoly, it may not extend the duration of a copyright beyond its expiration date.[46] In his view, the "limited Times" requirement acts as an essential element of the constitutional purpose of promoting the progress of science, and members of the public should have a right to rely on the expiration of copyrights at the time set forth in the grant.

> We have recognized that these twin purposes of encouraging new works and adding to the public domain apply to copyrights as well as patents. . . . And, as with patents, we have emphasized that the overriding purpose of providing a reward for authors' creative activity is to motivate that activity and "to allow the public access to the products of their genius after the limited period of exclusive control has expired." *Sony Corp. of America v. Universal City Studios, Inc.,* 464 U.S. 417, 429 (1984). *Ex post facto* extensions of copyrights result in a gratuitous transfer of wealth from the public to

---

[42]512 U.S. 622 (1994).

[43]123 S. Ct. at 789.

[44]*Id.*

[45]*Id.* at 789–90 (citing *Harper & Row*, 471 U.S. at 560, and *San Francisco Arts & Athletics, Inc. v. United States Olympic Comm.*, 483 U.S. 522 (1987)).

[46]123 S. Ct. at 790 (Stevens, J. dissenting).

> authors, publishers, and their successors in interest. Such retroactive extensions do not even arguably serve either of the purposes of the Copyright/Patent Clause.[47]

Responding to the Court's reliance on past congressional practice, Justice Stevens observed that "the fact that Congress has repeatedly acted on a mistaken interpretation of the Constitution does not qualify our duty to invalidate an unconstitutional practice when it is finally challenged in an appropriate case. . . . Regardless of the effect of unconstitutional enactments of Congress, the scope of '"the constitutional power of Congress . . . is ultimately a judicial rather than a legislative question, and can be settled finally only by this Court.' "'[48] Not even the early legislative efforts of the founding generation could substitute for that essential judicial function, he argued, because "'[i]t is obviously correct that no one acquires a vested or protected right in violation of the Constitution by long use, even when that span of time covers our entire national existence.' "'[49]

Turning to the merits of the Copyright Clause challenge, Justice Stevens rejected the argument that the retroactive extension of copyright terms provides "incentives to restore old movies," observing first that "such restoration and preservation will not even arguably promote any new works by authors or inventors," second, that such "justification applies equally to works whose copyrights have already expired," and third, that "the remedy offered—a blanket extension of all copyrights—simply bears no relationship to the alleged harm."[50]

He further noted that, regardless of congressional power to prospectively grant lengthy copyright terms, "a categorical rule prohibiting retroactive extensions would effectively preclude perpetual copyrights. . . . [U]nless the Clause is construed to embody such a categorical rule, Congress may extend existing monopoly privileges *ad infinitum* under the majority's analysis."[51]

---

[47] *Id.* at 793.

[48] *Id.* at 797 (quoting *United States v. Morrison,* 529 U.S. 598, 614 (2000) (quoting *Heart of Atlanta Motel, Inc. v. United States,* 379 U.S. 241, 273 (1964) (Black, J., concurring))).

[49] 123 S. Ct. at 797 (Stevens, J., dissenting) (quoting *Walz v. Tax Comm'n of City of New York,* 397 U.S. 664, 678 (1970)).

[50] 123 S. Ct. at 799–800 (Stevens, J., dissenting).

[51] *Id.* at 800–01.

Justice Breyer's dissent went further and took the position that the length of time tacked on to the existing lengthy copyrights added virtually no value and that the "economic effect of this 20-year extension—the longest blanket extension since the Nation's founding—is to make the copyright term not limited, but virtually perpetual. . . . And most importantly, its practical effect is not to promote, but to inhibit, the progress of 'Science'—by which word the Framers meant learning or knowledge."[52] He would have applied a more searching review of congressional judgments under the Copyright Clause given the countervailing First Amendment interests. Although such review would not rise even to the level of intermediate scrutiny, it would, in his view, be sufficient to invalidate the thin justifications used by Congress to support both the prospective and retrospective extension of copyright terms.

Applying his hybrid form of scrutiny, Justice Breyer would have found that "the statute lacks the constitutionally necessary rational support (1) if the significant benefits that it bestows are private, not public; (2) if it threatens seriously to undermine the expressive values that the Copyright Clause embodies; and (3) if it cannot find justification in any significant Clause-related objective."[53]

Central to Justice Breyer's analysis was the requirement that copyright statutes "must seek 'to promote the Progress' of knowledge and learning; and that they must do so both by creating incentives for authors to produce and by removing the related restrictions on dissemination after expiration of a copyright's 'limited Tim[e]'—a time that (like 'a *limited* monarch') is 'restrain[ed]' and 'circumscribe[d],' 'not [left] at large,' 2 S. Johnson, A Dictionary of the English Language 1151 (4th rev. ed. 1773)."[54] Applying that requirement, he concluded that "the partial, future uniformity [with EU copyright terms] that the 1998 Act promises cannot reasonably be said to justify extension of the copyright term for new works. And concerns with uniformity cannot possibly justify the extension of the new term to older works, for the statute there creates no uniformity at all."[55] Justice Breyer likewise rejected the "conflicting rationale that

[52]123 S. Ct. at 801 (Breyer, J., dissenting) (citation omitted).
[53]*Id.* at 802.
[54]*Id.* at 803–04.
[55]*Id.* at 810.

the publishers advance, namely that extension, rather than limitation, of the grant will, by rewarding publishers with a form of monopoly, promote, rather than retard, the dissemination of works already in existence" because the rationale was limitless in its application, because it conflicted with the Copyright Clause's embedded assumption that eventual entry into the public domain was the best means of promoting widespread distribution and use of works created with the incentive of copyrights, and thus such rationale "seems constitutionally perverse—unable, constitutionally speaking, to justify the blanket extension here at issue."[56]

Discussion

It is important to note from the outset that the question whether the text of the Copyright Clause or the First Amendment forbids retroactive extensions of existing copyrights is a fairly debatable issue on which reasonable jurists could differ. Although there are better and worse answers to that question—and in my view the Court elected a "worse" answer—the result in *Eldred* was hardly shocking or implausible. If the decision is to be criticized, then, it should not be on its outcome alone, but rather on the means the Court used to reach that outcome. The particular aspect of the opinion that I will focus on is the Court's reliance on a largely irrelevant and subtly distorted history to support its rather thin textual analysis of the Constitution. The problem is encapsulated in the Court's reliance on the questionable epigram that "'a page of history is worth a volume of logic.' "[57] That approach, in my view, gets it precisely backward and tends to undermine both the value of a written constitution and the role of the Court as the proper authority for interpreting such a constitution.

One of the very purposes of our written Constitution, as opposed to an evolving constitutional tradition, is to provide a definitive exposition of the powers and limits of government, and to stand as a bulwark over time against casual expansions of government power and encroachments on private liberty. Such purposes are thwarted whenever analysis of the terms of the Constitution is made secondary to the inherently biased practices of the government meant to be

[56]*Id.* at 811.
[57]123 S. Ct. 778 (quoting *New York Trust,* 256 U.S. at 349).

restrained by that Constitution. Indeed, precisely because our federal Constitution is one of *enumerated* powers (granting and limiting authority through the same language) and contains still further restraints on the exercise of those powers, deferring to Congress' interpretation of its own powers is akin to putting the fox in charge of the henhouse. Although comity undoubtedly counsels a healthy respect for the constitutional views of a coordinate branch of government, such respect must also be tempered by a proper skepticism of the political branches' inclination and ability to restrain themselves and Congress' seeming tendency to legislate first and ask constitutional questions later, if at all.

The judiciary's role as the last practical line of defense of our written Constitution is no less significant in connection with the Acts of earlier Congresses than it is in connection with more recent Congresses. Although some of the earliest members of Congress may indeed have had a greater familiarity with the then-fledgling Constitution, and may even have participated in its drafting, such backgrounds hardly suggest that, in their subsequent roles as legislators, they were any more willing or able than present-day legislators to interpret or abide by the restraints imposed upon them by the Constitution.

Once it is accepted that constitutional language and logic, and not mere historical practice, should govern constitutional analysis, the best approach is then to "start with first principles."[58] The first principles most significant to an analysis of the *Eldred* case are straightforward and uncontroversial: Constitutional interpretation begins with the actual language of the Constitution[59]; all such language is presumed to have meaning[60]; and the enumeration of certain powers presupposes powers outside the scope of the enumeration.[61] Those first principles lead to the conclusion that *all* of the language of the Copyright Clause in one way or another limits congressional authority, and that the First Amendment limits the copyright power just as it limits all other Article I powers.

---

[58]*United States* v. *Lopez*, 514 U.S. 549, 552 (1995).

[59]*Gibbons* v. *Ogden*, 22 U.S. (9 Wheat.) 1, 188–89 (1824).

[60]*Marbury* v. *Madison*, 5 U.S. (1 Cranch) 137, 174 (1803).

[61]*Gibbons*, 22 U.S. (9 Wheat.) at 194–95.

I. The Copyright Clause

Article I, section 8, clause 8, of the Constitution enumerates Congress' copyright and patent power:

> The Congress shall have Power . . . To promote the Progress of Science and useful Arts, by securing for limited Times to Authors and Inventors the exclusive Right to their respective Writings and Discoveries. . . .

Plainly read, the language of the Copyright Clause defines, and therefore delimits, congressional power as being "To promote the Progress of Science." The structure of the clause defines a power "to do X by means of Y." In the case of the copyright power, "X"—to promote the progress of sciences—not merely "preambular language," as the Court suggests[62]; it *is* the power granted to Congress. The remainder of the Clause—"by securing for limited Times," etc.—is not an affirmative grant; it is a negative limit on the *means* by which the power "[t]o promote" may be exercised.[63]

The actual language of the Copyright Clause thus determines the relevant inquiries when evaluating the CTEA: (1) Has Congress, in adopting the CTEA, acted to "promote the Progress of Science?; and (2) Has Congress done so through the prescribed means of securing to authors the exclusive right to their writings "for limited Times"?

A. The Nature of Limited Times

Regarding whether the CTEA's retrospective term extensions conflict with the "limited Times" requirement, the Court offered only a meager few sentences attempting to reconcile the CTEA with the language of the Constitution. Looking to dictionaries from both 1796 and 1976, the Court defined "limited" as "confine[d] within certain bounds," "restrain[ed]," "circumscribe[d]," "confined within limits," "restricted in extent, number, or duration."[64] Then, in what

---

[62]123 S. Ct. at 784.

[63]*See also, e.g.,* U.S. Const., Art. II, § 2, cl. 2 ("[The President] shall have the Power, *by and with the Advice and Consent of the Senate,* to make Treaties. . . ."); *id.,* Art. IV, § 1 (regarding full faith and credit for state acts, records, and proceedings, "Congress may *by general Laws* prescribe the Manner in which such Acts, Records and Proceedings shall be proved, and the Effect thereof"). The "by" language limits the means of exercising a particular authority; it does not imply that the language enumerating the power itself lacks any limiting function.

[64]123 S. Ct. at 778 (citations omitted).

constitutes the entirety of its textual analysis, the Court concluded that if the time span set out in the CTEA is "appropriately 'limited' as applied to future copyrights," then it "does not automatically cease to be 'limited' when applied to existing copyrights."[65]

But the Court's conclusion does not follow from the definitions it cited, and it certainly does not stand on its own. The problem with the CTEA's retrospective term extension is that it removed the restraint of existing copyright terms and made once-certain bounds uncertain. Indeed, even as applied to future copyrights, the extended term is certainly not confined within *certain* bounds or restricted in duration; it is subject to still further extension at Congress' whim, without any rationale as to where the "certain bounds" of copyright duration will lie. Absent such bounds, it cannot satisfy even the Court's own cited definition of "limited." The actual limit of a copyright thus remains "'[left] at large'" so long as the possibility of congressional extension remains.[66]

The notion that the Court was not *yet* confronted with a regime of perpetual copyright, or that Congress did not *intend* to secure such perpetual rights is wholly beside the point. Having offered no test for determining when a copyright becomes "perpetual," the Court's implicit definition of "limited" as meaning "not perpetual" simply begs the question. And if "perpetual" means only that a specific copyright term, on its face, literally extends forever, then the phrase "limited Times" in the Copyright Clause has no realistic function. A term of 1000 or 10,000 years is certainly not forever in the literal sense, but just as certainly it is not what the Framers could have meant when they permitted Congress to secure copyrights only for "limited Times."

Furthermore, when evaluating Congress' exercise of an enumerated power, the proper analysis is whether the *rationale* used by Congress to justify a statute is unlimited, not whether the exercise of such power in a specific instance is itself unlimited.[67] When defining a

---

[65] *Id.*

[66] 123 S. Ct. at 804 (Breyer, J., dissenting) (quoting 2 S. JOHNSON, A DICTIONARY OF THE ENGLISH LANGUAGE 1151 (4th rev. ed. 1773)).

[67] *See United States v. Lopez*, 514 U.S. 549, 564 (1995) (Congress may not justify an exercise of its commerce powers on a "rationale[ ]" that "would . . . authorize a general federal police power"); *id.* at 567 (rejecting "manner" of analyzing exercise of commerce power that "would bid fair to convert congressional authority under the Commerce Clause to a general police power of the sort retained by the States").

limited constitutional power, therefore, the Court looks to the larger *theory* used to justify the particular exercise of the power and asks whether that theory is limited, not whether the specific exercise of power involved the full application of that theory. So too, when evaluating whether copyrights are "limited" in time, the Court should have looked to whether the rationale for the extension had any limits that would prevent perpetual repetition, not whether this isolated extension failed to go all the way to perpetuity in a single step.

The approach taken by the Court regarding the limited times requirement lacked any rationale that would prevent Congress from repeatedly granting term extensions each time the latest extension neared completion. Indeed, the Court's suggestion—when discussing whether the CTEA promotes the progress of Science[68]—that all copyrights contain the implicit promise of the benefit of any future term extensions confirms that the duration of any copyright term under the Court's theory is anything but "confined within certain bounds." The nominal term of years granted by a copyright under the Court's rationale is not the *limit* of that term. Rather, it is merely the opening bid, subject to expansion (though presumably not contraction) at Congress' pleasure. The power to extend existing copyright terms, and all future terms subject to such power, renders such terms unlimited in that they are not subject to any "certain" bounds.[69]

As noted earlier, however, the deficiencies of the Court's reasoning do not necessarily demonstrate that its ultimate result was incorrect. Had the Court articulated a determinable outer limit to copyright terms (for example, that such terms could not exceed the rule against

[68]123 S. Ct. at 786.

[69]The Court's analysis perhaps can be understood in light of the challengers' supposed concession that the "CTEA's baseline term of life plus 70 years ... qualifies as a 'limited Tim[e]' as applied to future copyrights," thus leading the Court to assert that the same discreet time would likewise be limited even as applied to existing copyrights. 123 S. Ct. at 778. But such reasoning distorts petitioner's argument that a *fixed* term of life plus 70 years would be limited and evades the point that retroactive application of that new term removes the previous "limit" on existing copyright terms. The issue is not whether the facial amount of the baseline would be "limited" *if adhered to*, but whether the retroactive extension demonstrates that no term is limited if subject to retroactive revision. Thus understood, the CTEA's application even to future copyrights creates an unlimited term if that term is not certain and remains *subject to* still further extension.

perpetuities as it existed when the Constitution was written) then even retroactive term extensions within that outer limit might still be considered "limited Times" precisely because they could not be repeated indefinitely. Such outer limits would presumably set "certain bounds" for all present and future copyrights notwithstanding that the term of any given copyright might be somewhat of a moving target *within* those bounds. But the Court expressly refused to adopt any such outer boundary, or even to suggest a theory under which such a boundary could be determined in some later case.[70] Given the Court's highly deferential treatment of whether Congress had exercised its power rationally and of Congress's determinations of how best to promote the progress of science, it is far from clear how the Court would propose to draw any line between a limited and an unlimited copyright term. And insofar as the only term constraints the Court suggests are the due process limit that Congress exercise its powers rationally and the promote-progress limit from the remainder of the Copyright Clause, the phrase "limited Times" has no independent force, in violation of a first principle of constitutional construction that all the words have meaning.

In my view, the better construction would recognize that the Copyright Clause's use of the plural "Times" matches the plural "Writings and Discoveries," but that its use of the singular "the exclusive Right" suggests only a singular "Time[]" per each writing or discovery. That interpretation requires Congress to select a time and stick to it for copyrights already granted, though it could modify the "Time[]" prospectively as to any future copyright. It also has the benefit of avoiding the seriatim grant of supposedly limited copyright terms that could, as a practical matter, be repeated indefinitely. Absent that or some other theory limiting such repetition, the *Eldred* decision renders the "limited Times" language meaningless.

Without the essential foundation of a logical construction of the language of the Copyright Clause, the Court's reliance on historic congressional practice cannot support its decision. Furthermore, the Court's historical discussion is less than compelling even on its own terms. Most notable in that regard is the Court's attempt to channel the credibility of the Founders by relying on the 1790 Act creating

---

[70]123 S. Ct. 784 n. 17.

federal copyrights and its application to existing works protected by state or common-law copyrights.

While acknowledging the challengers' argument that "the 1790 Act must be distinguished from the later Acts on the ground that it covered existing *works* but did not extend existing *copyrights*," the Court refused to confront the implications of that argument as it related to understanding the phrase "limited Times" and instead offered the non sequitur that "the First Congress clearly did confer copyright protection on works that had already been created."[71] As Justice Stevens correctly observed, "the question presented by this case does not even implicate the 1790 Act, for that Act created, rather than extended, copyright protection. That this law applied to works already in existence says nothing about the first Congress's conception of their power to extend this newly created federal right."[72] The 1790 Act did not extend the terms of federal copyrights for the simple reason that no such copyrights even existed before the Act. And, even as to state-granted copyrights, not only did the 1790 Act not extend those copyrights, it instead replaced them with the newly enacted federal copyright that was, in many instances, *shorter* in term than the previously existing state copyrights.[73]

Absent any implicit support from the founding generation for its construction of the "limited Times" requirement, the Court can take little analytical comfort from the actions of subsequent Congresses in 1831, 1909, and 1976. The unarticulated construction of the Copyright Clause supposedly found in those Congresses' failure to restrain their own exercise of power is not based on any personal familiarity of the congressmen with the drafting of the Constitution or upon any "inside information" on the meaning of "limited Times."[74] If

[71] *Id.* at 776 n. 3.

[72] 123 S. Ct. at 795 (Stevens, J., dissenting); *see also id.* ("That Congress exercised its unquestionable constitutional authority to *create* a new federal system securing rights for authors and inventors in 1790 does not provide support for the proposition that Congress can *extend pre-existing* federal protections retroactively.") (emphasis in original).

[73] *Id.*

[74] Being slightly closer in time to the drafting of the Copyright Clause may have given earlier members of Congress a certain linguistic advantage based on familiarity with the speech patterns of the time, but, as the Court noted, 123 S. Ct. at 778, the meaning of the word "limited" has not changed, and hence that potential advantage does not bear on the issue in *Eldred*.

anything, those Congresses would be even less knowledgeable regarding the proper construction of the Constitution given the fewer judicial constructions and scholarly resources available to them and given the technological limits on accessing what information did exist at the time. Whatever added weight one might give to the constitutional understandings of the first Congress, such weight does not attach to the implied views of subsequent Congresses.[75]

B. Promoting the Progress of Science

Turning to whether the CTEA's retrospective extension of copyright terms "promote[s] the Progress of Science," the Court's opinion fails to offer any analysis of the meaning and limits of that constitutional language and frequently conflates the effects of the prospective lengthening of copyright terms and the quite different effects of the retrospective extension of existing copyrights. When the language of the Copyright Clause and the retrospective effects of the CTEA are properly analyzed, there is considerable reason to conclude that the retrospective extension of existing copyrights does nothing to induce the creation of new writings and hence does not "promote the Progress of Science."

As a precursor to this discussion, however, it is worth noting that the Court ducked the question of the independent force of the "promote the Progress of Science" language in the Copyright Clause, choosing instead to assume such a requirement and hold that it was met.[76] Unfortunately, by not confronting the question head on, the Court avoided a closer look at the language of that portion of the Clause, and its subsequent analysis of the merits suffered accordingly. As noted above, however, the initial language of the Copyright Clause is not merely a preamble, it is the very definition of the power granted to Congress, and thus some attention to the meaning of the enumerated terms of that power is warranted.[77]

---

[75] 123 S. Ct. at 798 (Stevens, J., dissenting) (presumption accorded historic practice "does not attach to congressional action in 1831, because no member of the 1831 Congress had been a delegate to the framing convention 44 years earlier").

[76] 123 S. Ct. at 784–787.

[77] The Court at least casually seemed to acknowledge the correct structural reading of the Copyright Clause by citing to its decision in the patent case of *Graham* v. *John Deere Co.*, 383 U.S. 1 (1966). *Eldred*, 123 S. Ct. at 784–85. In *Graham*, the Court stated regarding the patent Clause that the:

clause is both a grant of power and a limitation. This qualified authority ...
is limited to the promotion of advances in the "useful arts." ... The Congress in
the exercise of the patent power may not overreach the restraints imposed

The specific language of Congress's enumerated power is "To promote the Progress of Science." "Promote" means "to help forward," "to encourage."[78] "Progress" means "forward movement," "improvement, advancement."[79] Science, as used in the Constitution, was understood to mean all learning and knowledge, not merely the "sciences" as we more narrowly understand them today.[80] In combination, those definitions suggest that the copyright power must be used to induce new, and not merely to reward or sustain old, learning or knowledge.[81]

Many of the Court's arguments as to how the CTEA might encourage the creation of new works apply only to the prospective aspects of the term extensions, and have little or nothing to do with retrospective extensions of existing copyrights. For example, the claimed value of creating harmony with the EU's longer copyright terms is completely irrelevant to the bulk of the existing copyrights affected by the CTEA given that the Act does not even purport to create such uniformity for works published before 1978, for works-for-hire, and for anonymous and pseudonymous works.[82] And even as to the extension of existing copyright terms for post-1997 works by identified natural persons, there is precious little explanation of how such uniformity has any value for promoting progress beyond that promoted by the prospective creation of uniformity as to future works.

Likewise, the Court's discussion of the need for longer terms based on increased life expectancy, technological changes, and the need

---

by the stated constitutional purpose. . . . [A patent system] by constitutional command must "promote the Progress of . . . useful Arts." *This is the standard expressed in the Constitution and it may not be ignored.*
383 U.S. at 5–6 (emphasis added). If patent laws "must 'promote the Progress of . . . useful Arts,'" then copyright laws similarly "must" promote "the Progress of Science." The Court failed to take that final step, however, and thus neglected a closer discussion of the relevant language.

[78] NEW LEXICON WEBSTER'S DICTIONARY 800 (1994).

[79] *Id.* at 799.

[80] *Eldred*, 123 S. Ct. at 801 (Breyer, J., dissenting).

[81] *Cf. Sony Corp. of America* v. *Universal City Studios, Inc.*, 464 U.S. 417, 429 (1983) ("the limited grant [of monopoly privileges] is . . . intended to motivate the creative activity of authors").

[82] *Eldred*, 123 S. Ct. at 809 (Breyer, J., dissenting).

of authors to support their future efforts from the continuing proceeds of prior works generally serves as an explanation for longer terms for future copyrights, not retroactive extension of past copyrights. Indeed, the Court's argument regarding continuing creation by authors of earlier works is particularly odd.[83] Prior to the CTEA, existing copyrights for identified natural persons already extended well beyond the author's death, and the posthumous addition of 20 years to such copyrights could not possibly revive the creative flow from such authors.

In fairness, however, some of the Court's arguments might indeed apply to retroactive extensions. For example, the support-for-future-works rationale could apply where the author is not a natural person—for example, a corporate "author" of a work for hire—and thus may continue to exist and create further works for hire during the extended term. But the unconditional transfer of wealth to immortal authors represented by retroactive term extensions has only the most speculative connection to any future acts of creativity and thus drains much of the meaning from the word "promote." As the Supreme Court observed in *United States v. Morrison*, reasoning that follows a "but-for causal chain . . . to every attenuated effect" implicating an enumerated power is "unworkable if we are to maintain the Constitution's enumeration of powers."[84] Although it might be different if the retroactive extension were somehow conditioned on further acts of creativity, merely throwing monopoly rights at corporate "authors" in the attenuated *hope* they use the proceeds beneficially only mocks the constitutional enumeration that Congress actively "promote Progress." If such passive reliance on the positive consequences of corporate charity sufficed to promote science, then the language of the Copyright Clause has little meaning.

The same objection holds true for the Court's acceptance of the claim that retroactive extension encourages the preservation and dissemination of existing works. Because the retroactive extension is not conditioned on any further preservation or dissemination, there is no credible reason to believe that the extension will induce

[83]123 S. Ct. at 782 n. 15 ("'Authors would not be able to continue to create,' the Register explained, 'unless they earned income on their finished works. The public benefits not only from an author's original work but also from his or her further creations.'") (citations omitted).

[84]529 U.S. 598, 615 (2000).

owners to preserve any works that they have, by hypothesis, already neglected for years. The CTEA thus does not "promote" progress or anything else because the connection between the additional rights conferred and the supposed benefits is too attenuated and speculative.[85] The gift of 20 more years of exclusive rights for existing copyrights, without even requiring that the protected works be converted into a format that will be preserved *and available* for public use in the future, is not the promotion of progress, it is simply a transfer of wealth from the public to existing copyright holders. Furthermore, even if retroactive extensions promoted preservation, they do not promote the "Progress" of science. While "progress" involves forward movement, advancement, and creation, preservation involves the very different realm of stasis and avoidance of decay.[86] Although preservation might eventually *benefit* science or the public generally, authorizing the promotion of mere preservation would effectively nullify the word "Progress" and more broadly empower Congress to promote science *in toto*.

One argument that has a stronger theoretical appeal is the Court's characterization of the copyright quid pro quo as being understood by authors from the outset to include the retroactive application of any future extensions. If future extensions were understood as part of the original bargain, and hence the original incentive to create copyrightable works, then applying such extensions to existing works is simply the implementation of that bargain and, at a minimum, necessary and proper to the exercise of the copyright power. The trouble with that argument, insofar as the *Eldred* opinion itself is concerned, is that it is woefully underdeveloped and leaves unanswered a number of troubling questions. Thus, although it is true that Congress could have explicitly included in its definition of copyright terms a right to share equally in any future term extensions, it certainly did not do so in any of the copyright statutes it

---

[85] Also, it is highly doubtful whether Congress could grant a *new* copyright for the mere preservation of an existing work. Such a copyright would appear to violate the requirement of originality and the prohibition against removing works from the public domain. Yet that is precisely the effect of retroactively extending copyrights: Granting more years of exclusive rights in return for the hope of preservation of works that otherwise would enter the public domain in due course.

[86] *Compare* NEW LEXICON WEBSTER'S DICTIONARY 799 ("Progress" means "forward movement," "improvement, advancement"), *with id.* at 792 ("preserve . . . to keep up, maintain, prevent from ruin or decay").

has adopted. And implying such a promise into those past statutes is quite a stretch. Such a promise certainly would not be enforceable against the federal government or third parties had Congress elected *not* to extend the terms of existing copyrights, and surely would not constitute a sufficiently reasonable investment-backed expectation to sustain a takings claim for any failure to extend existing terms along with an extension of future terms. Insofar as copyright holders had nothing more than the unenforceable hope that they might be the beneficiaries of future extensions, fulfilling that unilateral hope surely does not qualify as either necessary or proper to fulfill Congress's side of the bargain struck when existing copyrights were initially issued.

Thus, although there are a smattering of arguments that might be stretched to support the Court's conclusion that retroactive term extensions are compatible with the "promote the Progress of Science" language of the Copyright Clause, accepting those arguments does considerable violence to the first principles of constitutional construction. The better interpretation would be to read "promote" as requiring an active incentive, in the form of an express quid pro quo for the creation of copyrightable works, and would read "Progress" as requiring the creation of something new in exchange for whatever benefits Congress bestows. Because the retroactive extension of existing copyright terms in the CTEA does not actively encourage the creation of any new works, it should have been held to violate the Copyright Clause.

The difficulties with the Court's analysis of the CTEA and the Copyright Clause once again leaves as the primary bulwark of the opinion the historical claim that Congress has consistently acted to promote the progress of science through the extension of increased benefits for existing works. That argument theoretically applies even to the 1790 Act given that the nonexistence of federal *copyrights* before 1790 is relevant only to the analysis of whether such copyrights are for limited times. In terms of promoting progress, it is the existence of the work itself that seems relevant—because the reward would go to a writing that is not "new"—not the existence of a federal copyright. But again, aside from the questionable abdication of interpretive authority even to the first Congress, the Court's reading of the historical record is a bit off. In claiming that the 1790 Act demonstrates that "the First Congress understood it could 'promote

... Progress' by extending copyright protection to existing works,"[87] the Court neglects to acknowledge that the original federal copyrights replaced and preempted state copyrights that in many instances would have provided *longer* protection.[88] Rather than extending the duration of author control over existing works, the retroactive application of the 1790 Act often hastened the entry into the public domain of those existing works. Such increased public access indeed would have been understood to promote the progress of science, but offers no support for the CTEA. And even as to existing works that may have received greater protection under the 1790 Act than under prior copyright law, there is no indication that the first Congress gave any consideration to whether such increased protection would promote the progress of science. It is far more likely that Congress, in creating a new federal copyright system, simply overlooked any such start-up problems or considered them sui generis rather than expressed an implied view on the matter of constitutional construction going forward.

Overall, therefore, an ambiguous history and the dubious inferences drawn from earlier Congresses' self-serving decisions to exercise power are no substitute for the logical analysis of the terms and implications of a written constitution. Such analysis is the province and duty of the courts, and should not be abdicated in favor of the historical practices of Congress.

II. The First Amendment

In addressing the First Amendment challenge to the CTEA, the Court again looked to history and observed that the "Copyright Clause and First Amendment were adopted close in time" thus reasoning that such "proximity indicates that, in the Framers' view, copyright's limited monopolies are compatible with free speech principles."[89] The Court then offered the additional analysis that the speech-promoting incentives of copyright law and the speech-protecting limits on copyright of the idea/expression dichotomy and the fair-use defense served generally to resolve most First Amendment questions in favor of copyright law.[90] Thereafter, while the Court

[87] 123 S. Ct. at 785 n. 19.
[88] 123 S. Ct. at 795 (Stevens, J., dissenting).
[89] 123 S. Ct. at 788.
[90] *Id.* at 788–89.

offered a welcome rejection of the D.C. Circuit's notion that copyright law was "'categorically immune from challenges under the First Amendment[,]' " it adopted the less-than-compelling alternative that "when, as in this case, Congress has not altered the traditional contours of copyright protection, further First Amendment scrutiny is unnecessary."[91]

In evaluating the Court's First Amendment reasoning, it is well to begin with a fundamental principle that the Court recently reiterated in another context: Article I powers do not supersede restrictions created by Amendments.[92] Rather, Amendments to the Constitution narrow congressional authority that would otherwise exist under Article I standing alone. The First Amendment question is whether government action is unconstitutional *despite* Congress's enumerated power. The constitutional hierarchy is no different in the case of copyright law. A law within Congress's copyright power may *still* be prohibited by the First Amendment.

That the Copyright Clause and the First Amendment were adopted close in time does nothing to mitigate the precedence of the First Amendment. The same proximity of adoption is equally true for all other Article I powers, yet that hardly raises the inference that all exercises of such powers are "compatible" with the First Amendment. Indeed, that the First Amendment was adopted at all suggests that the Framers understood that various exercises of congressional power could indeed abridge the freedom of speech, and hence that there was a need for still further limits operating *within* the scope of the limited enumerations of congressional power. There is no reason to think that the Copyright Clause involved less of a concern than any of the other Article I powers.

Ultimately, however, the Court in *Eldred* seemed to accept that the First Amendment indeed imposes some restraint on the copyright power. At that point, it was not enough simply to rely upon the idea/expression dichotomy and the fair-use defense, particularly

---

[91] *Id.* at 789–90.

[92] *See, e.g., Florida Prepaid Postsecondary Educ. Expense Bd. v. College Sav. Bank,* 527 U.S. 627, 635–36 (1999) (provision that "[a]ny State . . . shall not be immune, under the eleventh amendment of the Constitution of the United States or under any other doctrine of sovereign immunity, from suit in Federal court . . . for infringement of a patent" was unconstitutional, in part because "Congress may not abrogate state sovereign immunity pursuant to its Article I powers").

when evaluating a new statutory expansion of copyright's restrictions on speech rather than evaluating an individual copyright alone.
The notion that copyright only restricts particular expression, not the
underlying ideas, and hence has little impact on First Amendment
interests is mistaken. The First Amendment protects not only the
conveyance of concepts generally, but the particular *form* of expression as well. Thus, Paul Robert Cohen was constitutionally entitled
to display on his jacket a uniquely evocative disparagement of "the
Draft," not merely some alternative "expression" of the same basic
sentiment.[93] Indeed, the Court has recognized that protected expression "conveys not only ideas capable of relatively precise, detached
explication, but otherwise inexpressible emotions as well. In fact,
words are often chosen as much for their emotive as their cognitive
force."[94] It generally is left to the speaker to decide not merely what
to say, but also how to say it, and the First Amendment protects
the intangible value associated with a particular "expression" independently from the underlying idea.[95] Indeed, in the case of music
and much poetry and art, there may not be much of an underlying
"idea" at all beyond the descriptive beauty conveyed through the
particularized "expression." Yet such work is protected by the First
Amendment as well as by copyright, and the idea/expression dichotomy is insufficient to accommodate the First Amendment interests
at stake.

The fair-use defense likewise may mitigate the First Amendment
burden of copyrights generally, but it does not eliminate the substantial remaining burden on uses not subject to the defense. Activities
that would infringe authors' copyrights continue to have significant
value, as evidenced by the Framers' concern that copyrights remain
limited to relatively brief periods and their clear desire to expand
the public domain. The Framers understood that copyrights limited
access to protected works, and that fully free use of various works
would be a driving force for the progress of science. Fair use thus

[93] *See Cohen* v. *California*, 403 U.S. 15, 24 (1971) ("the usual rule [is] that governmental
bodies may not prescribe the form or content of individual expression").

[94] *Id.* at 26.

[95] The government could not, consistent with the First Amendment, restrict publication of works by Plato or Marx on the theory that the ideas could still be conveyed
through other "expression."

helps in the eventual balance, but fully *free* use is the First Amendment optimum, with anything less constituting a restriction on speech that should be analyzed accordingly.

As for the Court's refusal to engage in separate First Amendment balancing of new statutory restrictions added to copyright law that do not alter the "traditional contours of copyright protection,"[96] Justice Breyer correctly observed that "the sentence points to the question, rather than the answer."[97] The Court makes no attempt to explain why the term of copyrights is not part of the "traditional contours of copyright protection" or why a retroactive increase in term of 20 years—a substantial percentage of the term for any category of copyrighted works—is not a sufficiently significant alteration. Given the exceedingly trivial and speculative benefits from such retroactive extension and the palpable prolongation of copyright's burdens on fully free speech, surely the First Amendment balance will be different than it is for the prospective copyright protection previously analyzed by the Court.

The gain from such an extension does not involve any realistic *addition* to the incentive for prior authors to create new work, and the speech-promoting qualities of copyright therefore would not play a significant role in the balance. On the other side of the scale, an additional 20 years of retroactive monopoly is a significant burden on both First Amendment and copyright values. The extension will hinder access to numerous works that would soon enter the public domain and that need no additional incentive for preservation. And the CTEA will chill the public use of works having uncertain status or whose authors are not readily located because few persons will risk the criminal penalties for unauthorized use of such works. Categorically rejecting First Amendment balancing for statutory changes based on the conclusory assertion that such changes do not alter the traditional contours of copyright protection does a disservice to the fundamental priority of the First Amendment over Article I powers and avoids the Court's duty to enforce the Constitution when a case calls upon it to do so.

[96] 123 S. Ct. at 789–90.
[97] 123 S. Ct. at 812 (Breyer, J., dissenting).

Conclusion

The history of unchallenged congressional legislation relied upon by the Court to uphold the CTEA was inadequate for that purpose both in principle and in substance. Any defense of the CTEA should have started and ultimately ended with the words and logic of the Constitution itself. And by that measure, the opinion failed to persuade. Although the language and logic of the Constitution cannot be said to foreclose entirely the outcome reached by the Court, that language and logic certainly undermine many of the reasons given by the Court for its result and leave substantial doubts as to whether the CTEA could survive a logically rigorous examination under the Copyright Clause or the First Amendment. Regardless of the outcome, however, both the *Eldred* opinion and the jurisprudence it will influence would have been better served by an additional page or two of logic and a considerably smaller volume of history.

The Conservative Split on Punitive Damages
State Farm Mutual Automobile Insurance Co. v. Campbell

Robert A. Levy

I. Introduction

When a supposedly right-leaning court discovers that diversity is a compelling state interest,[1] reinforces an unenumerated right to privacy,[2] and expands the federal government's authority to override state sovereign immunity,[3] it is hard to find evidence that Republican-appointed justices did much to advance the party's conservative agenda. The most Republican-friendly of this term's opinions is probably the Court's reversal of a bloated $145 million punitive damages award against State Farm Insurance.[4] Ironically, that holding withstood separate dissents from the Court's conservative superstars, Justices Antonin Scalia and Clarence Thomas. Liberal Justice Ruth Bader Ginsburg also dissented. The same three justices had dissented from the Court's 1996 decision overturning a punitive damage award against BMW.[5] In that case, Chief Justice William H. Rehnquist dissented as well. But in *State Farm*, he switched sides without explanation.

That's a healthy sign, say many Court-watchers. It suggests that law and politics operate, as intended by the Framers, within separate realms. Perhaps so. An alternative explanation, however, is that the current Court has no ideological compass. That may be the lesson of the *State Farm* case, in which the Court grappled once again with

[1] Grutter v. Bollinger, 123 S. Ct. 2325 (2003).
[2] Lawrence v. Texas, 123 S. Ct. 2472 (2003).
[3] Nevada Dep't of Human Resources v. Hibbs, 123 S. Ct. 1972 (2003).
[4] State Farm Mutual Automobile Insurance Co. v. Campbell, 123 S. Ct. 1513 (2003).
[5] BMW of North America, Inc. v. Gore, 517 U.S. 559 (1996).

159

federal intervention, via the Fourteenth Amendment's Due Process Clause, to prevent states from violating substantive rights that some justices believe to be secured by the U.S. Constitution.

Contrasting the majority opinion in *State Farm* with the terse dissents by Scalia and Thomas, I hope to shed light on the battle between conservatives who want to rein in runaway punitive damage awards and other conservatives who find no federal judicial power to do so. First, I set the stage with a few comments on the purpose of punitive damages, the need for reform, and the Court's major stab at the problem in the *BMW* case. Then I summarize the facts in *State Farm*, the majority holding, and the Ginsburg dissent, which accuses the Court of usurping legislative powers. Next, elaborating on the Scalia and Thomas dissents, I explore the controversy over the Court's substantive due process jurisprudence. Finally, I offer a few recommendations to restore sanity in the punitive damages arena while honoring traditional notions of federalism.

II. Background

A. The Purpose of Punitive Damages

Compensatory damages are supposed to redress any loss that the plaintiff suffers because of the defendant's wrongful conduct. Punitive damages serve a different purpose. They "are aimed at deterrence and retribution."[6] The logic goes like this: A defendant whose misbehavior causes injury will neither be adequately punished nor deterred from similar misbehavior in the future if he is held accountable only for the losses he causes. That's because some wrongful acts are never litigated and others are incorrectly decided in the defendant's favor. Proper deterrence, therefore, has to make adjustments for an imperfect system of compensation. In *State Farm*, for example, the Utah Supreme Court relied on trial testimony indicating that "State Farm's actions, because of their clandestine nature, will be punished at most in one out of every 50,000 cases as a matter of statistical probability."[7]

Naturally, there are also errors that favor plaintiffs, including holding a defendant liable for conduct that is legally permissible. Prominent Washington, D.C., lawyer C. Boyden Gray describes the

---

[6]Cooper Industries, Inc. v. Leatherman Tool Group, Inc., 532 U.S. 424, 432 (2001).
[7]*Quoted in State Farm*, 123 S. Ct. at 1519.

ideal tort system, along with the risks of damage awards that are too low, too high, or capricious.

> [T]he tort system should perform two functions: compensate victims and deter potentially dangerous behavior. . . . If these principles are applied correctly, torts are minimized, because any benefits of such behavior would be eliminated by the expected costs of the damage award. When awards are too low, bad actors are not deterred. . . . Awards that are too large pose problems as well, as costs increase and products are no longer available. When awards are arbitrary, it becomes impossible to discern any relevant incentives from the pattern of damage awards, leaving businesses only to guess at what business practices will not instigate damage claims.[8]

Paradoxically, most states set no limit on punitive damages for civil acts, yet punishment for criminal acts is strictly limited. One would think that the goal of deterrence would be more compelling in the criminal sphere, where injuries to victims of murder, rape, and robbery are not ameliorated by the social utility of the acts committed. In the civil sphere, by comparison, the product or service that is deterred may have considerable value. Respected law and economics scholars have noted that "overdeterrence is a real danger when punitive damages are available. . . . A doctor who has been negligent once may nonetheless provide useful medical care."[9]

Moreover, when punitive damages are unbounded and unpredictable, many firms will avoid making rational risk-assessment calculations. That result—the suppression of cost-benefit analyses—is another downside of overdeterrence. "[A]ny consideration of risk in product design can later be interpreted by a jury as evidence that the firm knew it was producing a risky product and 'traded profits for lives.' "[10]

Thus, punitive damages can be an appropriate means of inhibiting injurious behavior or an inappropriate device that restrains trade in valuable goods and services. Tort reform advocates argue that judges

---

[8]C. Boyden Gray, *Damage Control*, WALL STREET JOURNAL, Dec. 11, 2002, at A18.

[9]Paul H. Rubin et al., *BMW v. Gore: Mitigating the Punitive Economics of Punitive Damages*, 5 SUPREME COURT ECONOMIC REVIEW 179, 184–85 (1997).

[10]*Id.* at 191.

and juries have allowed punitive damage awards to explode without regard to their harmful impact on the economy and without a rational link to the real need for deterrence. The evidence seems to support that view.

B. The Need for Reform

Consider the recent *Engle* tobacco class action litigation,[11] in which an inflamed Florida jury resolved to pilfer $145 billion in punitive damages from hapless cigarette companies. Trial judge Robert Kaye, in the face of a contrary opinion from the state's attorney general, permitted the jury to decide punitive damages for the entire class after hearing evidence on only three of the claimants.[12] The selected plaintiffs were not the designated class representatives; yet they were plucked from among the class members, with the judge's consent, because the lawyers knew that the three case histories would resonate with the jury.

No one knew the names of the other class members. No one even knew how many smokers were in the class; estimates ranged from 30,000 to nearly a million. No one knew anything about their alleged injuries or how much if any compensatory damages might be warranted. Yet Judge Kaye approved an award of punitive damages in the aggregate, as if it did not matter whether 50,000 plaintiffs had a raspy throat or 500,000 died from lung cancer, whether they started smoking as kids or as consenting adults, and whether they were ever influenced by the industry's so-called deceptive ads. Ultimately, a Florida appellate court decertified the class and reversed the punitive damages award because there had been no prior determination of compensatory damages. Still, the *Engle* case demonstrates the enormous potential for mischief when state courts impose punitive damages on out-of-state defendants.

If the *Engle* fiasco were the only evidence that punitive damage awards are out of control, that would be bad enough. But there's more. According to the *National Law Journal*, the largest punitive award in 2002 was $28 billion. Five verdicts exceeded $500 million

[11] *See* Liggett Group v. Engle, 2003 Fla. App. LEXIS 7500 (Fla. Dist. Ct. App. May 21, 2003).

[12] For further commentary on the *Engle* case, *see* Robert A. Levy, *Tobacco Class Decertified in Florida: Sanity Restored*, THE HILL, June 11, 2003, http://www.thehill.com/news/061103/ss_tobacco.aspx.

and 22 exceeded $100 million. The total of the top 100 verdicts for 2002 was nearly three-and-a-half times the total for 2001. Longer term, 38 verdicts topped $20 million in 1991; 66 verdicts were more than $20 million in 1996. But in 2002, $20 million did not make the top 100 list.[13] No doubt, nine U.S. Supreme Court justices were aware of the problem—if not the specifics, at least the general trend. Perhaps that's why, seven years ago, the Court took a first step toward reform.

C. BMW v. Gore

When Dr. Ira Gore discovered that his new BMW had been repainted, he sued the American distributor for fraud. BMW conceded that its policy was not to notify dealers or consumers if repairs for predelivery damage to a new car cost less than 3 percent of the suggested retail price. Gore's car, repainted for approximately $600, had originally cost $40,000. On the basis of testimony that a repainted car would lose 10 percent in value, an Alabama jury found BMW liable for $4,000 in compensatory damages, then imposed an additional $4 million in punitives, computed by multiplying the compensatory award by roughly 1,000 similar sales nationwide. On appeal, the Alabama Supreme Court concluded that only in-state sales should have been considered, then reduced the punitive award to $2 million, without explaining how it reached that result. The U.S. Supreme Court declared that state sovereignty and comity prevented one state from imposing its own policy choices on other states. In remanding the case, the Court held that the unwarranted award violated BMW's rights under the Due Process Clause of the Fourteenth Amendment.

First, said the Court, Gore's injury was purely economic. None of the aggravating factors associated with reprehensible conduct by the defendant was present. Second, the ratio of punitive damages to compensatory damages was 500 to 1, which was clearly outside the acceptable range. Third, Alabama's fine for comparable misconduct was only $2,000—an amount so much lower than the punitive award that out-of-state defendants would not have fair notice of their exposure to a multimillion dollar sanction.

---

[13] David Hechler, *Tenfold Rise in Punitives*, NATIONAL LAW JOURNAL, Feb. 3, 2003, at C3.

BMW's three-part test—"the degree of reprehensibility . . .; the disparity between the harm . . . suffered [and the] punitive damages award; and the difference between this remedy and the civil penalties authorized or imposed in comparable cases"[14]—provided the business community with a framework, however vague, and offered some hope that the punitive damages crisis was defused. Regrettably, it did not turn out that way. In the seven years since *BMW*, punitive awards have continued their upward spiral. The Court's initial step was not enough. It was time for a second intervention.

III. The State Farm Opinion

A. The Facts

Curtis Campbell, trying to pass six vans on a two-lane highway, faced a head-on collision with an oncoming car driven by Todd Ospital. To avoid a collision, Ospital swerved, lost control of his car, and hit Robert Slusher, who suffered permanent disabling injuries. Ospital was killed. Campbell was unharmed.

Campbell's insurer, State Farm, rejected settlement proposals from Ospital and Slusher for the policy limit of $50,000. Instead, State Farm decided to litigate, assuring Campbell and his wife that their "assets were safe," they had "no liability," and they did not need separate counsel. The jury had other ideas, however, and found the Campbells liable for roughly $186,000. Initially, State Farm refused to cover the excess liability of $136,000 and advised the Campbells to "put for sale signs on your property to get things moving." The Campbells then hired their own lawyer and appealed the jury verdict. They lost in the Utah Supreme Court, but State Farm changed its mind anyway and agreed to pay the entire judgment.

Still, the Campbells sued State Farm for bad faith, fraud, and intentional infliction of emotional distress. Because State Farm had ultimately paid the full $186,000, a Utah trial court ruled in favor of the insurer. That ruling was overturned on appeal and the case was returned to the trial court, which then determined that State Farm's refusal to settle was unreasonable.

Next, the trial court was to address fraud, emotional distress, and damages. But meanwhile the U.S. Supreme Court had decided *BMW*. In that case, the Court disallowed evidence of out-of-state conduct

[14]*BMW*, 517 U.S. at 575.

that was lawful where it occurred and had no impact on in-state residents. Based on *BMW*, State Farm asked the trial court to exclude evidence of conduct in unrelated cases outside of Utah. The court denied that request and proceeded to weigh State Farm's alleged fraudulent practices nationwide—in particular, the company's "Performance Planning and Review" (PPR) program that was designed to meet fiscal goals by capping payouts. Most of the PPR practices had nothing to do with third-party automobile insurance claims like those arising out of Campbell's negligence. Nonetheless, the jury awarded the Campbells $2.6 million in compensatory damages and $145 million in punitive damages, which the judge reduced to $1 million and $25 million, respectively. The Campbells and State Farm both appealed.

Purporting to apply *BMW*'s three guideposts, relying on evidence about State Farm's PPR policy, and considering State Farm's "massive wealth," the Utah Supreme Court reinstated the $145 million punitive damages award.[15]

B. The Majority Opinion

The reinstatement was short-lived. Justice Anthony Kennedy, writing for a six-member majority of the U.S. Supreme Court, put it bluntly: "[T]his case is neither close nor difficult. It was error to reinstate the jury's $145 million punitive damages award."[16] The high Court returned the case to Utah with this advice: "An application of the Gore guideposts to the facts of this case, especially in light of the substantial compensatory damages awarded (a portion of which contained a punitive element), likely would justify a punitive damages award at or near the amount of compensatory damages."[17]

Then Kennedy proceeded to address in some detail the first two guideposts of *BMW v. Gore*—the reprehensibility of the conduct and the ratio of punitive to compensatory damages. He also discussed at length the propriety of evidence related to the defendant's out-of-state conduct and net worth. As to *BMW*'s third guidepost, comparable fines, Kennedy quickly deduced that it provided no support for the *State Farm* award.

[15] Campbell v. State Farm Mutual Automobile Insurance Co., 65 P.3d 1134 (2001).

[16] *State Farm*, 123 S. Ct. at 1521.

[17] *Id.* at 1526.

> [W]e need not dwell long on this guidepost. The most rele-
> vant civil sanction under Utah state law for the wrong done
> to the Campbells appears to be a $10,000 fine for an act
> of fraud, an amount dwarfed by the $145 million punitive
> damages award. The Supreme Court of Utah speculated
> about the loss of State Farm's business license, the disgorge-
> ment of profits, and possible imprisonment, but here again
> its references were to the broad fraudulent scheme drawn
> from evidence of out-of-state and dissimilar conduct. This
> analysis was insufficient to justify the award.[18]

1. Reprehensibility and Out-of-State Conduct. To frame his discussion of reprehensibility, Kennedy first laid out the pertinent criteria:
whether the harm caused was physical as opposed to economic;
whether the wrongful behavior reflected an indifference to or a
reckless disregard of the health or safety of others; whether the
plaintiff was financially vulnerable; whether the conduct was recur-
ring or an isolated incident; and whether injury arose from intentional malice or mere accident.[19]

Weighing the various factors, Kennedy concluded that the Utah
courts were justified in awarding punitive damages, but "a more
modest punishment for this reprehensible conduct could have satisfied the State's legitimate objectives."[20] That conclusion stemmed in
major part from the state courts' misplaced reliance on State Farm's
dissimilar out-of-state conduct. Essentially, Kennedy agreed with
the stance taken by an alliance of insurance trade associations representing the major property and casualty insurers. In their friend-of-
the-court brief, the insurers cautioned, "When the punitive damage
case stops being about the harm done to a plaintiff and becomes an
indictment of an insurer's nationwide practices involving policy-
holders in other states, it essentially becomes a nationwide class
action without the class and without protections afforded to class
members and defendants."[21]

---

[18]*Id.* at 1526 (citation omitted).

[19]*Id.* at 1521.

[20]*Id.*

[21]*Quoted in* Charles E. Boyle, *Campbell vs. State Farm: U.S. Supreme Court May Resolve Issue,* INSURANCE JOURNAL, Sept. 16, 2002, http://www.insurancejournal.com/ magazines/west/2002/09/16/features/23288.htm.

Seven years earlier, the *BMW* Court had said in nonbinding language that punitive damages should not be used "with the intent of changing the [defendant's] *lawful* conduct in other states."[22] Kennedy followed that counsel; he reaffirmed that "A State cannot punish a defendant for conduct that may have been lawful where it occurred."[23] Then he addressed the question that *BMW* had not addressed: whether punitive damages could be used to deter *unlawful* conduct in other states. "Nor, as a general rule," stated Kennedy, "does a State have a legitimate concern in imposing punitive damages to punish a defendant for unlawful acts committed outside of the State's jurisdiction."[24]

In other words, out-of-state conduct should not itself be punished, whether lawful or unlawful. Nonetheless, Kennedy added, it may assist the judge or jury in assessing the reprehensibility of similar in-state conduct for which the defendant may be liable. "[O]ut-of-state conduct may be probative when it demonstrates the deliberateness and culpability of the defendant's action in the State where it is [unlawful], but that conduct must have a nexus to the specific harm suffered by the plaintiff."[25]

The key to Kennedy's reprehensibility analysis is the similarity between in-state and out-of-state acts. "A defendant should be punished for the conduct that harmed the plaintiff, not for being an unsavory individual or business," he remarked.[26] That does not mean recidivists must be treated the same as first-time offenders. Ordinarily, recidivism is evidence of reprehensible behavior. But, "in the context of civil actions courts must ensure the conduct in question replicates the prior transgressions."[27] While the prior acts do not have to be identical, noted Kennedy, the Utah court had allowed evidence "pertaining to claims that had nothing to do with a third-party lawsuit."[28] The Campbells had shown no conduct by State Farm similar to that which harmed them.

---

[22] *BMW*, 517 U.S. at 572 (emphasis added).
[23] *State Farm*, 123 S. Ct. at 1522.
[24] *Id.*
[25] *Id.*
[26] *Id.* at 1523.
[27] *Id.* (quoting *BMW*, 517 U.S. at 577).
[28] *Id.* at 1523.

2. The Punitive-to-Compensatory Ratio. Turning to the 145-to-1 ratio of punitive-to-compensatory damages, Kennedy made it clear that the Utah courts had overreached. He did not, however, impose a bright-line ratio, although he did volunteer that, "in practice, few awards exceeding a single-digit ratio between punitive and compensatory damages ... will satisfy due process."[29] That guideline is somewhat elastic. "[R]atios greater than those we have previously upheld may comport with due process where 'a particularly egregious act has resulted in only a small amount of economic damages.'... When compensatory damages are substantial, then a lesser ratio, perhaps only equal to compensatory damages, can reach the outermost limit of the due process guarantee."[30]

Applying that framework to the injuries suffered by the Campbells, Kennedy wrote:

> The compensatory award in this case was substantial; the Campbells were awarded $1 million for a year and a half of emotional distress. This was complete compensation. The harm arose from a transaction in the economic realm, not from some physical assault or trauma; there were no physical injuries; and State Farm paid the excess verdict before the complaint was filed, so the Campbells suffered only minor economic injuries for the 18-month period in which State Farm refused to resolve the claim against them.... Much of the distress was caused by the outrage and humiliation the Campbells suffered.... Compensatory damages, however, already contain this punitive element.[31]

Future plaintiffs will find little to cheer about in Kennedy's explanation. But he did hint at one qualification: The Court was dealing with a case in which only economic, not physical, harm had occurred. That suggests the Court might condone a more generous allowance for punitive damages in product liability cases involving injury or death. Nevertheless, if trial courts embrace the *State Farm* ratio guideline—punitive damages roughly bounded by an upper limit of 10 times compensatory damages—the impact on dollar awards could be substantial. Among the *National Law Journal*'s top 100 verdicts

[29] *Id.*

[30] *Id.* (quoting *BMW*, 517 U.S. at 582).

[31] *Id.* at 1524–25.

for 2001 and 2002, 31 percent of the punitive awards exceeded 10 times the corresponding compensatory award. In 2001, 24 percent of the 38 punitive awards had double-digit ratios, with a high of 500 to 1. In 2002, it was 39 percent of the 41 punitive awards, with a high of 1,145 to 1.[32]

3. Deep Pockets. One other aspect of the *State Farm* opinion has especially troubled plaintiffs' attorneys: the Court's apparent reluctance to consider the defendant's net worth. Trial lawyer Barry Knopf, interviewed just after the opinion was issued, said he was concerned that the high Court did not tie damage awards to the size of the defendant. "The purpose of punitive damages is to deter certain types of conduct . . . and what's important to a very small corporation is peanuts to State Farm," he said.[33]

True enough, at the margin, a dollar has less utility to a billionaire than to a blue-collar worker. Nevertheless, courts are probably ill-equipped to engage in the tricky business of comparing interpersonal utility functions. If courts were to perform that task, damages would be based not only on what the defendant did but on who he is. That said, courts are already in the business of measuring utility when they award compensatory damages for pain and suffering. For instance, a wrongful act resulting in the loss of a dog owned by a breeder would almost certainly not generate the same pain-and-suffering award as the same act causing the loss of a cherished pet.

The Court, in deemphasizing the importance of the defendant's net worth, neither accepted nor rejected utility as a basis for punitive damages. Instead, Kennedy adopted a more prosaic view of the matter: "[T]he presentation of evidence of a defendant's net worth creates the potential that juries will use their verdicts to express biases against big business, particularly those without strong local presences."[34] He also noted that State Farm's assets are what other insured parties in Utah and elsewhere must rely on for payment of

---

[32] Marcia Coyle, *New Battles to Come over Punitives Ruling*, NATIONAL LAW JOURNAL, Apr. 214, 2003, at A1.

[33] *Quoted in* Edward Walsh & Brooke A. Masters, *Justices Overturn Big Jury Award*, WASHINGTON POST, Apr. 8, 2003, at E1.

[34] *State Farm*, 123 S. Ct. at 1520 (quoting Honda Motor Co. v. Oberg, 512 U.S. 415, 432 (1994)).

claims. Accordingly, he concluded, "The wealth of a defendant cannot justify an otherwise unconstitutional punitive damages award."[35]

Kennedy's statement was promptly spotlighted by the media and legal practitioners. Respected *New York Times* reporter Linda Greenhouse proclaimed, "The most significant departure in the 6-to-3 decision was the court's declaration that juries should generally not be permitted to consider a defendant's wealth when setting a punitive damage award."[36] Evan Tager, a D.C. lawyer who helped write the amicus brief filed by the U.S. Chamber of Commerce, rejoiced, "The Court has basically rendered impotent the issue of wealth as a way to jack up awards."[37] *Findlaw* columnist Andy Sebok stated, less hyperbolically, "[S]ince the Court decided *BMW v. Gore*, the idea that punitive damages should be used to 'send a message' to corporate America has been used in closings in numerous jury trials around America. . . . *State Farm* should go a long way to slowing down that trend."[38]

Sebok's tempered perspective is probably more accurate. By declaring that a defendant's wealth cannot justify an otherwise unconstitutional punitive damages award, the Court left ample wiggle room for trial courts and juries. Even if Kennedy's 10-to-1 ratio of punitive-to-compensatory damages were a rigid upper constraint, an award somewhere between zero and ten times a dollar amount that included both economic losses and pain and suffering might still be deemed constitutional. Within that expansive range, net worth evidence can legitimately be used by a jury to decide on a specific punitive award.

If deterrence is a valid objective of tort law—a provocative topic for another day—then the defendant's wealth is a sensible factor to be weighed. In that respect, the Court may have gotten it right. Evidence of net worth is still admissible, but trial courts are on notice that appellate courts will scrutinize large punitive awards for

---

[35] *Id.* at 1525.

[36] Linda Greenhouse, *Justices Limit Punitive Damages in Victory for Tort Revision*, NEW YORK TIMES, Apr. 8, 2003, at A16.

[37] *Quoted in* Tony Mauro, *Damage Control on Punitives*, CORPORATE COUNSEL, June 2003, at 121.

[38] Anthony J. Sebok, *The Supreme Court's Recent Bombshell Punitive Damages Decision: Its Important Holdings and Implications*, FINDLAW'S LEGAL COMMENTARY, Apr. 21, 2003, http://writ.news.findlaw.com/sebok/20030421.html.

indications of anti-business bias, above all if the defendant is out of state.

C. *Ginsburg Charges Judicial Activism*

That brings us to the dissenting opinions. The longest of the dissents, by Justice Ginsburg, is discussed below. Then, in the succeeding section on "Substantive Due Process," the concerns of Justices Scalia and Thomas are addressed in some detail.

Justice Ginsburg raises two principal objections. First, she disagrees on the facts: "[O]n the key criterion 'reprehensibility,' there is a good deal more to the story than the Court's abbreviated account tells."[39] More specifically, said Ginsburg, the jury had ample basis to conclude that the Campbells' travails were directly related to State Farm's PPR profit scheme. Because of that connection, "it becomes impossible to shrink the reprehensibility analysis to this sole case."[40]

Second, Ginsburg balks at the "Court's substitution of its judgment for that of Utah's competent decisionmakers."[41] Referring back to her 1996 dissent in *BMW*, Ginsburg cautioned, "Even if I were prepared to accept the flexible guides prescribed in *Gore*, I would not join the Court's swift conversion of those guides into instructions that begin to resemble marching orders."[42] If the Utah legislature or the Utah Supreme Court had decided to set single-digit and 1-to-1 punitive damage benchmarks, she added, that would have been within their purview. But "a judicial decree imposed on the States by this Court . . . seem[s] to me boldly out of order."[43]

Undoubtedly, the Court does assume a quasi-legislative role when it establishes guidelines for punitive damages. That role evidently bothers some liberals, like Ginsburg, some of the time—like when a federal court overturns a state's huge award against a corporation that has plainly misbehaved. But concern over judicial usurpation of legislative authority is more often associated with conservatives who reflexively rail against "judicial activism." Columnist George Will, although not disposed to reflexive railing, puts it this way:

[39]*State Farm*, 123 S. Ct. at 1527 (Ginsburg, J., dissenting).

[40]*Id.* at 1530.

[41]*Id.* at 1527.

[42]*Id.* at 1531.

[43]*Id.*

"What, other than the justices' instincts, provides criteria of proportionality and arbitrariness? . . . And what principle makes the justices' instincts superior to the jury's . . .? Furthermore, even if the jury's award was unjust, the idea that 'unjust' and 'unconstitutional' can be synonymous gives [the Court] a license to legislate."[44]

Rigorously applied, however, the Will formulation might even preclude judicial review. Obviously, some unjust outcomes are also unconstitutional. Judicial restraint does not consist in deferring to a legislature that has exceeded its constitutional authority. Statutes that are unconstitutional cannot stand. Nor can unconstitutional outcomes imposed by trial judges or juries. Intervention by the U.S. Supreme Court is our final shield against abuse of government power and our final bulwark against violation of individual rights.

The crucial question, therefore, is whether the legislative enactment or the common law-based verdict of a federal or state court violates the U.S. Constitution. Ultimately, that determination is the job of nine justices. They should not impose their own policy preferences; rather, they should apply the Constitution, based on a proper theory of that document grounded in the Framers' notions of limited government, separation of powers, federalism, and individual liberty.

To the contrary, asserts Justice Scalia. "[A]pplication of the Court's new rule of constitutional law is constrained by no principle other than the Justices' subjective assessment of the 'reasonableness' of the award in relation to the conduct for which it was assessed."[45] Well, yes, judges are frequently called on to exercise a rule of reason. But, conceptually, an evaluation of reasonableness requires much the same thought process in the context of a punitive damage award as in the context of other murky terms throughout our statutes and Constitution—terms like cruel and unusual punishment, probable cause, unreasonable searches, and just compensation, which our courts must regularly interpret and apply.

If the justices decide that an egregious award breaches constitutional safeguards, they are authorized to do something about it. Their remedy might be couched in the broadest terms, as in *BMW*, or it might be somewhat more concrete, as in *State Farm*. Brighter-line

---

[44]George F. Will, *License to Legislate*, WASHINGTON POST, Apr. 17, 2003, at A23.
[45]*BMW*, 517 U.S. at 599 (Scalia, J., dissenting).

remedies, despite Justice Ginsburg's occasional distaste for them, do provide greater clarity to all litigants. If the legislature, previously acquiescent, wishes to reclaim its lawmaking role, a subsequent statute will ordinarily supersede the Supreme Court's default guidelines. The existence of those guidelines may even inspire long overdue legislation.

State Farm affords a particularly strong argument for judicial benchmarks. No statute dictated the outcome—just the common law of tort as construed by judge and jury. An appellate court is uniquely qualified to review the common-law decision of a lower court. So the real debate in *State Farm* does not center on separation of powers but on federalism. And that debate, in turn, recalls the muddle over substantive due process—the doctrine intermittently invoked by federal courts to prevent states from violating substantive rights presumably secured by the U.S. Constitution, applied to the states via the Due Process Clause of the Fourteenth Amendment.

IV. Substantive Due Process

The Court should not have imposed its judgment on Utah "under the banner of substantive due process," insisted Justice Ginsburg.[46] Predictably, her concern over the scope of that doctrine was echoed by Thomas and Scalia, both of whom cited Scalia's earlier dissent in *BWM*, which Thomas had joined. Virtually no scope best describes their view of substantive due process. Thomas's *State Farm* dissent is little more than one sentence: "[T]he Constitution does not constrain the size of punitive damage awards."[47] Scalia's dissent is not much longer: "[T]he Due Process Clause provides no substantive protections against 'excessive' or 'unreasonable' awards of punitive damages. I am also of the view that the punitive damages jurisprudence which has sprung forth from *BMW v. Gore* is insusceptible of principled application; accordingly, I do not feel justified in giving the case *stare decisis* effect."[48]

---

[46] *State Farm*, 123 S. Ct. at 1531 (Ginsburg, J., dissenting). Notably, Justice Ginsburg has been willing to invoke substantive due process in other contexts. *See, e.g.*, Lawrence v. Texas, 123 S. Ct. 2472 (2003), which she joined this term, holding that substantive due process protects an unenumerated right to privacy.

[47] *Id.* at 1526 (Thomas, J., dissenting) (quoting *Cooper Inds.*, 532 U.S. at 443 (Thomas, J., concurring) (citing *BMW*, 517 U.S. at 599 (Scalia, J., joined by Thomas, J., dissenting))).

[48] *Id.* at 1526 (Scalia, J., dissenting).

Scalia's second sentence says *BMW* is so poorly reasoned that the Court should not treat it as binding precedent, notwithstanding any reliance on its holding that may have evolved over the past seven years. As we shall see, Scalia's selective dismissal of *stare decisis* is an important adjunct to his substantive due process jurisprudence.

First, however, a celebrated statement from appellate judge Frank H. Easterbrook, who pithily captured the conservative perspective on substantive due process: "The fourteenth amendment contains an equal protection clause, and a due process clause, but no 'due substance' clause. The word that follows 'due' is 'process.' "[49] In a 1993 opinion concurring in a punitive damages award against TXO Production Corporation, Scalia elaborated on Easterbrook's point:

> To say (as I do) that "procedural due process" requires judicial review of punitive damages awards for reasonableness is not to say that there is a federal constitutional right to a substantively correct "reasonableness" determination. . . . Procedural due process also requires, I am certain, judicial review of the sufficiency of the evidence to sustain a civil jury verdict, and judicial review of the reasonableness of jury-awarded compensatory damages (including damages for pain and suffering); but no one would claim (or at least no one has yet claimed) that a substantively correct determination of sufficiency of evidence and reasonableness of compensatory damages is a federal constitutional right. So too, I think, with punitive damages: Judicial assessment of their reasonableness is a federal right, but a correct assessment of their reasonableness is not.[50]

In short, Scalia believes the U.S. Constitution guarantees defendants that the process followed in determining a punitive award will be reasonable, including judicial review, but not that the award itself will be reasonable. Assurances regarding the appropriate size of an award must come, if at all, from state statutes and constitutions. At first blush, the *TXO* majority opinion by Justice John Paul Stevens seemed to agree. But then Stevens distinguishes semantically between "unreasonable" awards, which are not foreclosed by the Constitution, and "grossly excessive" awards, which are foreclosed.

[49] McKenzie v. City of Chicago, 118 F.3d 552, 557 (7th Cir. 1997).

[50] TXO Production Corp. v. Alliance Resources Corp., 509 U.S. 443, 471 (1993) (Scalia, J., concurring in the judgment).

> Justice Scalia's assertion notwithstanding, we do not suggest
> that a defendant has a substantive due process right to a
> correct determination of the "reasonableness" of a punitive
> damages award. . . . [S]tate law generally imposes a require-
> ment that punitive damages be "reasonable." A violation of a
> state law "reasonableness" requirement would not, however,
> necessarily establish that the award is so "grossly excessive"
> as to violate the Federal Constitution.[51]

Stevens reminds us that "our cases have recognized for almost a
century that the Due Process Clause of the Fourteenth Amendment
imposes an outer limit on such an award."[52]

Interestingly, Kennedy's *TXO* concurring opinion rejected the distinction between "reasonable" and "grossly excessive" in no uncertain terms:

> To ask whether a particular award of punitive damages is
> grossly excessive begs the question: excessive in relation to
> what? . . . [W]e are still bereft of any standard by which to
> compare the punishment to the malefaction that gave rise
> to it. A reviewing court employing this formulation comes
> close to relying upon nothing more than its own subjective
> reaction to a particular punitive damages award in deciding
> whether the award violates the Constitution.[53]

Instead of a "grossly excessive" standard, Kennedy preferred to
focus on the jury's reasons for an award—that is, whether the "award
reflects bias, passion, or prejudice on the part of the jury, rather than
a rational concern for deterrence and retribution."[54] Fast forward
one decade. In *State Farm*, Kennedy now opts for benchmark ratios
and cites binding precedent that the "Due Process Clause of the
Fourteenth Amendment prohibits the imposition of grossly excessive or arbitrary punishments."[55]

Kennedy's earlier apprehension about unmanageable standards
like "grossly excessive" remains Scalia's concern today. But Scalia

[51] *Id.* at 458 n.24 (internal references omitted).

[52] *Id.*

[53] *Id.* at 466–67 (Kennedy, J., concurring in part and concurring in the judgment).

[54] *Id.* at 467.

[55] *State Farm*, 123 S. Ct. at 1520 (citing *Cooper Inds.*, 532 U.S. at 433; *BMW*, 517 U.S.
at 562).

goes further. He would deny substantive content to the Due Process Clause. He does, however, allow for this exception: "I am willing to accept the proposition that the Due Process Clause of the Fourteenth Amendment, despite its textual limitation to procedure, incorporates certain substantive guarantees specified in the Bill of Rights."[56]

On what principled basis does Scalia carve out that exception? Is his litmus test that the right be enumerated? He does say, after all, that the Due Process Clause is not "the secret repository of all sorts of other, unenumerated, substantive rights."[57] Yet that does not explain why he limits the clause to incorporating only *certain* provisions in the Bill of Rights. Moreover, the question of which substantive rights are encompassed by Due Process is quite different than the question of whether the Due Process Clause can be read to have any substantive content at all.

The answer, according to Harvard law professor Laurence H. Tribe, who argued *State Farm* before the Supreme Court on behalf of the Campbells, is that Scalia is simply relying on *stare decisis*— that is, respect for past decisions now well-settled in law.[58] That would explain why Scalia took care to say in his *State Farm* dissent, "*BMW v. Gore* is insusceptible of principled application; accordingly, I do not feel justified in giving the case *stare decisis* effect."[59]

By asserting that he can invoke *stare decisis* or not—presumably based on a set of neutral criteria that he claims to have formulated— Scalia leaves himself "open to the charge of importing his own views and values into his method of interpretation."[60] Perhaps that criticism unfairly assumes that Scalia cannot objectively apply his *stare decisis* criteria to determine whether an opinion has generated a sufficiently settled body of law, adequately woven into the fabric of society. Still, Scalia's peremptory refusal to invoke substantive due process in *State Farm* is difficult to square with a case dating back to 1907 holding that Due Process imposes substantive limits

---

[56] *TXO*, 509 U.S. at 470 (Scalia, J., concurring in the judgment) (internal references omitted).

[57] *Id.*

[58] Laurence H. Tribe, *Comment* in ANTONIN SCALIA, A MATTER OF INTERPRETATION: FEDERAL COURTS AND THE LAW 82–83 (1997).

[59] *State Farm*, 123 S. Ct. at 1526 (Scalia, J., dissenting).

[60] Tribe, *supra* note 58, at 83.

"beyond which penalties may not go."[61] Or a 1915 case in which the Court actually set aside a penalty because it was so "plainly arbitrary and oppressive" as to violate the Due Process Clause.[62]

Moreover, Scalia and Thomas might have sidestepped substantive due process by authorizing federal intervention on procedural rather than substantive grounds. Remember that the Court was dealing in *State Farm* with remedies, not with liability itself. Arguably, remedies have as much to do with procedure as with substance, in the following sense: Proper procedure requires advance notice of the law. Private parties must be able to determine which conduct is necessary to conform to the law's dictates; and legal outcomes must be reasonably predictable. As the Court stated in *State Farm*, "Elementary notions of fairness enshrined in our constitutional jurisprudence dictate that a person receive fair notice not only of the conduct that will subject him to punishment, but also of the severity of the penalty that a State may impose."[63] By violating those norms, outrageous punitive damages do not provide adequate notice and therefore offend procedural due process.

Finally, if the Court's conservatives are serious about resolving the substantive versus procedural quandary implicit in the Due Process Clause, maybe it is time for them to revisit the Fourteenth Amendment's nearly forgotten Privileges or Immunities Clause. Indeed, Justice Thomas and Chief Justice Rehnquist have indicated a willingness to do so "in an appropriate case."[64] Meanwhile, other conservatives, like former judge Robert Bork, demur because "we do not know what the clause was intended to mean."[65] Yet that critique is no more persuasive when applied to the Privileges or Immunities Clause than it would be if applied to the General Welfare Clause, the Necessary and Proper Clause, or the Commerce Clause. A compelling case can be made that the Court has misinterpreted

[61] Seaboard Air Line R. Co. v. Seegers, 207 U.S. 73, 78 (1907) (cited by *State Farm*, 123 S. Ct. at 454).

[62] Southwestern Telegraph & Telephone Co. v. Danaher, 238 U.S. 482 (1915) (cited by *State Farm*, 123 S. Ct. at 454).

[63] *State Farm*, 123 S. Ct. at 1520 (quoting *BMW*, 517 U.S. at 574).

[64] Saenz v. Roe, 526 U.S. 489 (1999) (Thomas, J., dissenting, joined by Rehnquist, C.J.).

[65] ROBERT BORK, THE TEMPTING OF AMERICA: THE POLITICAL SEDUCTION OF THE LAW 180 (1990).

each of those clauses, but no one has suggested that they not be interpreted at all.

In any event, probably the clearest discussion of the Privileges or Immunities Clause appears in a 1998 Cato Institute monograph by professor Kimberly Shankman and Cato scholar Roger Pilon. Here's their recap of the rise and fall of the clause:

> Shortly after the Civil War, the American people amended the Constitution in an effort to better protect individuals against state violations of their rights. Under the Privileges or Immunities Clause of the new Fourteenth Amendment, constitutional guarantees against the federal government could be raised for the first time against state governments as well. . . . But . . . in 1873, in the infamous *Slaughter-House Cases*,[66] a deeply divided Supreme Court effectively eviscerated the Privileges or Immunities Clause. Since then courts have tried to do under the Due Process and Equal Protection Clauses of the amendment what should have been done under the more substantive Privileges or Immunities Clause.[67]

As a result of *Slaughter-House*, conclude Shankman and Pilon, we now have "an essentially directionless body of Fourteenth Amendment jurisprudence that often reflects little more than each succeeding Court's conception of 'evolving social values.'"[68] By overturning *Slaughter-House* and reviving the Privileges or Immunities Clause, a more coherent doctrine of the Fourteenth Amendment and federalism is likely to emerge. Along the way, the debate over the substantive content of the Due Process Clause will inevitably diminish.

V. Recommendations and Conclusion

While we wait patiently for an "appropriate case" to revisit Privileges or Immunities, the problem of confiscatory state punitive damage awards need not be irreconcilable with dual sovereignty federalism. First, several remedies can be implemented by the states themselves, without federal involvement. Second, federal reform of long-arm jurisdiction and choice-of-law rules will curb punitive damage

---

[66] Slaughter-House Cases, 16 Wall. (83 U.S.) 36 (1873).

[67] Kimberly C. Shankman & Roger Pilon, *Reviving the Privileges or Immunities Clause to Redress the Balance among States, Individuals, and the Federal Government*, CATO INST. POL. ANALYSIS, no. 326, Nov. 23, 1998, at 1.

[68] *Id.* at 33.

abuse yet fit comfortably within a federalist regime. Although a full discussion of those reforms is beyond the scope of this paper, a brief summary—short of final endorsement—might be useful.

A. State Remedies

First, one cure for inflated punitive damage awards might be to take the dollar decision away from the jury. For example, the jury might be instructed to vote "yes" or "no" on an award of punitives, with the amount then set by a judge in accordance with preset guidelines. If the judge complied with the guidelines, an appellate court would grant deferential review. But should the trial court exceed the guidelines, appellate review would be more rigorous. The rationale for a diminished jury role, from a 1989 article by our current Solicitor General, goes like this:

> Juries are well constituted to perform as factfinders and determiners of liability. But here they are being given in effect the public function of sentencing—of deciding how high a penalty someone should pay for violating a public standard. Juries are remarkably ill-equipped for that task because they sit in only one case, hear evidence only in that case, and are then given very vague guidance with which to form a judgment. . . . Jurors are drastically swayed by such factors as the wealth, success, or personal demeanor of a defendant, even how far away the defendant lives from the location of the litigation. The jurors are frequently told to send a message back to such and such a corporate headquarters. After being instructed to set aside emotion, bias, and prejudice, juries are bombarded with arguments that are based almost exclusively on emotion, bias and prejudice.[69]

A similarly skeptical view of jurors' competence to assess punitive damages comes from attorney Mark Klugheit who specializes in class actions and mass tort litigation.

> Jurors are hardly expected to be experts in social engineering or economic analyses. They are not likely to understand, let alone apply, any kind of reason-based analyses to punitive damage determinations. Yet in most jurisdictions the law requires lay jurors to decide claims involving millions, or

[69] Theodore Olson, *Some Thoughts on Punitive Damages*, MANHATTAN INST. CIVIL JUSTICE MEMO, no. 15, June 1989, http://www.manhattan-institute.org/html/cjm_15.htm.

> sometimes billions, of dollars with virtually no guidance
> about how to translate abstractions like the need for punish-
> ment or deterrence into an appropriate verdict. Instructions
> predicated on amorphous concepts like 'punishment,' 'deter-
> rence,' and the 'public good,'. . . make the imposition of puni-
> tive damages a standardless, if not haphazard, exercise.[70]

Second, another suggestion for reform at the state level is to limit punitive damages to cases involving intentional wrongdoing or gross negligence. In fact, an even higher standard has had a salutary effect in Maryland, where punitive damages are permitted in a tort case only if the plaintiff has proved that the defendant acted with actual malice.[71] Whatever the heightened standard, the idea is that accidental injuries arising out of ordinary, garden-variety negligence are unlikely to require the deterrence for which punitive damages are designed.

Third, states might effect procedural guarantees similar to those inherent in criminal law. In *State Farm*, Kennedy observed that puni-tive awards "serve the same purposes as criminal penalties [but] defendants subjected to punitive damages in civil cases have not been accorded the protections applicable in a criminal proceeding."[72] Among the protections that might be offered:

- A higher burden of proof than the usual civil standard, which is preponderance of the evidence. Thirty-one states now require clear and convincing evidence for punitive awards.[73]
- No double jeopardy. Current rules allow "multiple punitive damages awards for the same conduct; for in the usual case nonparties are not bound by the judgment some other plaintiff obtains."[74] Victor Schwartz, a noted torts scholar, has proposed that "punitive damage awards be reduced by the sum of all

---

[70] Mark A. Klugheit. *Where the Rubber Meets the Road: Theoretical Justifications vs. Practical Outcomes in Punitive Damages Litigation*, 52 SYRACUSE LAW REVIEW 803, 806 (2002) (footnotes omitted).

[71] *See, e.g.*, Darcars Motors of Silver Spring v. Borzym, 818 A.2d 1159, 1164 (2003).

[72] *State Farm*, 123 S. Ct. at 1520.

[73] Martin F. O'Connor, *Taming the Mass Tort Monster*, NATIONAL LEGAL CENTER FOR THE PUBLIC INTEREST, Oct. 2000, at 21.

[74] *State Farm*, 123 S. Ct. at 1523.

previous awards for the same misconduct. The result would be what amounts to a single 'rolling' award."[75]

- No coerced self-incrimination, which criminal defendants can avoid by pleading the Fifth Amendment. In civil cases, however, compulsory discovery can be self-incriminating.

Fourth, the Eighth Amendment's prohibition of excessive fines could be applied to punitive damages. Presently, because the Eighth Amendment is primarily directed at prosecutorial abuse, the excessive fines provision does not cover civil damages. That principle was spelled out in the *Browning-Ferris* case.[76] But Justice Sandra Day O'Connor's dissent,[77] covering the history of fines, convincingly showed that punitive damages, unless they were merely symbolic, were always treated as fines. Moreover, after *Browning-Ferris*, several states modified their statutes to provide that punitives would, in part, be payable to the state.[78]

Indeed, making punitive awards payable to the state is a fifth possible reform. Because the purpose of punitives is deterrence, not compensation for injury, the identity of the recipient is irrelevant to that purpose, and receipt by the plaintiff is beyond what is necessary to make him whole. Of course, adequate incentive must be provided for the plaintiff's attorney to seek punitive damages. That incentive might be in the form of court-ordered attorneys' fees with the amount set by a judge. Much of the abuse that now exists can be traced to enormous contingency-based fees paid not to "public officials, who are accountable to the citizenry and have a long tradition of ethics and restraint, but private citizens and lawyers whose only interest is the size of the award they can bring in."[79]

B. Federal Reform of Long-Arm Jurisdiction

Apart from state imposed constraints on punitive damage awards, there are at least two areas in which the federal government can

---

[75] O'Connor, *supra* note 73, at 23.

[76] *See* Browning-Ferris Industries of Vermont, Inc. v. Kelco Disposal, Inc., 492 U.S. 257 (1989).

[77] *Id.* at 282 (O'Connor, J., concurring in part and dissenting in part).

[78] *See, e.g.,* Roy C. McCormick, *Punitive Damages Defined and Reviewed for Questions and Changes Ahead,* ROUGH NOTES, Nov. 1995, at 68.

[79] Olson, *supra* note 69.

intervene without intruding on long-established state prerogatives. The guiding principle is that federal legislatures and courts are authorized to act when there is a high risk that state legislatures or courts will systematically appropriate wealth from the citizens of other states. One federal reform that is consistent with that principle is to amend the rules that control state exercise of so-called long-arm jurisdiction over out-of-state businesses.

Rather than apply the Due Process Clause to the size of a punitive damages award, a federal court could, for example, use that clause to preclude a local court from hearing a case unless the defendant engages directly in business activities within the state. Sensible rules should protect a firm from being hauled into court unless the firm does in-state business. Those same rules would give firms an exit option—that is, if they withdrew from a state, they could avoid the risk of an unrestrained in-state jury. Unfortunately, federal limits on long-arm statutes remain lax or ambiguous. Perhaps that helps explain the Supreme Court's recent punitive damage jurisprudence. Instead of reining in state jurisdiction, the Court may have resolved cases like *BMW* and *State Farm* with a view toward approximating the same result by other means.[80]

Unpredictable or unclear federal guideposts for punitive damages may not resolve the problem, however. Law and economics scholars Paul Rubin, John Calfee, and Mark Grady argue that the Court should address the jurisdiction problem head-on.

> If Alabama juries demonstrate bad judgment in pharmaceutical cases, manufacturers might refuse to sell in Alabama, denying Alabamians drugs that expose the manufacturer to inappropriate punitive damages awards. Middlemen, however, might fill this lacuna by purchasing and reselling drugs in Alabama at a higher cost to compensate for liability, and manufacturers might not be able to escape liability under existing long-arm statutes.[81]

An overhaul of the Court's jurisdictional rules would entail a significant shift in its prior case law. First, under *International Shoe Co. v. Washington*,[82] the Court held that an out-of-state corporation

---

[80] *See* Rubin et al., *supra* note 9, at 179.

[81] *Id.* at 203–04.

[82] International Shoe Co. v. Washington, 326 U.S. 310 (1945).

could be sued within the state if the corporation had "minimum contacts" in-state. International Shoe was sued in Washington even though it had no office and made no contracts there to buy or sell merchandise. Because the company employed salesmen who resided and solicited business in Washington, it was subject to the jurisdiction of the state's courts.

Encouragingly, thirty-five years later, in *World-Wide Volkswagen Corp. v. Woodson*,[83] the Court signaled that state jurisdiction triggered by nominal ties might violate the Due Process Clause. The Robinsons purchased an Audi from a New York dealership that had acquired the car from a regional distributor. Later, the Robinsons were injured when their car was involved in an accident in Oklahoma, where neither the dealer nor the distributor did business. The Court said the defendant might have foreseen that an automobile bought in New York would be driven through Oklahoma. But that noncommercial contact with the state was insufficient to confer jurisdiction on Oklahoma's courts.

That hopeful outcome was mostly undone by the Court's 1987 opinion in *Asahi Metal Industry Co., Ltd. v. Superior Court of California*.[84] Valves made by Asahi, a Japanese corporation, were installed by another company on Taiwanese tires that were involved in a California accident. The Court refused to confer jurisdiction on the California courts, mainly because the burden on Asahi of litigating in California outweighed the state's interest in adjudicating the case. But Justice O'Connor could not command a majority of the Court to support this more restrictive proposition: "[A] defendant's awareness that the stream of commerce may or will sweep the product into the forum State does not convert the mere act of placing the product into the stream into an act purposefully directed toward the forum State."[85] If that rule had won the day, exit from a state with a confiscatory tort regime would be feasible. But only four justices agreed.

Rubin, Calfee, and Grady conclude that "the economically harmful effects of excessive punitive damages awards by unrestrained juries in particular states could . . . largely be ameliorated by a clear and

---

[83] World-Wide Volkswagen Corp. v. Woodson, 444 U.S. 286 (1980).

[84] Asahi Metal Industry Co., Ltd. v. Superior Court of California, 480 U.S. 102 (1987).

[85] *Id.* at 112.

realistic 'minimum contacts' doctrine. Justice O'Connor's opinion in *Asahi* suggests how such a doctrine could be formulated, but the Court has not accepted her approach."[86]

C. Federal Choice of Law

Because the Supreme Court continues to apply capacious jurisdictional rules, oppressive state tort laws remain a threat to out-of-state defendants. If manufacturers could avoid unfair tort regimes—for example, by not doing business in a particular state—juries would not be able to impose their punitive damage awards extraterritorially. Then, consumers in each state would decide whether they want confiscatory tort law or plentiful goods and services. But to the extent that manufacturers cannot avoid a state's jurisdiction—for example, because long-arm statutes overreach—a different remedy is necessary. The remedy that raises the fewest federalism concerns is a federal choice-of-law rule,[87] which would allow manufacturers to exert some control over governing law. Here's how that might work:

Basically, choice of law is the doctrine that determines which state's laws control the litigation. There are a number of different rules used by courts to decide choice-of-law questions. Federal courts must apply the choice-of-law rules in the state in which the federal court is sitting. Generally, plaintiffs can and will select the most favorable forum state, based in part on its choice of law. The resultant tort law will no doubt be least hospitable to the defendant and might even be contrary to the defendant's home-state law in important respects. That leaves the defendant at the mercy of the plaintiff.

Of course, there would be no involuntary extraterritoriality and less of a liability crisis if consumers and sellers could choose both their forums and their law by contract. Transacting parties should be able to designate the state whose laws will govern any disputes arising out of their agreements. Unfortunately, however, many transactions are not covered by written agreements and choice-of-law clauses in consumer contracts are generally unenforceable.[88]

---

[86] Rubin et al., *supra* note 9, at 210.

[87] *See, e.g.*, Michael McConnell, *A Choice-of-Law Approach to Products-Liability Reform*, *in* NEW DIRECTIONS IN LIABILITY LAW 90 (Walter Olson ed., 1988).

[88] *See* Michael Greve, *Eulogy for a Lost Clause*, NATIONAL LAW JOURNAL, May 26, 2003, at 27.

Accordingly, if the forum state's rules call for applying the law of the state in which injury occurred, out-of-state manufacturers will have difficulty avoiding oppressive regimes. But suppose a federal choice-of-law rule were enacted for those cases in which the plaintiff and defendant were from different states. Suppose further that the applicable law were based on the location where the product was originally sold. A manufacturer could thus stamp products by state-of-sale and price them differentially to allow for anticipated product liability verdicts.

Alternatively, the applicable law might be based on the state in which the manufacturer was located.[89] That would obviate the need to identify where the sale occurred. A manufacturer could decide where to locate and its decision would dictate the applicable legal rules. Consumers, in turn, would evaluate those rules when deciding whether to buy a particular manufacturer's product.

Would there be a race to the bottom by manufacturers searching for the most defendant-friendly tort law? Probably not. More likely, states would balance their interest in attracting manufacturers against the interest of in-state consumers who want tougher product liability laws to ensure adequate redress for injuries. In effect, healthy competition among the states would enlist federalism as part of the solution rather than raise federalism as an excuse for failing to arrive at a solution.

D. Conclusion

By tightening state long-arm jurisdiction and federalizing choice-of-law rules in multistate litigation, the national government would be broadening the procedural guarantees of the Due Process Clause. At the same time, it would be acting pursuant to unambiguous authority under the Commerce Clause to prevent states from using their tort law in a manner that impedes the free flow of trade among the states. Those remedies, which circumvent the difficult controversy over substantive due process, are perfectly consistent with time-honored principles of federalism.

The touchstone of federalism is not states' rights but dual sovereignty—checks and balances designed to promote liberty by limiting excessive power in the hands of either state or federal government.

---

[89] *See* William Niskanen, *Do* Not *Federalize Tort Law*, 18 REGULATION, no. 4 (1995).

When a state exercises jurisdiction beyond its borders to impose grossly excessive punitive damages on out-of-state businesses, and applies laws that deny both procedural and substantive protection against quasi-criminal punishment, the federal government not only may, but must, intervene. Otherwise, federalism becomes a pretext for constricting rather than enlarging liberty.

Campaign Finance Reform: Searching for Corruption in All the Wrong Places

Bradley A. Smith

Introduction

In the autumn of 2000, Harvey Bass, the owner of Harvey Bass Furniture and Appliance in the west Texas town of Muleshoe, painted "Save our Nation: vote Democrat; Al Gore for President" on the side of a leftover refrigerator shipping box. Bass left the homemade sign on the porch of his business on State Highway 214, to be seen by passersby. Soon another local resident, Bill Liles, "got tired of looking at it, especially the 'Save our Nation' part." Liles and a friend, one Mark Morton, decided to make a sign supporting Gore's rival, Texas Governor George W. Bush. The two decided that their sign "should be bigger and better." They obtained a large plywood board, hired a professional sign painter, and mounted the finished product on the side of a cotton trailer obtained from another local resident, Don Bryant. They parked the trailer, with its sign, across the street from Mr. Bass's store. "As word spread the sign became a topic of conversation at local gathering places. Mostly the Spudnut Shop on Main Street and the Dinner Bell Café on Highway 84. People started coming by and donating to help pay for the cost of the sign."

This spontaneous burst of political activity ended when another Muleshoe resident, Don Dyer, filed a complaint with the Federal Election Commission against Liles, Morton, Bryant, and one of their "contributors." Though Dyer apparently had no difficulty uncovering who was behind the sign, he complained that the sign lacked disclaimers required by the Federal Election Campaign Act. In due course the Commission's General Counsel dutifully recommended that the Commission find "reason to believe" that the Muleshoe Four, as we might call them, had violated 2 U.S.C. § 441d(a), by failing to include a disclaimer on the sign stating who had paid for it, and whether or not it was authorized by the candidate.[1] However, many other potential violations were not considered at all. For example, if the group spent in excess of $250 (quite likely when one includes the cost of the wood, the in-kind value for the use of the cotton trailer, and the cost of hiring a professional sign painter) the group would also have violated 2 U.S.C. § 434(c)(1) by failing to file reports with the Federal Election Commission. If any of the men contributed in excess of $200 in cash or in-kind value, even if it was later repaid from donations, they might also have violated the reporting requirements of 2 U.S.C. § 434(c)(2). If the group spent more than $1,000 on the activity—unlikely in this case, but not at all impossible when one adds in the rental value of the trailer, in-kind contributions of gas to haul the sign, and other costs, and certainly an amount that similar spontaneous activity might exceed—then it would have also violated 2 U.S.C. §§ 432(a)-(h), 433(a)-(b), and 434(a) and (b) by failing to register as a political committee, name a treasurer, and file more detailed reports. In this case, if any individual donated in excess of $50, it would have violated the limit on anonymous contributions, and if any individual had donated in excess of $1,000, it would have violated 2 U.S.C. § 441a(a). If Mr. Bryant's cotton trailer was titled in the name of a corporation—perhaps his own Subchapter S corporation—lending it to the group would have violated the prohibition on corporate contributions of 2 U.S.C. § 441b. Total statutory penalties could have easily exceeded $25,000. The Commission eventually chose not to find "reason to believe," but two of the six Commissioners dissented and even those voting to take no action on the complaint were forced to admit that the respondents had, in fact, violated the law.[2]

---

[1] The case of the "Muleshoe Four" is Federal Election Commission Matter Under Review (MUR) 5156. A Statement of Reasons by Commissioner Scott E. Thomas is available on the Web at www.fec.gov/members/thomas/thomasstatement44.html. Other documents are on the public record.

[2] See MUR 5156, Statement of Reasons of Commissioner Daryl R. Wold, Mar. 22, 2002, at. 4; Statement of Reasons of Chairman David M. Mason and Commissioner Bradley A. Smith, April 25, 2002. One dissenter felt strongly enough about the dismissal to write a lengthy dissent. See Statement of Reasons of Commissioner Scott E. Thomas, July 15, 2002, at 3. As to other potential violations, Commissioner Wold estimated that the cost of the sign would have been "a few hundred dollars, at most," but did not consider other cost such as use of the trailer and costs for hauling. Wold, supra at 3, n.3.

At about the same time that Liles and Morton were preparing their sign, a group of law students in Columbus, Ohio, decided to launch an organization called "Law Students for Bush-Cheney." As they made preparations for their first meeting, the group's faculty adviser cheerfully mentioned their plans in a casual conversation with a lawyer familiar with federal election law. "Well, be careful not to spend more than $250 advocating their election," said the latter, "or you'll have to file reports with the Federal Election Commission." Planning for the group ground to a halt.[3]

In the summer of 2000 Mike Ferguson's aging and ill parents established a trust fund, providing for substantial sums to go to each of their four children upon the attainment of 30 years of age, the completion of a bachelor's degree, and marriage. Shortly thereafter, Ferguson became the first of the siblings to qualify for trust distributions, and he promptly spent a substantial sum of this inheritance on his campaign for Congress. A prominent political operative for the opposing party then filed charges with the FEC, alleging that because the trust was not established until after the November 1998 start of the 2000 election cycle, the funds constituted an illegal contribution from Ferguson's parents to his congressional campaign. The Commission agreed and found probable cause that Ferguson had violated the law. Facing civil prosecution by the federal government, Ferguson agreed to pay a $210,000 fine to the Federal Election Commission. Ferguson's case is not unique. In fact, in recent years the FEC has, with some regularity, fined parents for contributing too much to their children, children for contributing too much to their parents, and husbands for contributing too much to their wives.[4]

At a time when flag burning, Internet pornography, and commercial speech enjoy unprecedented First Amendment protection,[5] why

[3]The formation of Law Students for Bush-Cheney was told to the author by Professor David Mayer of Capital University Law School. Professor Mayer was the group's faculty adviser. The lawyer in question is the author. The reporting violation is 2 U.S.C. § 434(c).

[4]MUR 5138, Mike Ferguson; *See also* MUR 4568 (mother and father-in-law made excessive contribution); MUR 5348 (excessive contribution by parents); MUR 4568 (excessive contribution by son of candidate); MUR 5049 (excessive contribution by spouse of candidate).

[5]*See* United States v. Eichman, 496 U.S. 310 (1990) and Texas v. Johnson, 491 U.S. 397 (1989) (holding that burning the United States flag is a form of protected speech under the First Amendment and striking down laws prohibiting flag burning); Reno v. ACLU, 521 U.S. 844 (1997) (striking down Communications Decency Act, limiting pornography transmitted to minors over the Internet); Greater New Orleans Broadcast

would core grassroots political activity, or gifts from parents to children to use for political activity, be subject to civil and even criminal penalties?

Federal Election Commission v. Beaumont,[6] decided near the close of last term, is a little case dealing with issues on the margin of the complex doctrine that the Supreme Court has thrown up in the area of campaign finance law. In a typical term, the case would draw notice from only a handful of campaign finance reform lobbyists, campaign lawyers, and First Amendment specialists. When decided in June of 2003, however, *Beaumont* drew much attention of a possible harbinger of things to come in *McConnell v. Federal Election Commission.*[7] *McConnell* was the long-awaited constitutional challenge to the constitutionality of the Bipartisan Campaign Reform Act of 2002, popularly known as "McCain-Feingold" after its lead Senate sponsors. But *Beaumont*'s real value may be less as a leading indicator of the case to come than as a classic example of the intellectual confusion at the heart of the Court's campaign finance jurisprudence.

Part I of this essay reviews the setting for and result of the Supreme Court's landmark decision in *Buckley v. Valeo.*[8] Part II discusses how *Beaumont* fits into the "patternless mosaic"[9] of judge-made law that has followed *Buckley.* Part III attempts to set forth the options available to the Supreme Court, and the likely consequences of each.

Part I: Getting to *Buckley*: The Corruption of Politics

A. Early Days

Until perhaps 35 years ago, it was possible for a young man or woman to launch a campaign for the United States Congress without

---

Association v. United States 527 U.S. 173 (1999), Rubin v. Coors Brewing Company, 514 U.S. 476 (1995), and Edenfield v. Fane, 507 U.S. 761 (1993) (state must demonstrate real harm, not merely potential or perceived harm, before regulating commercial speech), and 44 Liquormart v. Rhode Island, 517 U.S. 484 (1996) (government regulation of commercial speech must directly advance the interest asserted).

[6] 123 S. Ct. 2200 (2003).

[7] McConnell v. Federal Election Commission, 251 F. Supp. 2d 176 (D.D.C. 2003); *prob. juris. noted*, 123 S. Ct. 2268 (2003). On September 8, 2003, a month before the usual opening of the term, the Supreme Court heard an unusually long four hours of oral argument in *McConnell v. FEC*.

[8] Buckley v. Valeo 424 U.S. 1 (1976).

[9] *See* Daniel H. Lowenstein, *A Patternless Mosaic: Campaign Finance and the First Amendment after Austin*, 21 CAP. U. L. REV. 381 (1992).

contacting a lawyer. Indeed, before 1897 there were no state or federal laws directly regulating campaign finance. In 1896, however, Republican William McKinley's skilled campaign manager, Mark Hanna, had deftly organized the business community behind McKinley's candidacy. Spending a then unheard of $7 million, mostly solicited from corporations, McKinley defeated prairie populist William Jennings Bryan. In response, Bryan's home state of Nebraska, plus three other pro-Bryan states with large Democratic majorities in their legislatures, Missouri, Florida, and Tennessee, passed laws barring corporate contributions to political campaigns. The federal government did not get involved until the passage of the Tillman Act in 1907, which banned corporate contributions in federal elections. The Tillman Act, however, and its various successors, never amounted to much. For example, there was not a single prosecution under the Federal Corrupt Practices Act, the primary law governing federal campaign finance, from its enactment in 1925 until its repeal in 1971. Disclosure reports were haphazardly completed, haphazardly filed, and almost impossible to find, let alone use—they gathered dust and mold in a file room in the Capitol. The ban on corporate contributions was routinely flaunted, in part by corporations simply reimbursing managers for their individual contributions. When Republicans seized control of Congress in 1947 after sixteen years of Democratic rule, one of their first acts was to attempt to stem the flow of union money that had become a bulwark of Democratic control since passage of the Wagner Act in 1933 by banning direct union contributions. Unions responded by establishing "political action committees" (PACs), funded by automatic checkoffs negotiated into union contracts. The end result was to institutionalize what had previously been ad hoc union involvement in politics. State laws were similarly flouted or ignored. For example, in California, donor disclosure sometimes consisted of nothing more than an unalphabetized list of donor names. Thus, the de jure laissez faire system that ruled from 1787 until 1907 was replaced by a de facto laissez faire system that lasted from 1907 until 1971.[10]

B. *The Federal Election Campaign Act and Buckley v. Valeo*

With the passage of the Federal Election Campaign Act of 1971 (FECA), and substantial amendments to that Act in 1974, the United

---

[10] *See* BRADLEY A. SMITH, UNFREE SPEECH: THE FOLLY OF CAMPAIGN FINANCE REFORM 22–31 (2001), and sources cited therein.

States embarked on what is now a thirty-year experiment with serious campaign finance regulation. The basic framework of FECA included reporting requirements for contributions and expenditures and a ban on direct corporate and union contributions. Individual contributions were limited to $1,000 per election when made to candidates, $5,000 per calendar year when made to a PAC, and $20,000 per calendar year when made to a national party, with an aggregate cap of $25,000 per calendar year. PACs, in turn, were limited to contributing $5,000 to a candidate for office, or $15,000 to a party. Spending by candidates was limited, and spending by individuals or groups independent of a candidate was limited to just $1,000 if such spending was "relative to" a federal election. The Act also provided for taxpayer financing of the presidential elections. Finally, for the first time, an effective enforcement mechanism was established, through the creation of the FEC.[11]

This framework was immediately challenged on First Amendment grounds,[12] reaching the Supreme Court in the landmark decision of *Buckley v. Valeo*.[13] Here the Court eschewed a straightforward reading of the First Amendment ("Congress shall make no law . . . abridging the freedom of speech,"[14]), choosing instead to engage in one of the complex balancing tests that has so enamored the Court in the post-World War II era. The Court recognized that important First Amendment interests were involved, with the restrictions falling on political speech and association at the core of the First Amendment.[15] Therefore, the Court held that any statutory regulation must be subject to an "exacting" and "rigorous" standard of review.[16] Importantly,

[11] *See Buckley*, 424 U.S. 1, 7 (1976).

[12] The Supreme Court had earlier interpreted Article I, Section 4 of the Constitution ("The Times, Places and Manner of holding Elections for Senators and Representatives, shall be prescribed in each State by the Legislature thereof; but the Congress may at any time by Law make or alter such Regulations. . .") and Article II, Section 1, Para. 4 ("The Congress may determine the Time of chusing the Electors, and the Day on which they shall give their votes,") as encompassing the ability of Congress to regulate campaigns for federal offices beyond the time, place, and manner of holding elections. *See* Burroughs v. United States, 290 U.S. 534 (1934) (presidential elections); Newberry v. United States, 256 U.S. 232 (1921) (congressional elections).

[13] 424 U.S. 1.

[14] U.S. CONST. amend. I.

[15] *Buckley*, 424 U.S. at 14, 25.

[16] *Id.* at 16, 29.

Buckley rejected the idea that the state could limit political participation, in the form of contributions and expenditures to promote some version of political equality. To allow the government to limit speech on the basis of such judgments would all but eviscerate the First Amendment because it would allow the government to restrict speech based on who had spoken too much, been heard too much, or was too persuasive. The theory was rejected in the strongest possible terms: "The concept that government may restrict the speech of some elements of our society in order to enhance the relative voice of others is wholly foreign to the First Amendment."[17] But it went on to find that the government had a "compelling interest" in preventing the dangers of "corruption or the appearance of corruption" in government, and that large campaign contributions clearly posed that danger. Then it began dissecting the Act.

The Court held that a limitation on spending "relative to" a clearly identified candidate was a phrase both vague and overly broad. It had the potential to make almost all talk about issues and ideas subject to regulation, regardless of any potential danger of corruption, given that

> the distinction between discussion of issues and candidates and advocacy of election or defeat of candidates may often dissolve in practical application. Candidates, especially incumbents, are intimately tied to public issues involving legislative proposals and governmental actions. Not only do candidates campaign on the basis of their positions on various public issues, but campaigns themselves generate issues of public interest.[18]

To avoid vagueness problems, the Court held that to be covered under the Act, political speech must be limited to communications that not only advocated the election or defeat of a candidate, as the Court of Appeals had held,[19] but which "include explicit words of advocacy of election or defeat of a candidate." In a footnote, the Court explained that this would limit application of the Act to communications containing such phrases as " 'vote for,' 'elect,' 'support,' 'cast your ballot for,' 'Smith for Congress,' 'vote against,' 'defeat,'

[17] *Id.* at 48.
[18] *Id.* at 42.
[19] Buckley v. Valeo, 519 F. 2d 821, 852–53 (D.C. Cir. 1975).

'reject.' ''[20] Such phrases would eventually become known as "express advocacy, and subject to regulation." Political communications not using such phrases would eventually become known as "issue advocacy," and would not generally be subject to regulation.

The Court went on, however, to hold that even so construed, the Act's limitations on expenditures impermissibly burdened First Amendment rights. First, such limits directly served to suppress the amount of speech.[21] Second, when expenditures were made independently of the candidate, it alleviated the danger that those expenditures would be made in return for an explicit quid pro quo from the candidate.[22] This was not only because the lack of discussion between speaker and candidate made an explicit quid pro quo exchange less likely, but also because such independent expenditures might not be helpful, and might even be harmful, to a candidate.[23] Similarly, the Court found that limits on the candidate's own expenditures, whether from personal or campaign funds, simply were not tailored to address the problem of corruption, as the danger of corruption came in the exchange of favors for contributions, not in spending funds rightly obtained.[24]

However, the Court upheld the Act's contribution limits. The Court recognized that contribution limits burdened the First Amendment rights of both speech and association. They implicate the former because contributions are made for the purpose of funding speech, and they implicate the latter because by contributing to a campaign or committee, citizens are exercising their rights of association to achieve political goals.[25] But the Court nonetheless discounted the

[20] *Buckley*, 424 U.S. at 43, n. 51.

[21] *Id.* at 19–20, 47–51.

[22] *Id.* at 47.

[23] *Id.* The phenomenon may be observed yet today. *See e.g.* Pam Belluck, *Feingold Defies Party and Retains Senate Seat*, N. Y. TIMES, Nov. 4, 1998, at B4 (describing how Senator Feingold asked Democratic National Senatorial Committee to stop running independent ads intended to assist his 1998 reelection bid). Indeed, the *Buckley* court might well have remembered this lesson from firsthand experience. A major problem for Barry Goldwater's 1964 presidential campaign, in which a young William Rehnquist was heavily involved as a strategist and sometime speechwriter, was trying to either control or disassociate from the campaign groups trying to act in support of Goldwater. *See generally* RICK PERLSTEIN, BEFORE THE STORM: BARRY GOLDWATER AND THE UNMAKING OF THE AMERICAN CONSENSUS 409–515 (2001).

[24] 424 U.S. at 53.

[25] *Id.* at 15–19.

First Amendment rights involved, arguing that the speech entailed in a contribution was merely the symbolic act of contributing, a "general expression" of support that did not significantly vary with the amount involved. And whether any further message would result from the contribution, argued the Court, depended on whether someone other than the contributor would turn the contribution into speech.[26] Both points are questionable, at best. For contributors, the goal is to speak not only through the act of contributing but also through the ultimate message that the contribution will help to finance. Most Americans cannot, for example, afford to pay for a full-page ad in a major daily newspaper, let alone commercial television advertising, but must pool their resources to buy time and have someone else do the actual speaking for the group.[27] In any case, the Court also found that contribution limits were justified by the interest in preventing, "the actuality and appearance of corruption," as they directly targeted quid pro quo exchanges of campaign contributions for government favors.[28]

Finally, the Court upheld a scheme of taxpayer financing for presidential elections, provided that participation was not mandatory or accompanied by mandatory limits on expenditures.[29]

II. The Corruption of *Buckley v. Valeo*

A. *Buckley's Definition*

The *Buckley* decision turned on three key holdings. First, limits on contributions and expenditures burdened fundamental First Amendment rights, and were subject to "rigorous" and "exacting" scrutiny. Second, the government's interest in promoting equality was not sufficient to justify suppressing political speech. Third, despite these First Amendment constraints, the government's interest in preventing corruption or the appearance of corruption could justify some level of speech suppression.

Given the importance of the government interest in preventing corruption or its appearance, one might have expected the Court to devote considerable attention to defining the term, but it did not.

[26] *Id.* at 21.

[27] *See id.* at 22; Nixon v. Shrink Missouri Government PAC, 528 U.S. 377, 415 (Thomas, J. dissenting).

[28] *Buckley*, 424 U.S. at 26.

[29] *Id.* at 90–107.

The 143-page per curiam majority opinion devotes just three short paragraphs to the issue. The Court made clear that by "corruption" it meant more than personal enrichment in return for favors, noting that "laws making criminal the giving and taking of bribes deal only with the most blatant and specific attempts of those with money to influence government action."[30] But what, then, did constitute "corruption," if not bribery? The term was defined in a single sentence: "To the extent that large contributions are given to secure political quid pro quo's from current and potential office holders, the integrity of our system of representative democracy is undermined."[31] That is, a direct promise of official action for campaign support would constitute "corruption."

Given that definition, the Court's distinction between expenditures, which generally may not be regulated, and contributions, which may be restricted, is not wholly nonsensical. Expenditure limitations directly limit the amount of political speech. Contribution limits, however, only limit the total amount of speech indirectly. True, if set low enough, they may limit the total amount of speech considerably. But they may not limit the total at all, if the candidate is still able to raise as much money as he desires to spend in smaller increments, and if his donors use excess funds they might have contributed to the campaign to make independent expenditures, either by themselves or through participation with other groups. In reality, contribution limits almost certainly do limit the total amount of speech, simply by discouraging some speakers, generally raising the costs of pooling funds, and imposing additional legal requirements on speech. But this need not happen in every single case, and the effect is probably less than it would be with direct expenditure limitations.

Perhaps more important, there is truth in the Court's assertion that large expenditures, by themselves, cannot result in quid pro quo corruption. An independently wealthy candidate spending his own money is promising no quos in return for quid. Similarly, a candidate who raises large sums in small contributions is not likely to make quid pro quo promises to donors before he spends the

---

[30] *Buckley*, 424 U.S. at 27–28.
[31] *Id.* at 26–27.

money—that promise would necessarily take place at the time the money is raised.

But to focus on the distinctions that might justify treating expenditure limitations and contribution limitations differently is to pass over the primary question: Regardless of how expenditures are treated, are limits on contributions justified? Overlooked in the Court's analysis is that contribution limitations themselves are hopelessly overbroad.

One need not assert that a large contribution can never influence an officeholder to grant a special favor in order to recognize that the vast majority of large contributions do not result in the quid pro quo granting of favors. For example, Steven Kirsch, a wealthy Silicon Valley entrepreneur, each year, directly and through his foundation, contributes large sums to a variety of groups on the political left such as the Center for Responsive Politics, People for the American Way, and the Natural Resources Defense Council.[32] Kirsch's large soft money donations to the Democratic party, and contributions to liberal Democratic candidates for office, seem quite obviously to flow from the same ideological commitment. Likewise, the financial support that the DeVos family, founders of Amway, give to conservative causes and candidates is rather clearly based on ideological commitment, not the hope of some quid pro quo favor. Similarly, when Mike Ferguson's parents established a trust that eventually provided Ferguson with money he spent on his congressional campaign, they were not attempting to gain a political favor. In fact, had they sought a political favor, it would have made more sense to keep the money, with the threat of writing young Ferguson out of the will, than to give him the money and lose control over his conduct. Oddly enough, this course would have been perfectly legal.

It is difficult to determine when or whether an officeholder takes, or fails to take, action due to the effect of a large campaign contribution. Thus any studies of the issue are vulnerable to the critique that they simply failed to catch the "corruption" that is taking place. Nevertheless, literally decades of studies have consistently failed to find evidence that campaign contributions purchase special favors

---

[32] *See* Kirsch Foundation 2003 Grants *available at* http://www.kirschfoundation.org/done/2003.html#Anchor-Politica-29211, viewed July 25, 2003.

on any type of systematic basis.[33] Supporters of the "contributions as corruption" thesis continue to produce anecdotal evidence of specific episodes of "corruption."[34] Anecdotal evidence, however, is generally viewed by the Supreme Court as inadequate to support the infringement of a fundamental right such as speech.[35] But leaving that aside, the failure of serious study to find a cause-and-effect relationship and the continued reliance by regulatory advocates on anecdotal stories—which are often contested[36]—supports the position that most large contributions are neither intended to nor result in the granting of political favors. Thus, while contribution limits may stop some episodes of quid pro quo corruption, they do so at the expense of limiting a great deal of speech that is unrelated to quid pro quo corruption. Most donors simply do not seek any particular action, or even access, in exchange for their contributions. Most donors never seek, let alone obtain, a meeting with the office-holder. And as the Court recognized that contribution limits do burden speech, albeit perhaps less so than spending limitations, this overbreadth should pose a serious constitutional problem.

An equally fundamental problem is that the Court did not attempt to explain why it chose the definition of "corruption" that it did, or why such behavior constituted "corruption." The Court defined corruption not only to include the use of office for personal gain but also to include the exchange of "political" favors. But this is a very broad understanding of "corruption," indeed. Traditionally, "corruption" meant the exchange of official favors for personal gain, not support for reelection. Politics is full of exchanges for political favors that are not generally described as "corrupt." When a popular politician endorses a candidate on the understanding that he will

[33] *See* Stephen Ansolabehere, John M. de Figueiredo, and James M. Snyder, Jr., *Why Is There So Little Money in U.S. Politics?*, 17 J. ECON. PERSPECTIVES 105, 113, Table 1 (2003) (summarizing results of 36 major studies). *See also* Bradley A. Smith, *supra* n. 10 at 127–28 (summarizing studies). Beyond compiling a quarter century of studies by others, Ansolabehere conducts added statistical analysis and concludes that, "after controlling for legislator ideology, these contributions have no detectable effects on the behavior of legislators." Ansolabehere, *supra* at 117.

[34] *See e.g.* LARRY MAKINSON, SPEAKING FREELY: WASHINGTON INSIDERS TALK ABOUT MONEY IN POLITICS (2003).

[35] *See e.g.* Board of Trustees v. Garrett, 531 U.S. 356, 370 (2001).

[36] Smith, *supra* n. 10, at 54, 126–27.

be appointed to some office in the event of victory, or at least have a say in patronage appointments, we have a political quid pro quo. When a union promises that its members will drive voters to the polls or engage in other get-out-the-vote activity if the candidate will promise to fight for tariffs on imported goods, there is a promise of official action in return for campaign assistance. When a popular singer or actor endorses a candidate or appears at a fund raiser on his behalf, with the understanding that she will be able to send political memoranda outlining her views to the White House or to testify at a Congressional hearing, we witness an exchange of favors for support. When a candidate urges voters in a town to elect him to office because he will fight to make sure that the Navy continues to build submarines in its obsolete shipyards, he is offering the voters a quo for their quid: "vote for me, and although it is not the most efficient use of taxpayer dollars, I will try to keep your government contracts." When a reporter implies a flattering story will be forthcoming in exchange for an exclusive interview, a quid pro quo exchange has occurred. The Court has never attempted to explain, in *Buckley* or elsewhere, why granting a political favor in exchange for funds that might help in a campaign, like any of the inducements discussed above, constitutes corruption. These funds may not be used for personal enrichment, but are used to attempt to convince voters of the candidate's merit. They are used for speech.[37] The question as to whether campaign contributions are truly different than other favors that may have some potential to result in political quid pro quos goes beyond the scope of this article.[38]

---

[37] At the time *Buckley* was decided, a candidate or officeholder could keep leftover campaign funds and convert them to his personal use. Thus, at the time of *Buckley*, campaign funds could, at times, be used in much the same way as outright bribes for the personal gain of the officeholder. Since 1991, officeholders have not been able to convert leftover funds to personal use.

[38] Nor have commentators explored the issue as thoroughly as one might expect. For a smattering of some of the better literature, *see* John Copeland Nagle, *The Recusal Alternative to Campaign Finance Legislation*, 37 HARV. J. ON LEGIS. 69 (2000); David A. Strauss, *What is the Goal of Campaign Finance Reform?* 1995 U. CHI. LEGAL F. 141 (1995); Daniel Hays Lowenstein, *Campaign Contributions and Corruption: Comments on Strauss and Cain*, 1995 U. CHI. LEGAL F. 163 (1995); Daniel Hays Lowenstein, *On Campaign Finance Reform: The Root of All Evil is Deeply Rooted*, 18 HOFSTRA L. REV. 301 (1989); David W. Adamany and George E. Agree, POLITICAL MONEY (1975); Brief for Amici Curiae Cato Institute and Institute for Justice at 6–11, McConnell v. Federal Election Commission, 251 F. Supp. 2d 176 (D.D.C. 2003); *prob. juris. noted*, 123 S. Ct. 2268 (2003); *see also* Bradley A. Smith, *Hamilton at Wits End: The Lost Discipline of the Spending*

The key point for our immediate purposes is that the Court has never really attempted to clarify the evil it thinks limitations on campaign contributions prevent. Therefore, not surprisingly, its standard is malleable.

Finally, to compound the problem, the Court allowed that the mere "appearance" of corruption could serve as a proxy for corruption itself in justifying regulation. This is a standard the Court has not otherwise accepted in the First Amendment realm,[39] and with good reason—it has no objective meaning. The "appearance of corruption" can mean anything. What percentage of people must share this perspective? What if they mean different things by "corruption?" Suppose they continue to think politics is "corrupt" even if the law restricting contributions is passed? Suppose the appearance comes only from the mistaken belief that campaign contributions may be diverted to a candidate's personal use? In the 1950s and 1960s, before the regulatory regime of FECA was ushered into place, and when public opinion polling showed trust in government was at its peak, roughly thirty percent of poll respondents thought that government was run for the benefit of a few big interests, and considered "quite a few" or "all" politicians to be corrupt.[40] It is almost impossible to conceive of a democracy in which a substantial percentage of the population did not tend to see the system, or at least the party holding power, as corrupt. If the "appearance of corruption" is sufficient to justify regulation, the practical effect is to eliminate the need for the government to show any justification for the regulation in question. In short, the appearance of corruption is not merely a blank check, but an endlessly refilled bank account for those who seek greater regulation.

In fact, no sooner had the Bipartisan Campaign Reform Act (BCRA) become law then the same groups and institutions that had

---

Clause vs. the False Discipline of Campaign Finance Reform, 4 CHAPMAN L. REV. 117, 128–36 (2001); Smith, supra n. 10 at 222.

[39] See Greater New Orleans Broadcast Association v. United States, 527 U.S. 173 (1999) (harms needed to justify regulation of speech must be "real"); Rubin v. Coors Brewing Company, 514 U.S. 476 (1995) (proof of actual harm "critical"); Edenfeld v. Fane, 507 U.S. 761 (1993).

[40] Karlyn Bowman and Everett Ladd, WHAT'S WRONG: A SURVEY OF AMERICAN SATISFACTION AND COMPLAINT (1998).

promoted its passage, in order to end "the appearance of corruption," resumed their drumbeat. The *Washington Post*, for example, called for new regulation of campaign fundraisers, arguing that the lack of regulation was a "glaring omission."[41] Charles Lewis of the Center for Public Integrity complained about George W. Bush's ability to raise funds in small contributions from individuals, saying, "they're the most well-heeled interests, with vested interests in government," while columnist Bob Hebert continued to call these small donors "fat cats." Commentator Norm Ornstein called Bush's success at raising money in small contributions "not healthy."[42] None of the three suggested that any quid pro quo had taken place, or was much of a possibility among such small contributors. But like the *Post*, all sought to describe, if not create, an "appearance of corruption."

Three consequences flow from *Buckley*'s treatment of the "corruption" issue. First, by rejecting the equality argument as a justification for reform, *Buckley* requires equality advocates to shoehorn their arguments into the guise of anti-corruption arguments. Second, by creating a legal standard that encompasses a great deal of activity whose regulation rather obviously cannot be justified by the stated purpose of the regulation, it opened the door to regulating far more political activity than the Court may have intended. Finally, by failing to more precisely define the evil to be prevented, it opened up the system to manipulation.

B. Confusing Equality and Corruption

A particular conception of equality lurks behind many if not all efforts to regulate campaign finance. This definition equates speech to votes, and holds that the speech of some must be suppressed to guarantee some level of equal opportunity to speak. It is the definition unequivocally struck down in *Buckley* as "wholly foreign" to the First Amendment.[43] Nevertheless, it dominates the arguments

---

[41]Editorial, *Name Those Fundraisers*, Wash. Post, July 2, 2003, at A22 (and further arguing that with soft money eliminated, it is "even more critical now" that the individuals who help raise small contributions for a campaign by soliciting friends, neighbors, and acquaintances, be further regulated).

[42]Norman Ornstein, *Next for CFR Backers: Fixing the Presidential Campaign System*, ROLL CALL, June 25, 2003, p. 7; Rich Lowry, *Campaign Finance Reform Benefits Bush*, SEATTLE POST-INTELLIGENCER, July 15, 2003 at B6 (quoting Lewis and Hebert).

[43]*Buckley*, 424 U.S. at 48.

for reform in the academy,[44] and also appears frequently in Congress and in the more popular press.[45]

Indeed, during the debate over BCRA in 2003, direct references to equality were as common as concerns about "corruption." Senator Susan Collins expressed her support for the bill by noting her commitment to assuring that "all Americans have an equal political voice," and her support for "a tradition where those who have more money do not speak any louder or have any more clout than those who have less money."[46] Senator Paul Wellstone, a key cosponsor, complained about that portion of BCRA raising the individual contribution limit from $1,000 to $2,000, stating that

> during the last election 4 citizens out of every 10,000 Americans made contributions greater than $200. Only 232,000

[44] For a small sampling of the literature, *see e.g.* Burt Neuborne, *Toward a Democracy Centered Reading of the First Amendment*, 93 Nw. U. L. Rev. 1055 (1999); Richard L. Hasen, *Campaign Finance Laws and the Rupert Murdoch Problem*, 77 Tex. L. Rev. 1627 (1999) (arguing for limits on institutional press to promote equality); Richard L. Hasen, *Clipping Coupons for Democracy: An Egalitarian/Public Choice Defense of Campaign Finance Vouchers*, 84 Cal. L. Rev. 1 (1996) (arguing that individuals should be limited to contributing an amount given to them by the government); Ronald Dworkin, *The Curse of American Politics*, N. Y. Rev. of Books, Oct. 17, 1996, at 19; Cass Sunstein, *Political Equality and Unintended Consequences*, 94 Colum. L. Rev. 1390 (1994); Edward Foley, *Equal Dollars per Voter: A Constitutional Principle of Campaign Finance*, 94 Colum. L. Rev. 1204 (1994) (arguing that the Constitution requires limiting all political contributions to an amount presented to each voter by the government, in order to promote equality); Jamin Raskin and Jon Bonifaz, *Equal Protection and the Wealth Primary*, 11 Yale L. & Pol'y Rev. 273 (1993) (arguing that the 14th Amendment makes privately financed campaigns unconstitutional); Owen Fiss, *Free Speech and Social Structure*, 71 Iowa L. Rev. 1405, 1425 (1986) ("we may sometimes find it necessary to restrict the speech of some elements of our society in order to enhance the relative voices of others").

[45] For a few recent examples, *see e.g.* Bruce Ackerman and Ian Ayres, *Patriot Dollars Put Money Where Votes Are*, Los Angeles Times, July 17, 2003 at B15 (calling for reform to "allow ordinary Americans to compete effectively with the rich"); Neely Tucker, *Poor Say Campaign Reforms Help Rich*, Orlando Sentinel, Dec. 6, 2002 at A3 (quoting Jon Bonifaz of National Voting Rights Institute that less than one percent of population contribute most campaign funds); Editorial, *Shays-Meehan Moment*, Boston Globe, Feb. 12, 2002 at A16 ("Elimination of soft money is only a start, but there can be no reform without it. Regular voters, too long drowned out by big money, are crying for an equal voice."); *CNN Late Edition*, Feb. 10, 2002, remarks of Rep. Charles Rangel (Transcript # 021000CN.V47, available at Lexis) (supporting BCRA to "level the playing field").

[46] 148 Cong. Rec. 2133 (2002).

Americans gave contributions of $1,000 or more. That was one-ninth of 1 percent of the voting-age population. By bumping the spending limits up, I think we just simply further maximize the leverage and the influence, and, frankly, the power of the wealthiest citizens in the country.[47]

Similar expressions were equally common in the House. For example, Rep. Fortney Stark called for a "level playing field."[48] Rep. John Dingell voiced concern about the percentage of funds coming from a small number of donors.[49]

But because equality is not a sufficient justification for the First Amendment infringements entailed, such sentiments had to be expressed as "corruption." Thus, when Senator Jean Carnahan claimed that the new law would, "make it possible for the voices of ordinary Americans to be heard. No longer will wealthy special interest groups have an advantage over average, hard-working citizens," she described this, in a ritual bow to *Buckley*, as "cleaning up" the system.[50] Similarly, Rep. John Lewis explained his support for the law by arguing that "it is time to let all our citizens have an equal voice," but labeled this inequality "corruption."[51] Like many of his colleagues, Rep. Bob Borski complained about voices being "drowned out," and called this egalitarian interest "corruption." Still, there was no mistake but that the crux of his argument was egalitarian—it just wasn't fair that so few could have more influence.[52] And so it went throughout.

While the Court itself has not officially deviated from its *Buckley* holding that equality is not an adequate ground to uphold the suppression of speech, in fact it has held just that, and done so through the same slight of hand: simply by referring to inequality as "corruption." This process started in *FEC v. Massachusetts Citizens for Life*, wherein the Supreme Court, in the course of striking down a portion of FECA on an as-applied basis, noted that corporate contributions "are not an indication of the popular support for the corporation's

[47] *Id.* at 2097.
[48] *Id.* at 348.
[49] *Id.* at 349.
[50] *Id.* at 2100.
[51] *Id.* at 342 (2002).
[52] *Id.*

ideas."[53] Relying on this language, four years later the Court upheld a Michigan statute restricting independent expenditures by a corporation in *Austin v. Michigan State Chamber of Commerce*.[54] The Court argued that it was addressing

> A different type of corruption in the political arena: the corrosive and distorting effects of immense aggregations of wealth that are accumulated with the help of the corporate form and that have little or no correlation to the public's support for the corporation's political ideas.[55]

But can this reasonably be called "corruption" at all? Before this pronouncement, it seems unlikely that anyone had ever seriously considered it "corruption" when the amount of one's speech did not correlate with popular support for that speech. Certainly such a pronouncement is at odds with *Buckley*'s fundamental holding that limits on independent expenditures, or expenditures from a candidate's personal funds, are not corrupting, since neither would necessarily correlate with public support for the ideas expressed. Nor is there any reason why the amount of speech should correspond to popular sentiment. Such an assertion misconstrues the entire purpose of the political campaign, which is to persuade and change minds. Political fund raisers have long noticed that a group's fund raising often increases after a political defeat, as members and supporters devote more resources to promoting their vision to recapture lost ground or stave off further defeat. Certainly the mere disequilibrium between the determination of a speaker to speak and the level of preexisting support for the ideas expressed does not amount to a quid pro quo.

Austin's rationale, then, hinges not on a concern for the granting of political favors in return for campaign contributions, but rather on the concern that corporations might have too much political influence generally—the quintessential argument for equality. Whether or not there are particular reasons for limiting the speech of citizens who join together using the corporate form, particularly where, as in *Austin*, the corporation is not in business for primarily

---

[53] Federal Election Commission v. Massachusetts Citizens for Life, 479 U.S. 238, 258 (1986).

[54] Austin v. Michigan State Chamber of Commerce, 494 U.S. 652 (1990).

[55] *Id.* at 660.

commercial purposes, is highly debatable. True, the citizens involved receive the benefits of limited liability and perpetual life, yet whatever benefits one group may gain from the corporate form are, of course, available to others, even individuals through the creation of Subchapter S corporations. Moreover, the Court has long held that the receipt of government benefits cannot be predicated on the recipient's relinquishing fundamental constitutional rights.[56] Certainly many other speakers have unfair advantages, often derived from the state. An individual may amass great personal wealth through business dealings conducted through the corporate form. Other individuals will benefit from elements of the tax code, or from the receipt of government contracts. For the government to enter into this fray and decide who has spoken too much and who too little is the element that the Court in *Buckley* correctly recognized as "wholly foreign to the First Amendment." Merely calling it "corruption" doesn't change the underlying constitutional problem. That the Court allowed such a broad, vague, changing definition of "corruption" stems from the underlying failure of the Court to identify precisely the alleged evil it sought to address.

C. Defining Corruption Down

A second problem with *Buckley* is that, by defining "corruption" to include an exchange of political favors in the normal ebb and flow of policymaking, mediating among interests, and seeking popular support, it allows a good deal of regulation of activity having little to do with either corruption or equality. This is true of both small time grassroots activity, such as that of Law Students for Bush-Cheney, and also for most large donors, of which the Fergusons are merely an easy case. These flaws first became evident in *Buckley* itself.

Buckley operated on the presumption that any large contribution could lead to "corruption" or "the appearance of corruption," even though the vast majority of contributions are clearly not corrupting, either in intent or in fact. As a result, *Buckley* concluded that contributions from immediate family members could be banned.[57] As a professor, and more recently as a member of the Federal Election Commission for more than three years, I have spoken to thousands of

---

[56] *See e.g.* Legal Services Corporation v. Velazquez, 531 U.S. 533 (2001); Nollan v. California Coastal Commission, 483 U.S. 825 (1987).

[57] *Buckley*, 424 U.S. at 53, n. 59.

people, and written numerous articles in which I routinely note the inappropriateness, if not absurdity, of the government's regulating contributions by immediate family members. I have never had a person approach me to suggest otherwise. This is not to say that they do not exist, but that clearly the risk of family contributions resulting in the quid pro quo exchange of political favors is simply not perceived by most Americans. Certainly, at a minimum, most family members have more persuasive means at their disposal.

Similarly, *Buckley* upheld reporting thresholds and contribution limitations generally at levels that would seem to offer little risk of corruption, such as the $250 reporting threshold for independent expenditures.[58] Certainly there is some merit in the Court's determination not to micromanage legislative judgments. But as states pass increasingly restrictive laws, in some cases limiting contributions for statewide office to as little as $400,[59] and requiring disclosure of amounts as low as $10,[60] the courts must eventually be drawn into that fight. But if it is inevitable that the courts will at some point have to determine that a contribution threshold is too low to meet any legitimate anti-corruption rationale, why not make the determination earlier? A $2,000 contribution, currently the limit under BCRA, is well under one-half of one percent of the amount generally necessary to run a serious campaign for a seat in the U.S. House, and much less for most senate seats. Even accepting that campaign contributions may be regulated due to the fear of political favors granted in return, it is hard to argue that such amounts could result in such quid pro quo exchanges.

A prime example of how the Court has allowed noncorrupting, egalitarian activity to be regulated is *Federal Election Commission v. National Right to Work Committee* (hereinafter *NRWC*),[61] a case of no

---

[58] For example, the $1000 contribution threshold long in effect in FECA, 2 U.S.C. 441a(a), was, by 2002, less than two-tenths of one percent of the $600,000 to $1 million generally considered necessary to run a serious race for the U.S. House. Independent expenditures had to be reported once they topped just $250, 2 U.S.C. 434(c), an amount that seemed to serve little purpose other than to harass grassroots politickers such as the "Muleshoe Four," *see* text *supra*.

[59] *See e.g.* Vt. Stat. Ann. Tit 17, § 2805 (2001).

[60] *See e.g.* Fla. Stat. § 106.07(1) (2002).

[61] Federal Election Commission v. National Right to Life Work Committee, 459 U.S. 197 (1982).

small importance for the decision in *Beaumont*. Pursuant to the law, a corporation may not make contributions to candidates or independent expenditures in support of candidates, but it may use its general treasury funds to pay the administrative fees of a political action committee, which may make contributions to candidates and independent expenditures.[62] A nonprofit corporation with a PAC may only solicit contributions to the PAC from its "members."[63] The National Right to Work Committee (NRWC), an incorporated nonprofit group formed to lobby for laws prohibiting compulsory unionism, had established a PAC into which it solicited individual contributions, subject to the limitations of FECA, and made contributions to candidates, also subject to the limitations of FECA. NRWC defined its members as anyone who had previously contributed to the organization.[64] The Supreme Court held that the people solicited by NRWC for contributions to its PAC were not "members" as defined in the law, and therefore that NRWC had violated FECA. The Court went on to hold that the statute did not violate the First Amendment rights of free speech and association of NRWC or its donors.[65]

While the Court recited the magic words of "corruption" and "apparent corruption," it chose not to actually analyze the words at all, merely noting that the Court would not "second-guess" Congress on the need for "prophylactic" protection.[66] But what was corrupt, and what was the "prophylactic" law preventing? The contributions to the PAC came in limited amounts, and the contributions from the PAC to candidates were in limited amounts. They were not, by definition, the large contributions that Congress determined posed some danger of corruption and so had outlawed under FECA. Moreover, because contributors are subject to an overall limit on contributions to PACs and candidates,[67] there existed no danger of evading the statute by creating numerous PACs into which donors might contribute. And because the contributions were voluntary,

[62] 2 U.S.C. §§ 441b(a), 441b(b)(2)(C) (2002).
[63] 2 U.S.C. § 441b(b)(4)(C) (2002).
[64] *FEC*, 459 U.S. at 200–201.
[65] *Id*. at 203–210.
[66] *Id*. at 210.
[67] 2 U.S.C. § 441a(a)(3) (2002).

from individuals, there was not even the *Austin*-like specter of "accumulated corporate wealth." Any exchange of political favors would merely have represented the determination of a candidate to respond to the large number of small contributors supporting the NRWC PAC, whose contribution could not, by law, exceed $5,000. But if adopting a legislative position in exchange for the assistance of large numbers of people with one's campaign—or alternatively, exchanging campaign support for a pledge to adopt one's favored positions—is "corrupt," what is left of pluralist democratic theory? However, by defining the issue as one involving "contribution limitations," and having decided that contributions posed an inherent danger of corruption or the appearance of corruption, the Court found such grassroots rallying to be subject to limits despite the First Amendment.

Similarly in *Federal Election Commission v. Colorado Republican Federal Campaign Committee*[68] the Court found "corruption" in the ordinary give and take of politics. In *Colorado Republican II*, the question before the Court was whether a political party had a constitutional right to coordinate expenditures with its candidates. Under *Buckley*, of course, expenditures could be made independently of a candidate without limit, and this holding had later been expressly extended to political parties.[69] However, such expenditures, if "coordinated" with a candidate's campaign, were treated as contributions, and subject to limitation.[70] Here the parties sought to claim a right to make unlimited coordinated expenditures from contributions received subject to the limits of the law. As in *NRWC*, all of the funds were therefore solicited from individuals in amounts that, by definition, were not large contributions of the sort that would lead to "political favors." The donors were united in contributing for the purpose of electing Republicans—indeed, the primary if not sole purpose of their association was to elect Republicans. How the Republican Party could "corrupt" individuals who already declared themselves members of the same group was generally unclear. The

[68] Federal Election Commission v. Colorado Republican Federal Campaign Committee, 533 U.S. 431 (2001).

[69] Colorado Republican Federal Campaign Committee v. Federal Election Commission, 518 U.S. 604 (1996).

[70] *Buckley*, 424 U.S. at 46. *See* 2 U.S.C. § 431(17) (2002).

Court suggested that the parties might serve as "conduits,"[71] but conduits of what? Of public support? Of small, individual contributions in amounts that Congress had determined were not corrupting? The Court didn't say. Instead, it rotely upheld a "contribution" limitation, with no serious look at the alleged evil of the speech being suppressed.

What we see is that the Court, having decided in *Buckley* that some contributions create the danger of "corruption," has been willing to uphold most anything that comes before it labeled as a "contribution limitation," regardless of whether the particular type of transaction really raises a danger of corruption. Thus, at the extremes we find the FEC policing gifts from husbands to wives and from parents to children, and every day we find the agency pursuing violations against citizens who thought that they were doing their civic duty by being involved in political affairs, with no intent to corrupt anyone.

D. Manipulating the Rules

Perhaps the biggest problem with the Supreme Court's failure to precisely define "corruption" is that the constitutional standard for protecting free speech and association has become subject to manipulation through the incantation of the magic words, "corruption or the appearance of corruption."

Buckley argued that "large campaign contributions [are] the narrow aspect of political association where the actuality and potential for corruption have been identified."[72] And it described corruption as "political favors" given in return for financial campaign support. But as we have seen, *Buckley* failed to analyze why adopting an official position in exchange for speech supporting one's campaign— for it recognized that that is what campaign contributions make possible—is corrupting at all, or if monetary support is corrupting in some way that other types of support are not, why that is. Thus, both legislatures and courts have found it relatively easy to manipulate the standards of *Buckley* to limit disfavored speech, either under rationales *Buckley* supposedly rejected, or by the discretionary labeling of some types of activities as "corrupt."

---

[71] *Colorado Republican*, 533 U.S. at 459–60.
[72] 424 U.S. at 28.

For example, in the district court litigation of *McConnell v. Federal Election Commission*, litigating the constitutionality of the McCain-Feingold act, the three-judge panel, with each judge attempting to apply the principles of *Buckley* and its progeny, came to three differing conclusions about the constitutionality of the law. One judge found almost the entire law to be unconstitutional; a second found almost all of the law was constitutional; and the third found parts constitutional and other parts unconstitutional, often for differing reasons than those offered by whichever of his colleagues was in agreement on the provision at issue. Given that all three judges acted in good faith, we can see that the rules are open to judicial manipulation.[73]

The Supreme Court itself has reached results at odds with the stated rationale of *Buckley*. We have seen, for example, that the Court in *Austin* allowed the suppression of speech to equalize voices merely by describing that quintessential equality argument as "a different type of corruption." Similarly, we have seen how the Court was prepared, in *NRWC* and *Colorado II*, to accept limitations on political activity that bear little or no chance for corruption as *Buckley* attempted to describe it.

In *Nixon v. Shrink Missouri Government PAC*,[74] plaintiffs attempted to force the Court to flesh out the nature of "corruption." Pointing to a paucity of evidence, plaintiffs argued that Missouri's limitations on contributions were set at a level far below that needed to prevent "corruption" or "the appearance of corruption."[75] In *Buckley* the Court had required the government to justify the law under a standard of "rigorous" and "exacting" scrutiny.[76] The Court had upheld contribution limits on the grounds that they were less of a burden on First Amendment rights than expenditure limits, and that the state interest in contribution limitations was more compelling than its interest in expenditure limitations. But at no point did the Court suggest that a lesser degree of scrutiny applied to contribution limitations. In *Shrink PAC* the Court rejected this exacting standard for

---

[73] McConnell v. Federal Election Commission, 251 F. Supp. 2d 176 (D.D.C. 2003); *prob. juris. noted*, 123 S. Ct. 2268 (2003).

[74] 528 U.S. 377 (2000).

[75] *Id.* at 384.

[76] *Buckley*, 424 U.S. at 15–16, 29.

contribution limitations, instead adopting a new constitutional standard, not named, but which would allow a statute regulating contributions to survive constitutional scrutiny if "closely drawn."[77] The Court went on to reject the notion that the state actually had to prove that "corruption" or its appearance existed, so long as its explanation had "plausibility."[78] "Since contribution limitations could not satisfy the rigors of strict scrutiny (particularly since contribution limitations do not seem to be narrowly tailored to the problem of eliminating corruption), the Court simply lowered the bar."[79]

The ability to manipulate judicial results when one is not exactly clear what is the evil to be eliminated, or why, is seen in a remarkable *Shrink PAC* concurrence by Justice Breyer. Justice Breyer suggested that it might be possible to regulate expenditures by a candidate from his personal funds, as they "might be considered contributions to their own campaigns."[80] Of course, this is just semantic word play. New labels are not a good substitute for a clear idea as to why the law is as it is. If expenditures by a candidate from his own funds are not corrupting, they are not corrupting, regardless of whether one chooses to call them expenditures or "contributions to his own campaign." But if it is not clear why we have defined a particular type of exchange as "corrupting," it is a simple matter to reach a desired result through word games.

The dangers of the Court's imprecise analysis are greater still at the legislative level. Under *Shrink PAC*, if the state can come up with a plausible explanation for its speech limitations—the magic words "corruption or appearance of corruption" will do—it is free to limit most anything except expenditures by a candidate or expenditures made independently of a campaign, unless the latter are made by a corporation, in which case they too can be limited pursuant to *Austin*.

It has been amply demonstrated, however, that campaign finance laws are not neutral in application. Certain types of restrictions on contributions will benefit incumbents. Some groups will be harmed

---

[77] *Nixon*, 528 U.S. at 387–88.

[78] *Nixon*, 528 U.S. at 391.

[79] J. Clark Kelso, *Book Review: Mr. Smith Goes to Washington*, 1 J. ELEC. L. 75, 78 (2002).

[80] *Shrink PAC*, 528 U.S. at 405 (Breyer, J. concurring).

by a ban on "bundling" of contributions,[81] others by limitations on voter "scorecards," and this will often vary by the nature and make-up of the groups' membership. On the one hand, "bundling" is a tactic that has proven very effective for the liberal women's PAC Emily's List, and for trial lawyers. Both groups represent high-income individuals with a high degree of political involvement. These individuals are sophisticated enough to understand how to maximize their political voice, and have disposable income to make contributions up to the limit. Scorecards, on the other hand, tend to work effectively for right-to-life groups or groups such as the Christian Coalition, whose members have lower incomes but a built-in distribution network through churches. Simply knowing how a particular group attempts to influence the political system allows lawmakers to target hostile groups for speech suppression.

We noted that the very first campaign finance laws were intended to strike at the Republican power base in the corporate community. Little has changed in the past 100 years. For example, after Emily's List contributed mightily to Democrat Debbie Stabenow's U.S. Senate victory in 2000, Michigan Republicans sought to ban the practice of "bundling," used so effectively by Emily's List.[82] As the McCain-Feingold bill drew near to final Senate passage, sponsor Russ Feingold remarked on the Senate floor how the bill had changed over time, in part to build a coalition sufficient for passage.[83] As Senator Feingold's remarks indicate, the very act of drafting campaign finance legislation and gathering supporters must involve decisions by individual legislators as to the relative political advantages of different provisions of the law. To give just one example, lawmakers apparently decided that it was important to preventing the appearance of corruption that any broadcast advertisements mentioning a candidate within 60 days of an election should be limited,[84] but that it would not create an appearance of corruption if the contribution limit for incumbent senators facing a wealthy challenger was raised

---

[81] Bundling is the practice of directing members of a group to write checks directly to targeted campaigns, then delivering them to the candidate in a "bundle."

[82] See Chris Christoff, *State GOP Flexes Muscles of Power: Last Minute Legislation Gives Democrats Fits*, DETROIT FREE PRESS, Dec. 15, 2001, at 1A.

[83] 148 Cong. Rec. 2096 (2002).

[84] See 2 U.S.C. § 441b(c) (2002).

to $12,000.[85] Of course, it should not be necessary for Congress to attack all potential sources of corruption in order to attack one of them. But the Court's lack of rigorous scrutiny for congressional action amounts to a green light to engage in speech regulation for the express purpose of silencing one's political enemies, or otherwise enhancing one's reelection prospects. In fact, in lobbying for passage of BCRA, advocates of the bill specifically tried to recruit Republican votes by noting that the law would harm Democrats as much or more than Republicans, and help incumbents at the polls.[86] It would seem that preventing this type of partisan self-dealing or rigging of the system is just what the First Amendment should aim to prevent.

III. *Beaumont* and the Future of Reform

A. *The Case*

All of these consequences are visible in *Federal Election Commission v. Beaumont*. Beaumont was an officer of North Carolina Right to Life, Inc. (NCRL), a not-for-profit corporation organized under North Carolina law. Its funding came almost entirely from donations from individual members, but it also accepted a small amount in corporate donations. NCRL used its general treasury funds to make both independent expenditures and contributions to candidates for state office, as allowed by North Carolina law. NCRL challenged the federal prohibition on contributions from its treasury to candidates for federal office.[87]

NCRL based its challenge on *Federal Election Commission v. Massachusetts Citizens for Life*.[88] In *MCFL*, the Supreme Court had held that restrictions on independent expenditures by certain nonprofit groups violated the First Amendment. The Court held that limitations on corporate expenditures generally were "a substantial" restriction on political speech, notwithstanding the ability of a corporation to establish a "separate segregated fund," that is, a political

---

[85] *See* 2 U.S.C. § 441a(h) (2002).

[86] *See e.g.* Peter H. Stone, *Soft Money and the Senate*, BALTIMORE SUN, Jan. 7, 2001 at 1M (quoting McCain advisor Trevor Potter and Brennan Center lobbyist E. Joshua Rosenkranz.)

[87] Federal Election Commission v. Beaumont, 123 S. Ct. 1220 (2003).

[88] 479 U.S. 238 (1986).

action committee, or PAC.[89] The Court noted that the burdens of operating a separate PAC were significant, and that such burdens created a "disincentive for such organizations to engage in political speech."[90] Further, the Court heartily rejected the notion that a non-profit, ideological group such as MCFL posed any threat of "corruption" at all:

> It is not the case, however, that MCFL merely poses less of a threat of the danger that has prompted such regulation. Rather, it does not pose such a threat at all. Voluntary political associations do not suddenly present the specter of corruption merely by assuming the corporate form.[91]

The Court cited three "essential" features of MCFL: first, it was formed for the purpose of promoting political ideas, and did not engage in business activities; second, it had no shareholders or others with a claim to its assets or earnings; and third, it was not formed by a corporation, and had a policy against accepting corporate contributions.[92]

Lower courts had over the years extended *MCFL*'s reach, holding that engaging in nonpolitical as well as political activities, failing to maintain a formal policy against accepting corporate contributions, receiving *de minimis* amounts of corporate donations, and engaging in incidental business activities did not prevent a group from qualifying for the "*MCFL* exemption" from the prohibition on corporate expenditures.[93] In each case, the courts chose not to focus solely on

[89] *Id.* at 252.

[90] *Id.* at 254.

[91] *Id.* at 263.

[92] *Id.* at 263–64.

[93] *See* Federal Election Commission v. National Rifle Association, 254 F. 3d 173 (D.C. Cir. 2001) (sponsorship of non-political activities, provision of non-political goods and services such as magazines and accident insurance to members, lack of policy against corporate contributions, and actual receipt of up to $1000 in corporate contributions did not place incorporated advocacy group outside scope of *MCFL*); North Carolina Right to Life, Inc. v. Bartlett, 168 F. 3d 705 (4th Cir. 1999), *cert. denied* 528 U.S. 1153 (2000) (lack of policy against corporate donations and receipt of up to 8% of organization's revenue from corporations did not prevent corporation from claiming *MCFL* exemption); Federal Election Commission v. Survival Education Fund, 65 F. 3d 285 (2nd Cir. 1995) (lack of policy against corporate contributions and actual receipt of up to 1% of funds from corporations did not place group outside scope of *MCFL*); Day v. Holahan, 34 F. 3d 1356 (8th Cir. 1994), *cert. denied* 513 U.S. 1127 (1995) (lack of policy against corporate donations and engaging in "incidental" business activities did not put group outside *MCFL* exemption).

the corporate form of the organization, but rather conducted an inquiry into the actual threat of "corruption" posed by the nonprofit membership corporations at issue. Guided by *MCFL* and four U.S. Courts of Appeal, both the District Court and the U.S. Court of Appeals for the Fourth Circuit agreed that NCRL had a constitutionally protected right to make contributions to candidates.[94] The Court of Appeals, noting that NCRL posed neither a threat of quid pro quo activity, as outlined in *Buckley*, nor "distortion" as discussed in *Austin*,[95] held that contributions by such a group, like independent expenditures, fell within the *MCFL* exception to prohibitions on corporate activity.

Rather than analyze the case under *MCFL*, the Supreme Court considered *National Right to Work Committee* to be the controlling precedent. Interpreting *NRWC* as standing for "the practical understanding that [a] corporation's capacity to make contributions was limited to indirect donations within the scope allowed to PACs,"[96] the Court held that under the lower level of scrutiny given to contribution limitations, the prohibition on corporate contributions extended to corporations eligible for the *MCFL* exception on the expenditure side. It reversed the Court of Appeals.

Beaumont neatly captures many of the contradictions and problems of the Supreme Court's campaign finance jurisprudence. Most obvious is its malleability. First, the Court extended to contribution prohibitions its *Shrink PAC* holding that contribution limitations would no longer be subject to *Buckley's* "rigorous" and "exacting" standard of review.[97] The Court argued that "it is not that the difference between a ban and a limit is to be ignored; it is just that the time to consider it is when applying scrutiny at the level selected, not in selecting the standard of review itself."[98] But of course, selecting the level of scrutiny often determines the outcome—as we have noted, there is strong reason to think that *Shrink PAC* would have come out the other way had the Court applied "exacting" and "rigorous"

---

[94] Beaumont v. Federal Election Commission, 137 F. Supp. 2d 648 (E.D.N.C. 2000), *aff'd* 278 F. 3d 261 (2002).

[95] *Austin*, 278 F. 3d at 272.

[96] *Beaumont*, 123 S. Ct. at 2208.

[97] *Id.* at 2210.

[98] *Id.*

scrutiny, even after considering the differences between contributions and expenditures. Subjected to a higher level of scrutiny, it is equally doubtful that the statute in *Beaumont* could have withstood the Court's review. So the question is, is there a valid reason for subjecting the political activity of a small, voluntary, political nonprofit group such as NCRL to the same level of scrutiny as the political activity of corporations such as Coca-Cola, or wealthy millionaires? This can only be determined if we understand why an exchange of political favors for contributions is evil—assuming such exchanges take place regularly enough that the law is not hopelessly overbroad in any case. For as we have seen, politicians routinely exchange political favors for campaign support. Is the problem merely that money is involved? But if any money creates the danger of corruption, why allow individual or PAC contributions? Is it that a large amount of money is involved? Is $5,000—the maximum at issue in *Beaumont*—a large amount? Is the problem that the money comes from a corporation rather than an individual? If so, does it nonetheless make sense to treat NCRL the same as Coca Cola or Microsoft? Is a $5,000 donation from NCRL inherently more capable of creating "corruption or the appearance of corruption" than a promise from a labor union to put 100 flushers and drivers on the streets on election day?[99] More "corrupt" than a promise made to unemployed workers to support higher unemployment benefits if elected? More "corrupting" than $1 million in independent expenditures? The Court has no coherently stated theory as to why some exchanges of political promises for campaign support are "corrupt" and others are not. Hence, its rulings lack coherency and a sense of legitimacy. Similarly, lacking any strong notion of what evil the government is attempting to prevent, there is no particularly principled reason for picking either *MCFL* or *NRWC* as the controlling precedent. Either was available to the Court, and absent some thought as to why some types of contributions lead to exchanges that are particularly "corrupting," whereas others do not, the Court's analysis as to why these contributions should be banned is unconvincing.

---

[99] "Flushers" are people who look for eligible voters likely to support the preferred candidate, but who have not yet voted. Drivers then collect these people and take them to the polls.

Beaumont also exemplifies the specific problems of post-*Buckley* law. The Court expresses considerable angst about "political war chests" that corporations may amass, and follows *Austin's* bastardized, equality-based definition of "corruption" to inherently include corporate activity, given that corporations may have "advantages" over other groups—even if those groups could themselves incorporate.[100] The Court did not much consider how a corporation such as NCRL might build a "war chest" (small, voluntary donations) or why the presence of a "war chest" is corrupting. And like the case on which it relies, *National Right to Work Committee,* the court expresses fears of quid pro quo corruption without suggesting that North Carolina Right to Life actually posed any such dangers. Indeed, the Court claimed that the "details of corporate form," "affluence of particular corporations," the absence of "the evil that contributions by traditionally economically organized corporations exhibit," and the lack of "vast reservoirs of capital" were irrelevant to its determination that NCRL posed a threat of corruption.[101] If this is truly so, what is the Court's view of the danger posed by NCRL?

Finally, the Supreme Court tossed in another argument for good measure, one that was not briefed by the government, arguing that limits on corporate contributions protected shareholders from having their funds used to support candidates they opposed.[102] In so doing, the Court quietly, but not explicitly, overruled *First National Bank of Boston v. Bellotti.*[103] Bellotti had 25 years earlier rejected that same argument because of the voluntary nature of corporate association, an argument with particular force when applied to an inherently political organization such as NCRL. *Beaumont* sent it packing.

B. *Beaumont: Foretelling the Future*

As we noted at the outset, *Beaumont* is not, by itself, a case of earthshaking proportions, at least not given the broader restrictions on political speech enacted by Congress and accepted by the *Buckley* paradigm. Any effort to extract from this small case a prediction of where the Court will go when it decides the challenge to the Bipartisan Campaign Reform Act is risky at best. Those who hope to see

[100] *Beaumont,* 123 S. Ct. at 2209.
[101] *Id.* at 2208.
[102] *Id.* at 2206.
[103] First National Bank of Boston v. Bellotti, 435 U.S. 765 (1978).

the provisions of BCRA struck down have downplayed *Beaumont* for precisely these reasons. Nevertheless, *Beaumont* may be analyzed as part of a broader trend, and so analyzed, it does not bode well for defenders of unfettered political speech.

First, of course, is the lopsided 7-to-2 vote. Justice Kennedy's concurrence indicated, however, strong disagreement with the authorities on which the majority relied, and suggested that "were the whole scheme of campaign finance regulation under review," he might have joined Justices Thomas and Scalia in dissent.[104] Even then, the majority opinion successfully relies on *Austin v. Michigan Chamber of Commerce* without losing the support of Justice O'Connor, a dissenter in *Austin*. The opinion includes the de facto overruling of *Bellotti*. And the opinion's inclusion of a sweeping, largely inaccurate, and generally unnecessary review of congressional and judicial regulation in the field indicates an intellectual confidence in the Court's majority.

Much of the decision in *McConnell* may turn on whether or not the court considers large contributions to political parties, for purposes other than expressly advocating the election or defeat of a candidate, to pose a danger of corruption. With that in mind, it is interesting that the *Beaumont* majority refers to limits on "direct" corporate contributions at least 13 times, contrasting them with "indirect" corporate contributions in the form of administrative support for PACs. This, some argue, could at least suggest a willingness to strike down limits on corporate contributions or large individual contributions to political parties. The costs of PAC administration are not insignificant—many corporations and unions spend an amount upward of fifty percent of PAC revenue on administration. A PAC supported by corporation or union dollars is able to use 100 percent of its individual receipts for political contributions and expenditures. By comparison, under McCain-Feingold a political party must use a substantial percentage of its receipts merely to cover overhead and administration. Arguably, corporate and union support, or large donations, for such overhead expenses would be constitutionally protected because they are not "direct" support to candidates.

This theory faces two big problems, however. First, nothing in *Beaumont* suggests that the Court sees such "indirect" contributions

---

[104] *Beaumont*, 122 S. Ct. at 2212 (Kennedy, J., concurring).

as a constitutional right. The Court plays them up in *Beaumont*, it seems, precisely to downplay the magnitude of the speech restrictions it upholds. But the Court's rationale offers no support for the idea that some outlet must exist for corporate speech, and the notion is certainly not essential to the holding. The second problem is the Court's emphasis on preventing the use of nonprofits as "conduits" for large contributors,[105] a concern also expressed in *Colorado Republican II*,[106] despite that in neither case was there evidence of such a problem on the record, and despite the fact that such "conduit" contributions are otherwise illegal under the FECA.[107] The Court could choose to see such administrative and overhead support as a mere "conduit" allowing greater "direct" contributions, and thus not protected by the First Amendment.

Another possibility is that the *Beaumont* Court's emphasis on "direct" contributions foreshadows a breakdown of the long-standing demarcation between contributions and expenditures generally. In line with Justice Breyer's concurrence in *Shrink PAC*, the Court's majority may be ready, if asked, to simply reclassify many expenditures as "indirect contributions," thus opening them to the lower standard of review for contributions already announced in *Shrink PAC* and seconded in *Beaumont*. This would pave the way for a backdoor overruling of *Buckley's* distinction between contributions and expenditures.

Indeed, if there are tea leaves to be read in *Beaumont*, it may be that the Court already considers *Buckley* obsolete. As we have seen, *Buckley's* requirement of "rigorous" and "exacting" scrutiny, at least as applied to contribution restrictions, has already been abolished through *Shrink PAC* and *Beaumont*. This leaves the *McConnell* plaintiffs with the arduous task of showing that the regulation is not "closely drawn." This is a near impossibility given the Court's willingness to rely, in both *Colorado Republican II* and *Beaumont*, on fears of "conduits" and "evasion," even absent record evidence of same. Here, too, *Beaumont* chips away at *Buckley*. In *Buckley*, loophole closing was generally frowned upon as a justification for regulation.[108]

---

[105] 123 S. Ct., 2209–10.

[106] *Colorado II*, 533 U.S. at 458–460.

[107] *See* 2 U.S.C. § 441a(a)(8).

[108] *See Buckley*, 424 U.S. at 45–46 (disallowing restrictions on independent expenditures as a loophole closing measure).

In *Beaumont* and *Colorado Republican II*, it becomes the prime justification for regulation.

Meanwhile, the nebulous "appearance of corruption" standard will do as a sufficiently compelling government interest to justify suppression. *Buckley*'s core holding, that "corruption" or the "appearance of corruption," not equality, justified suppression of political speech, appears to be foundering in the wake of *Austin*, *NRWC*, and *Beaumont*. *Austin* specifically upholds an equality rationale that *Buckley* rejected, at least where corporations are concerned, even while calling it "corruption," whereas cases such as *NRWC* and *Beaumont* apply the corruption standard so rotely as to make it meaningless. Also fallen by the wayside is *Bellotti*'s rule that shareholder protection is not a valid basis for limiting corporate speech. Add to this *Colorado Republican II*'s view that political parties are little more than conduits for corruption, rather than the traditional view that parties are mediators in political struggles and builders of coalitions, and it is hard to see restrictions on soft money being stricken on constitutional grounds. In *NRWC*, *Austin*, and now *Beaumont*, the Court has expressed a view that corporate activity—even that of nonprofit membership corporations that merely bring together thousands of concerned citizens to participate in politics—can be regulated with little concern for overbreadth. This suggests that what may be McCain-Feingold's most notorious provision, the prohibition of any corporate or union ad that so much as mentions a federal candidate within sixty days of an election,[109] may well pass the Court's "closely drawn" scrutiny as well.

The lead plaintiffs in *McConnell* have argued that following *Buckley v. Valeo*, most provisions of BCRA should be struck down.[110] They may find that they are trying to call back a ship that has already sailed.

IV. Conclusion

Before 1974, federal elections were substantially unregulated, first as a matter of law, and later as a matter of fact. *Buckley v. Valeo*, the

---

[109] 2 U.S.C. §§ 34(f)(3) and 441a(a)(7).

[110] *See generally* Brief for Appellants Senator Mitch McConnell *et al.*; Brief for Appellants Republican National Committee *et al.*, 251 F. Supp. 2d 176 (D.D.C. 2003); *prob. juris. noted*, 123 S. Ct. 2268 (2003). It should be noted that there are some 80 plaintiffs in the case, many of whom do challenge the doctrine of *Buckley*.

judicial response to the wave of regulation ushered in after 1972, attempted to strike a balance between concern over the role of money in politics and the First Amendment protections of free speech and association. Whether *Buckley's* distinctions between contributions and expenditures, between express advocacy and issue advocacy, and between voluntary tax financing and mandatory tax financing were correct is a subject of long debate. The years since *Buckley* have led to a series of further hairsplitting decisions by the high Court, yielding what one perceptive observer has described as a "patternless mosaic."[111] Not-for-profit corporations have more protection than for-profit corporations, but only when spending money, not when contributing it. However, within that mix, giant media conglomerates have more protection than membership organizations. Massachusetts Right to Life, Inc., was protected as an ideological corporation, while the Michigan Chamber of Commerce was given less protection as a "non-political" organization, a description that would have stunned most observers of Michigan politics. Spending on ballot measures has more protection than spending on candidate races.[112]

These patternless distinctions are reflected, with even less order, in the legislatures. McCain-Feingold, for example, places limits on a group such as the Sierra Club or NRA spending $10,000 on broadcast ads, but would allow spending $100,000 on billboards and print ads.[113] *Shrink PAC's* lowered level of scrutiny, combined with the poorly thought-out magic words "corruption or appearance of corruption," are increasingly able to justify regulatory infringements on routine political activity. In such an atmosphere, incumbent self-dealing and efforts to gut the fund-raising ability of one's opponents run rampant. Meanwhile, the truest grassroots activity, such as that of the "Muleshoe Four," the Law Students for Bush-Cheney, or the Ferguson family, is caught up in a Byzantine web of regulation. This regulation is fostered, ironically enough, by a well-financed lobby that relies heavily on corporate contributions.[114]

[111] Lowenstein, *The Root of All Evil, supra* n. 38, 382–386.

[112] *See* Smith, *supra* n. 10 at 134.

[113] *See* 2 U.S.C. § 441a(a)(7) and 434 (f)(3) (2002).

[114] Groups urging greater regulation of campaign speech were, in the late 1990s, spending approximately $25 million a year, mostly in grants from large foundations, to promote their agenda. *See* Cleta D. Mitchell, Who's Buying Campaign Finance Reform? (2001); *see also* Bradley A. Smith, *The Gaggers and the Gag-making*, NATIONAL REVIEW, March 11, 2002 at 33 (discussing Mitchell report); and *id.* at 36 (providing example of contributions by large corporations).

Beaumont on its own is not particularly significant, but combined with other recent cases, most notably *Shrink PAC* and *Colorado Republican II*, it is significant indeed. Whatever its flaws, *Buckley* provided a reasonably broad area in which political speech could flourish. These protections for political speech are now being rapidly eroded. This trend will continue so long as a large segment of the public, and an apparent majority of the Supreme Court, see corruption, rather than virtue, in the routine give and take of democratic elections.

Eleventh Amendment Sovereignty: Much Ado about Nothing?

James E. Bond

The Supreme Court's decision in *Nevada v. Hibbs*[1] is the latest skirmish in the current Supreme Court's bitter internecine battle over the constitutional scope of a state's sovereign immunity. That battle is but the most recent phase in a two-hundred-year war over the appropriate, respective roles of the state and national governments in America's compound republic. That war dominated the debate over the ratification of the Constitution, fueled the Civil War, pitted the Reconstruction radicals against the defiant apologists for the Old South, underlay the seventy-five-year political struggle between increasingly conservative Republicans and ever more progressive Democrats that ended in the triumph of the New Deal; and it continues to divide those who prize individual liberty and advocate limited government from those who favor group rights and demand the regulatory state. One might plausibly argue that the history of America is largely the history of this war between these partisans over whether the national government or the states should dominate the making of public policy.[2]

The battle over the constitutional scope of a state's sovereign immunity began quietly enough thirty years ago. Only three years after his confirmation as an associate justice, Rehnquist, in a lonely dissent, articulated the theoretical basis for the Court's current sovereign immunity doctrine, which seeks to preserve the constitutional prerogatives of the states. Objecting to his brethren's acquiescence in the federal government's imposition of wage and price controls on the states, Rehnquist acknowledged that the Union was indestructible but questioned whether the states were any longer indestructible; and he asserted that the states had an "affirmative defense

---

[1]Nevada v. Hibbs, 123 S. Ct. 1972 (2003).
[2]JAMES BRYCE, THE AMERICAN COMMONWEALTH (1896).

against a congressional act that infringed their retained sovereignty."[3] He also explained a practical reality that would be repeatedly emphasized in subsequent cases: "[W]here the Federal Government seeks not merely to collect revenue as such, but to require the State to pay out its moneys to individuals at particular rates, not merely state revenues but also state policy choices suffer."[4] An important prerogative of state sovereignty is deciding how to spend its tax revenues, and interference with the exercise of that prerogative necessarily circumscribes the state's power to implement its public policies.

Four years later in *Nevada v. Hall*[5] Rehnquist again unfurled the banner of sovereign immunity, arguing that "unconsenting states are not subject to the jurisdiction of the Courts of other states."[6] This time he was not alone. Chief Justice Burger joined his dissent, and the "Sovereign Immunity Cavalry" was born.

Not until 1996, however, did Chief Justice Rehnquist rally a majority to his crusade to protect the states' sovereign immunity from an intrusive, overbearing national government. From 1996 through 2002, the Court decided a series of 5-to-4 cases in which the majority protected and arguably expanded the states' sovereignty immunity.[7] Each case involved plaintiffs who sued under a congressional act that authorized them to sue in state court for remedial damages caused by the state's violation of the act's guarantees. In each case, the five-person majority uttered the same battle cry: "Not without the State's consent." The Chief Justice forcefully and succinctly articulated the point in *Seminole Tribe of Florida v. Florida*,[8] declaring that "the Eleventh Amendment prevents congressional authorization of suits by private parties against unconsenting States."[9]

---

[3] Fry v. United States, 421 U.S. 542, 544 (1975).

[4] *Id.* at 545.

[5] Nevada v. Hall, 440 U.S. 410 (1979).

[6] *Id.* at 437 (Rehnquist, J., dissenting).

[7] Seminole Tribe of Florida v. Florida, 517 U.S. 44 (1996); Florida Prepaid Postsecondary Education Expense Board v. College Savings Bank, 527 U.S. 627 (1999); College Savings Bank v. Florida Prepaid Postsecondary Ed. Expense Bd., 527 U.S. 666 (1999); Alden v. Maine, 527 U.S. 706 (1999); Kimmel v. Florida Board of Regents, 528 U.S. 62 (2000); Board of Trustees of University of Alabama v. Garrett, 531 U.S. 356 (2001).

[8] *Seminole Tribe*, 517 U.S. 44 (1996).

[9] *Id.* at 53 (1996).

In *Nevada v. Hibbs,* however, the Chief deserted his troops. Leaving Justices Kennedy, Scalia, and Thomas to warm their hands around the perhaps flickering federalism campfire, Rehnquist and his law school classmate Justice O'Connor joined the "Anti-Sovereign Immunity Four" to hold that Congress could in some circumstances authorize damage suits against state governments even though the state had expressly refused to waive its sovereign immunity.

Does the Court's Opinion Clarify the Scope of a State's Sovereign Immunity?

Before *Nevada v. Hibbs,* the black letter law of sovereign immunity seemed clear, if controversial. Basically, the "Sovereign Immunity Cavalry" argued that the Eleventh Amendment was intended by those who framed and ratified it to guarantee each state sovereign immunity, including immunity from suit by its citizens unless it waived that immunity. As Justice Kennedy observed in *Alden v. Maine,* "[States] are not relegated to the role of mere provinces or political corporations. . . ."[10] That pronouncement is consistent with James Madison's broader description of the states' retained sovereignty in Federalist No. 45: "[The] powers reserved to the several States will extend to all objects, which, in the ordinary course of affairs concern the lives, liberties and properties of the people; and the internal order, improvement and prosperity of the State."[11] Moreover, the specific constraints on state sovereignty contained in Section 10 of Article I of the Constitution impliedly presuppose the existence of state sovereignty at least as broad as Madison acknowledges in No. 45.

Notwithstanding Chief Justice Stone's cavalier dismissal of the Tenth Amendment as a mere "truism,"[12] that amendment would also seem to confirm Madison's original understanding of a state's sovereign immunity. Madison was, after all, the author of the Bill of Rights, which was intended in part to assuage anti-federalist concerns that the new Constitution would strip the states of their sovereignty. During the ratification debates Madison had emphasized that the powers of the national government were few and

---

[10] Alden v. Maine, 527 U.S. 706, 715 (1999).
[11] THE FEDERALIST NO. 45 (MADISON) 241.
[12] United States v. Darby 312 U.S. 100, 124 (1941).

defined, while state governments enjoyed many and often undefined powers.[13] So, too, did his ardent nationalist collaborator Alexander Hamilton, who denied that the federal courts would have any power to breach the sovereign immunity of a state, which he described as a preexisting right of state governments.[14] More particularly, Hamilton insisted that "[i]t is inherent in the nature of sovereignty not to be amenable to the suit of an individual without its consent."[15]

Consequently, the "Sovereign Immunity Cavalry" have insisted over the last seven years that Congress can abrogate the states' retained sovereign immunity only if it is validly exercising its Fourteenth Amendment enforcement power, and then only if it expressly states that it intends to abrogate the states' immunity. The Court enunciated the governing test for evaluating the validity of a congressional attempt to abrogate a state's sovereign immunity in the exercise of its power to enforce the guarantees of the Fourteenth Amendment in *City of Boerne v. Flores*.[16] *Boerne* involved a challenge to the 1993 Religious Freedom Restoration Act, which prohibited the states from "substantially burden[ing]" the free exercise of religion unless the states could demonstrate that the burden furthered a "compelling state interest" by the "least restrictive means."[17] Relying on the Act, a San Antonio church challenged a historic preservation regulation that prohibited it from enlarging its chapel. One might have predicted that the conservative majority, which has been generally more sympathetic to the claims of the religious than was the Warren Court, would have blessed Congress's deferential acquiescence to the interests of the religious. One would have been wrong.

While conceding that Congress had broad enforcement powers under Section 5 of the Fourteenth Amendment, the Court majority, per Justice Kennedy, worried that acquiescence in its exercise here would permit Congress to define the substantive scope of the Fourteenth Amendment. If Congress could define the substantive scope of the rights guaranteed in Section 2, "it is difficult to conceive of a principle that would limit congressional power."[18]

---

[13] THE FEDERALIST NO. 81 (HAMILTON) 423.

[14] *Id.*

[15] *Id.*

[16] *Boerne*, 521 U.S. 507 (1997).

[17] *Id.* at 515–6.

[18] *Id.* at 529.

Although ostensibly interested in policing Congress's power, the Court majority was also determined to protect its own power. The Religious Freedom Restoration Act (RFRA), which was passed unanimously in the House and 93 to 7 in the Senate, intended to overrule the Court's prior decision in *Employment Division Department of Human Resources v. Smith*.[19] Congress could not do that. Perhaps a constitutional amendment could. But absent that, the Court alone determined the scope of constitutional rights: '[t]he power to interpret the constitution . . . remains in the judiciary."[20] Moreover, the Court insisted that the scope of any remedy had to be "congruent and proportional" to the nature of the violation, a standard that is a gloss on Congress's Article I, Section 8 "necessary and proper" authority to implement its Article I powers.

John Marshall would have been proud. The *Boerne* rule echoed the proclamation of *Marbury v. Madison* that '[i]t is emphatically the province and duty of the judicial department to say what the law is"[21] and his oft-repeated declaration in *McCulloch v. Maryland* that so long as "the end be legitimate . . . [and] within the scope of the constitution . . . all means which are appropriate and plainly adopted to, which are not prohibited, but consist with the letter and the spirit of the constitution, are constitutional."[22]

Nevada v. Hibbs may nevertheless confuse the clarity of the Court's prior sovereign immunity doctrine because the "Sovereign Immunity Cavalry" (the Chief Justice and Justices Kennedy, O'Connor, Scalia, and Thomas) split. To the surprise of some Court-watchers, the Chief and Justice O'Connor joined the "Anti-Sovereign Immunity Four" in finding no sovereign immunity bar to a citizen suing his state in federal court, at least where certain constitutional rights are at stake. This potential confusion is compounded by the fact that Rehnquist's opinion for the Court appears to reflect only Justice O'Connor's and his judgment, and the rule of the case is thus difficult to discern.

The "Anti-Immunity Four" clearly repudiate the Court's opinion even as they concur in its result. Justice Souter emphasized, for

---

[19] *Employment Division* 494 U.S. 872 (1990).

[20] *Id.*

[21] Marbury v. Madison, 5 U.S. 137, 177 (1803).

[22] McCulloch v. Maryland, 17 U.S. 316, 420 (1819).

example, that the same result would follow from the reasoning of the dissenting positions of Justices Breyer, Stevens, and himself in prior sovereign immunity cases. He stated, "I join the Court's opinion here without conceding the [principles of those] dissenting opinions."[23] Justice Stevens, concurring separately, scornfully asserted that "the plain language of the Eleventh Amendment poses no barrier" to Congress's abrogation of Nevada's sovereign immunity because the state's defense was "based on what I regard as the second [judge made] Eleventh Amendment."[24] In other words, the Amendment—by its own terms—simply does not apply to suits involving a state and its own citizens. The "Anti-Sovereign Immunity Four" thus adhere in *Hibbs* to their consistent position that the Eleventh Amendment embodies a concept of sovereign immunity no broader than that a state may not be dragged into federal court by a citizen of another state or a foreign state.

It is consequently the disagreement among the "Sovereign Immunity Cavalry" that is critical to deciding whether *Nevada v. Hibbs* clarifies or confuses the preexisting law. The scope and nature of their disagreement can only be understood in light of the facts of the case. The critical facts are undisputed. In 1993 Congress passed the Family and Medical Leave Act (FMLA),[25] granting eligible employees up to 12 weeks of unpaid leave annually for, among other reasons, a "serious health condition" suffered by an employee's parent, spouse, or child. FMLA grants aggrieved employees a private right of action "against any employer (including a public agency) in any Federal or State court of competent jurisdiction."[26] Congress adopted FMLA to eliminate gender discrimination in the workplace.

Nevada, however, had enacted a gender-neutral family leave policy. Indeed, Mr. Hibbs had received 500 days leave under the state act. Insisting that FMLA gave him yet more leave time, he refused to return to work after he was warned, following a state hearing on his claim, that he would lose his job if he did not. Following his

---

[23]*Hibbs*, 123 S. Ct. at 1984 (Souter, J., concurring).

[24]*Id.* at 1985 (Stevens, J., concurring in the judgment).

[25]29 U.S.C. § 2601.

[26]29 U.S.C. § 2617(a)(2).

termination, Mr. Hibbs sued to vindicate his rights in Nevada's Federal District Court.

While all the justices who wrote opinions appeared to agree that Congress had the authority to pass FMLA under its power to regulate interstate commerce, the Court's controlling precedents made it clear that Congress's Commerce Clause powers did not include the authority to abrogate a state's sovereign immunity. Consequently, Congress rested its authority to impose FMLA upon the states on its power under Section 5 of the Fourteenth Amendment to enforce the substantive provisions of Section 1, which prohibit the states from (1) abridging the privileges or immunities of citizens and (2) denying persons the equal protection of the laws and due process of law. Thus, the issue before the Court was the scope of Congress's enforcement powers under Section 5 of the Fourteenth Amendment. More particularly, the question was whether Congress's abrogation of Nevada's sovereign immunity was a "proportional and congruent remedy" for a persistent pattern of gender discrimination in the workplace.

This phrasing of the issue highlights the two determinative questions in *Hibbs*. First, what factual predicate must Congress establish to justify abolition of a state's sovereign immunity in the exercise of its Section 5 enforcement powers? Chief Justice Rehnquist dwelled at length on the evidence Congress weighed in reaching its conclusion that the states had engaged in a persistent pattern of gender discrimination in the workplace. He concluded that "the States' record of unconstitutional participation in, and fostering of, gender-based discrimination in the administration of leave benefits is weighty enough to justify the enactment of prophylactic § 5 legislation."[27]

The Chief Justice explained that his rejection of analogous congressional justifications in *Board of Trustees v. Garrett*[28] and *Kimmel v. Board of Florida Regents*[29] reflected the different nature of the interest Congress sought to protect in *Hibbs*. In *Garrett* and *Kimmel* Congress had sought to protect the aged and the disabled, neither of whom belongs to a "protected" class. In *Hibbs* it sought to protect women

---

[27] *Hibbs*, 123 S. Ct. at 1981.

[28] *Garrett*, 531 U.S. 356 (2001).

[29] *Kimmel*, 528 U.S. 62 (2000).

and men from discrimination based on their gender, which the Court recognized in *United States v. Virginia*[30] as a "semi-suspect" and thus "protected" class.

Normally, the significance of the distinction between the general run of legislative classifications and semi-suspect and suspect classifications is that the Court scrutinizes more carefully the government's regulation of the latter two classes to ensure, in the case of semi-suspect classifications, that the classification serves "important governmental objectives" in a manner "substantially related to the achievement of those objectives."

Here, however, the significance of the nature of the class subject to regulation appears to be that the Court will give greater deference to Congress's judgment that it must abrogate a state's sovereign immunity to protect a semi-suspect (or, one presumes, a suspect) class from discriminatory state legislation. In any case, Chief Justice Rehnquist was satisfied that Congress had met its evidentiary burden:

> Congress responded to this history of discrimination by abrogating States' sovereign immunity in Title VII of the Civil Rights Act of 1964, 78 Stat. 255, U.S.C. § 2000e-2(a), and we sustained this abrogation. . . . But state gender discrimination did not cease. It can hardly be doubted that . . . women still face pervasive, although at times more subtle, discrimination . . . in the job market. According to evidence that was before Congress when it enacted the FMLA, States continue to rely on invalid gender stereotypes in the employment context, specifically in the administration of leave benefits. Reliance on such stereotypes cannot justify the States gender discrimination in this area. The long and extensive history of sex discrimination prompted us to hold that measures that differentiate on the basis of gender warrant heightened scrutiny; here . . . the persistence of such unconstitutional discrimination by the States justifies Congress' passage of prophylactic § 5 legislation.[31]

The majority's apparent deference to congressional fact-finding may mitigate Judge Noonan's fear that the "proportional and congruent" test invites the justices to usurp the role of Congress and substitute

---

[30] *United States v. Virginia*, 518 U.S. 515 (1996).

[31] *Hibbs* at 1978–9.

their value judgments for those of the House and Senate, at least where Congress is exercising its Fourteenth Amendment enforcement powers.[32]

The dissenting members of the "Sovereign Immunity Cavalry" clearly rejected such deference, however; and they reviewed the congressional record almost as if it were a trial transcript. They first challenged the factual nexus that Congress asserted between the alleged pattern of gender discrimination in the states and the Equal Protection Clause. Even the Court of Appeals had conceded that much of the evidence upon which Congress relied did "not document a widespread pattern of precisely the kind of discrimination prohibited by § 2612 (a)(1)(c) of FMLA."[33] Justice Scalia framed the factual predicate which would justify abrogation of a state's sovereign immunity in such circumstances very narrowly and clearly articulated its relationship to the range of remedies that Congress might employ:[34]

> The constitutional violation that is a prerequisite to "prophylactic" congressional action to "enforce" the Fourteenth Amendment is a violation by the State against which the enforcement action is taken. There is no guilt by association, enabling the sovereignty of one State to be abridged under §5 of the Fourteenth Amendment because of violations by another State, or by most other States, or even by 49 other States.

Under that standard, the generosity of Nevada's gender-neutral family leave policy would seem to preclude any justification for Congress's subjecting it to FMLA. In other words, the factual record did not show that Nevada had violated the substantive guarantees of Section 1 of the Fourteenth Amendment.

The second determinative question was thus whether Congress's remedy was proportional and congruent to the violation revealed by the facts. Justice Scalia sarcastically emphasized the cut of this rule in *Hibbs* by citing *City of Rome v. United States*[35] as evidence that

---

[32] JOHN NOONAN, NARROWING THE NATIONS POWERS: THE SUPREME COURT SIDES WITH THE STATES 145–8 (2002).

[33] 273 F.3d 844, 859 (9th Cir. 2001).

[34] *Hibbs* at 1985 (Scalia, J., dissenting).

[35] 446 U.S. 156 (1980).

"Congress has sometimes displayed evidence of this self-evident limitation" because there it restricted "the most sweeping provisions of the [1965] Voting Rights Act" to "seventeen states" with a demonstrable history of intentional racial discrimination in voting.[36] Because there was no evidence that all states had discriminated against women in family leave policies, Congress's remedy was not proportional.

Justice Kennedy shared Scalia's concern, asserting that the majority had failed to show "that States have engaged in a pattern of unlawful conduct which warrants the remedy of opening state treasuries to private suits."[37] But Kennedy added another, more nuanced objection. Characterizing FMLA as "a welfare benefit" rather than "a remedy for discrimination," he insisted that that categorical distinction "demonstrate[s] the lack between any problem Congress had identified and the program it mandated."[38] If Kennedy's characterization is correct, the congressional remedy is plainly not congruent; and he pointed out that FMLA was thus not structured "as a remedy to gender-based discrimination in family leave." Rather, it was a "Congressional attempt to define the scope of the Fourteenth Amendment." Here Justice Kennedy cited, not *City of Boerne*, but Justice Harlan's dissent in *Katzenbach v. Morgan*[39] where he would have invalidated the federal ban on literacy tests in New York because there was no evidence that the state had used them for discriminatory purposes. Thus, the ban was not, in his view, an "appropriate remedial measur[e] to redress and prevent the wrongs" but an impermissible attempt to define the *substantive* scope of the Amendment.[40]

It would appear then that this much can be said about the clarity of the Court's sovereign immunity doctrine, post *Nevada v. Hibbs*. While the generally applicable "rule" remains the same, the factual nexus that Congress must establish to justify enacting remedial legislation to address violations of Section 1 of the Fourteenth Amendment is now uncertain. Arguably, on the one hand, the opinion of the

---

[36] *Hibbs* at 1981 (Scalia, J., dissenting).

[37] *Hibbs* at 1987 (Kennedy, J., dissenting).

[38] *Id.* at 1991.

[39] 384 U.S. 641 (1966).

[40] *Id.* at 666 (Harlan, J., dissenting).

Court signals a willingness on the part of the otherwise mismatched majority to defer to congressional findings of fact in this area, much as Chief Justice Burger once suggested was appropriate in *Fullilove v. Klutznick.*[41] On the other hand, such deference might seem more appropriate under a "rational basis test" than a "narrowly tailored" test. Indeed, a week later Chief Justice Rehnquist himself seemed less disposed to defer to legislative findings in *Grutter v. Bollinger,*[42] though there it was a state university, not the Congress, that was making the judgment; and the impacted class was a suspect rather than a semi-suspect one.

The first distinction made all the difference to Chief Justice Burger in *Fullilove.* Why it should make such a difference to Chief Justice Rehnquist, the patron saint of state sovereignty, is less clear. Perhaps the explanation is that Rehnquist was simply engaged in damage control. Once Justice O'Connor deserted, the Chief Justice may have felt that he faced a Hobson's choice: dissent, where he could only cry foul, or join the majority, where he could assign himself the opinion and at least seize the opportunity to cite the VMI case without repeating Justice Ginsburg's "exceedingly persuasive" language, which had caused some analysts to speculate that gender classifications might soon be subject to strict rather than intermediate scrutiny. More important, he could make the result in *Hibbs* appear to turn on a particularized assessment of the factual record before Congress rather than on some broader principle of constitutional law enunciated by the "Anti-Sovereign Immunity Four" and thus maintain doctrinal fluidity while awaiting the appointment of new recruits to his "Sovereign Immunity Cavalry."

The dissenters' insistence that Congress cannot cloak its redefinition of a constitutional guarantee as a remedy for an assumed violation of that guarantee suggests a much less deferential view toward congressional findings of fact. The rigorous application of that dissenters' rule would presumably require, not deference to Congress's stated factual conclusions, but a searching inquiry to determine their accuracy and perhaps even to assess Congress's "real" intent. Generally, the Court has refrained from such inquiries. Whether such an inquiry would be consistent with the respect one branch of the

---

[41] 448 U.S. 448 (1980).
[42] 123 S. Ct. 2325 (2003).

national government ought to practice toward a coordinate branch is a fair and complex question. Whether such an inquiry is necessary if the sovereign immunity of the states is to be protected is an equally fair and complex question, as Professor Richard Epstein, a confessed "Doubting Thomas" on the wisdom of the Court's current sovereign immunity doctrine, conceded in a recent review of Noonan's book. Epstein nevertheless concludes that Judge Noonan "does not come anywhere near proving that the Court's invocation of sovereign immunity usurp[s] Congress' legislative powers."[43]

Is the Doctrine of State Sovereignty a Substantial Contribution to Our Enduring Understanding of Federalism?

From the political left, the answer is a resounding no. Their view, reflected within the Court most clearly in the dissents of Justice Breyer, is that modern America is a post-federal polity whose institutions have superceded the quaint antebellum political structures within which states enjoyed substantial discretion to regulate the health, welfare, and morals of their citizens. Consequently, the national government should have the authority to impose its public policy choices on the states, despite the Tenth Amendment's clear reservation of traditional police powers to the states. In *United States v. Lopez*,[44] Justice Breyer argued, on the one hand, that Congress might reasonably have concluded that many school children were traumatized by their knowledge that persons carried guns near schools. Accordingly, those children dropped out of school and deprived America of their latent skills. As a result, America would be unable to compete in the global economy. He then concluded:[45]

> In sum, a holding that a particular statute before us falls within the commerce power would not expand the scope of that Clause. . . . It would recognize that, in today's economic world, gun-related violence near the classroom makes a significant difference to our economic, as well as our social well-being.

---

[43] Richard Epstein, *A Federal Case*, NATIONAL REVIEW 50, 52 (October 28, 2002).
[44] United States v. Lopez, 514 U.S. 549, 616 (1995) (Breyer, J., dissenting).
[45] *Id.* at 624–5.

Chief Justice Rehnquist, on the other hand, recognized the impact of such reasoning in *United States v. Morrison*,[46] where he pointed out:

> The reasoning that petitioners advance seeks to follow the but-for causal chain from the initial occurrence of violent crime (the suppression of which has always been the prime object of the States' police power) to every attenuated effect upon interstate commerce. If accepted, petitioners' reasoning would allow Congress to regulate any crime as long as the nationwide, aggregated impact of that crime has substantial effects on employment, production, transit, or consumption. Indeed, if Congress may regulate gender-motivated violence, it would be able to regulate murder or any other type of violence since gender-motivated violence, as a subset of all violent crime, is certain to have lesser economic impacts than the larger class of which it is a part.

The Chief Justice's reasoning in *Morrison* is difficult to reconcile with his *Hibbs* opinion. In *Morrison*, Rehnquist rested his conclusion on the national government's constitutional obligation to respect the reserved powers of the states. One of those powers, implicit in Rehnquist's pre-*Hibbs* view of the Eleventh Amendment, is a state's authority to prevent citizens from suing it without its consent.

Perhaps Rehnquist's arguable inconsistency merely reflects the ambivalence of the political right, which is curiously divided over whether the Court's sovereign immunity doctrine is a substantial contribution to our enduring understanding of federalism. Conservatives and libertarians alike generally embrace traditional notions of federalism because it is one of the institutional structures that they believe both permit diverse communities to flourish and, equally important, protect the liberties of the people from overweening governmental power. As Judge Alex Kozinski and Professor Steven Engel point out, "dividing sovereignty fundamentally changed the business of government by introducing competition into that oldest of monopolies."[47]

And yet some on the right dismiss the Court's sovereign immunity doctrine as "federalism lite" at best and pernicious at worst. Robert

[46] *United States v. Morrison*, 529 U.S. 598, 615 (2000).

[47] Alex Kozinski and Steven A. Engel, *Recapturing Madison's Constitutionalism Without the Blank Check*, in JAMES MADISON AND THE FUTURE OF CONSTITUTIONAL GOVERNMENT 13 (John Samples, ed. 2002).

Levy, a senior fellow in constitutional studies at the Cato Institute, insists that "[w]hen sovereign immunity is used, supposedly to reinforce federalism, it constricts rather than enlarges personal liberty."[48] The doctrine of sovereign immunity is rooted in the assumption that "the king can do no wrong." All history demonstrates that kings not only can do wrong but, if given an opportunity, will do wrong. The founders understood that history. They had lived it, as the Declaration's searing indictment of King George so clearly demonstrates. Mr. Levy is thus correct when he points out that the founding generation knew that governments could and would do wrong. And state governments are no exception to that rule, as Clint Bolick has so chillingly described in the aptly named *Grassroots Tyranny*.[49]

Mr. Levy may be mistaken, however, when he argues that the Founders' concept of sovereign immunity must be construed narrowly—bounded by the express text of the Eleventh Amendment.[50] While the Declaration makes clear that ultimate sovereignty rests in the people, that fact scarcely supports the conclusion that the Framers rejected a broader concept of sovereign immunity, including the perceived need for governmental immunity. They were not all libertarians. Thomas Paine's *Common Sense* may have fueled the revolutionaries' fervor that ignited their revolt, but its libertarian, anti-government bias did not dominate discussions in the constitutional convention or in the subsequent ratification debates. Rather, those debates focused, first, on which level of government—state or national—would enjoy predominant governmental power and its implied handmaiden, sovereign immunity, and, second, on what allocation of power between the two would best protect the liberties of the people.

There is also good reason to question the prudence of Mr. Levy's rejection of state sovereign immunity. Adherence to the original understanding is essential to the preservation of the rule of law, the interpretive lodestar of the political right; and while there may be

---

[48] Robert Levy, *People v. State*, LEGAL TIMES 74 (June 16, 2003).

[49] CLINK BOLICK, GRASSROOTS TYRANNY: THE LIMITS OF FEDERALISM (1993).

[50] *But see* CLYDE E. JACOBS, THE ELEVENTH AMENDMENT AND SOVEREIGN IMMUNITY (1972) (state sovereign immunity is inconsistent with both the original understanding and the nature of the government established in the Constitution).

room for different assessments of the original understanding of the scope of the Eleventh Amendment, there is much less reason to doubt the accuracy of Justice Thomas's understanding of the founding generation's concept of state power and the scope of sovereign immunity, which that power included.

Dissenting in *U.S. Term Limits, Inc. v. Thornton*, Justice Thomas succinctly described the original understanding of the peoples' ultimate sovereignty and the constitutional division of powers between the national and state governments.

> In each State, the remainder of the people's powers—"t[he] powers not delegated to the United States by the Constitution, nor prohibited by it to the States," Amdt. 10—are either delegated to the state government or retained by the people. The Federal Constitution does not specify which of these two possibilities obtains; it is up to the various state constitutions to declare which powers the people of each State have delegated to their state government. As far as the Federal Constitution is concerned, then, the States can exercise all powers that the Constitution does not withhold from them. The Federal Government and the States thus face different default rules: Where the Constitution is silent about the exercise of a particular power—that is, where the constitution does not speak either expressly or by necessary implication—the Federal Government lacks that power and the States enjoy it.[51]

In other words, if the states retained the traditional authority to deny citizen suits against themselves, the federal government could not abridge that dimension of a state's sovereign immunity.

In contrast to Mr. Levy, some observers on the political right bubble with optimism about the future foreshadowed by the Court's statutory federalism decisions. Michael Greve, director of the American Enterprise Institute's Federalism Project, wrote:

> The Rehnquist Court's statutory federalism decisions have had a real effect. They have measurably increased the autonomy of state and local governments, diminished the role of special-interest advocacy groups, and increased the accountability of Congress. That shift spells neither the end of the welfare state nor an "activist" judicial arrogation of power.

[51] U.S. Term Limits v. Thornton, 514 U.S. 779, 847–8 (1995) (Thomas, J., dissenting).

> The central theme of the Rehnquist Court's statutory federal-
> ism is democratic responsibility and accountability. Congress
> remains free to create private entitlements and to impose
> corresponding mandates on the states—so long as it clearly
> informs the states of their obligations. If Congress lacks the
> will or the votes to expose states to private enforcement, it
> can provide for enhanced federal agency oversight over the
> states or else administer welfare statutes with the federal
> government's own money and bureaucrats.[52]

While Mr. Greve is doubtless correct that the Court's statutory federalism decisions have protected the states' fiscal autonomy, no one can
contemplate with equanimity the "Big Brother" alternative means of
enforcement that he acknowledges the federal government might
employ.

We may take heart from the anti-federalists, who rightly insisted
that the people are the best guardians of their liberty. The fact that
states enjoy sovereign immunity does not preclude their citizens, in
whom ultimate sovereignty does rest, from defining the scope of
governmental immunity narrowly under state law. Acting through
the political processes established in their state constitutions and
statutes, they can secure legislation or amendments that redefine
the scope of their state's sovereign immunity.

In addition, state court judges may appropriately construe their
respective state constitutions in ways that curtail a state's powers.
Indeed, one distinguished state court jurist has recently made that
very point emphatically and persuasively:

> To the extent a state government exercises its power to under-
> take activities beyond those necessary to protect and main-
> tain individual rights, courts must look for specific manifesta-
> tions of the people's consent that evidence constitutional
> grants of that authority. But, where a legislature acts without
> express or necessarily implied authorization of the constitu-
> tion, it exceeds its authority—even if there is no constitu-
> tional provision barring such actions.[53]

Justice Sanders then draws the obvious conclusion:

---

[52] MICHAEL S. GREVE, *Federalism, Yes. Activism, No*, AEI PUBLIC POLICY RESEARCH, No.
7 at 5 (July 2001).

[53] RICHARD SANDERS AND BARBARA MAHONEY, *Restoration of Limited Government: A
Dissenters' View*, 59 NEW YORK UNIVERSITY ANNUAL SURVEY OF LAW 269, 270 (2003).

The practice of interpreting state constitutions as granting the state legislature plenary power except where such power has been expressly limited by the constitution presumes that state governments have inherent powers that sovereignty resides with the servant rather than the popular masters. However, this presumption contradicts the basic premise of American government that all power resides in the people except as it has been delegated to the government. Because courts have uniformly and uncritically adopted this presumption, they have interpreted state constitutions contrary to the clear meaning of the text and allowed an unwarranted expansion of state power that threatens individual rights. Once this presumption is debunked, a defensible theory of constitutional interpretation emerges that embodies that principle of limited government expressed by the people who ratified their state constitutions.[54]

Simultaneously, one can hope that the Supreme Court will follow Justice Sanders' advice in its own construction of Congress's enumerated powers. The truth is that the Rehnquist Court has demonstrated an instinct for the capillaries rather than the jugular when it comes to federalism questions and the preservation of the states' police powers. The jugular is the forgotten or ignored concept of enumerated powers. The national government continues to expand in lockstep with the Court's ever more expansive readings of Congress's enumerated powers, most especially its power to regulate interstate commerce. Unfortunately, the Court has not succeeded in reining in those powers, notwithstanding *United States v. Lopez*[55] and *United States v. Morrison*.[56] Until the Court retreats from its general latitudinal "anything Congress wants to do, it can" approach to interpreting Congress's Article I powers, federal power will continue to expand.

In a recent article on enumerated powers, Roger Pilon made this very point, demanding that courts man the batteries against such political assaults on the principle of enumerated powers.[57] Madison had also stressed the power and obligation of the courts to enforce

---

[54] *Id.*

[55] *Lopez*, 514 U.S. at 549 (1995).

[56] *Morrison*, 529 U.S. at 598 (2000).

[57] ROGER PILON, *Madison's Constitutional Vision: The Legacy of Enumerated Powers*, in JAMES MADISON AND THE FUTURE OF LIMITED GOVERNMENT 25 (John Samples, ed. 2002).

the principle of enumerated powers in his veto of an act to promote internal improvement:[58]

> Such a view of the Constitution [as the bill contemplated] would have the effect of excluding the judicial authority of the United States from its participation in guarding the boundary between the legislative powers of the General and the State Governments, inasmuch as questions relating to the general welfare, being questions of policy and expediency, are unsusceptible of judicial cognizance and decisions.

Madison's emphasis on the inappropriateness of the courts policing legislative judgments on questions of "policy and expediency" arguably reinforces the importance of confining the national government to its enumerated powers rather than attempting to preserve state police powers by employing the general doctrine of sovereign immunity to curtail federal power. Only Justices Thomas and Scalia, however, appear ready to take the doctrine of limited enumerated powers seriously by overruling prior precedents. Justice Thomas made his position clear in his concurring opinion in *Lopez*:

> Although we have supposedly applied the substantial effects test for the past 60 years, we always have rejected readings of the Commerce Clause and the scope of federal power that would permit Congress to exercise a police power; our cases are quite clear that there are real limits to federal power. . . . In an appropriate case, I believe that we must further reconsider our "substantial effects" test with an eye toward constructing a standard that reflects the text and history of the Commerce Clause without totally rejecting our more recent Commerce Clause jurisprudence.[59]

Thomas's colleagues have also been conspicuously unresponsive to his plea to reexamine and rationalize the "dormant commerce clause" doctrine, which has generally inhibited the states from exercising their traditional police powers.[60] In a withering assessment of the Court's federalism cases, Professor Earl Maltz ties the Court's

[58]JAMES MADISON, *Veto Message*, March 3, 1817, MIND OF THE FOUNDER 308 (MARVIN MEYERS, ed. 1981).

[59]*Lopez*, 514 U.S. at 584 (Thomas, J., concurring).

[60]*See* Camps Newfound Owatonna, Inc. v. Town of Harrison, 520 U.S. 564, 609–20 (1997) (Thomas, J., dissenting).

sovereign immunity cases to those dormant commerce clause cases. While conceding that "Justice Kennedy's opinions in *City of Boerne* . . . and *Lopez* . . . demonstrated that he had at least some concern for the preservation of state decision-making authority,"[61] Professor Maltz points out that in *U.S. Term Limits, Inc. v. Thornton*[62] Kennedy refused to recognize state sovereignty over the number of terms its U.S. senators and representatives could serve. Even more disturbing, according to Maltz, Justice Kennedy has routinely invoked the dormant commerce clause as a justification for invalidating "even-handed state regulations" where the magnitude of the state interests does not, in the Court's judgment, justify the burden on interstate commerce. Maltz concludes:[63]

> The preservation of state autonomy in the federal system requires more than judicial protection of the structure of state governments or even the enforcement of constitutional limitations on the power of Congress; it also requires that the Supreme Court itself adopt a restrained posture in reviewing the enactments of state governments. Justice Kennedy quite obviously has failed to grasp this fundamental truth; thus, his strong endorsement of the concept of state sovereignty in *Alden* has a hollow ring.

Whatever the legal, historical, and policy merits of this two-century-long war, two underlying facts are clear. One, the "Sovereign Immunity Calvary's" earlier attempts to cut back the ever expanding power of the national government proved short-lived[64] and may suggest that hydraulic pressures to expand government are built into a postmodern technological society. That is the implicit thesis of Professor Rossum's lament over the adoption of the Seventeenth Amendment, which abolished the system under which state legislatures elected Senators:

---

[61] EARL MALTZ, *Justice Kennedy's Vision of Federalism*, 31 RUTGERS L.J. 761, 762 (2000). See also LINO GRAGLIA, *United States v. Lopez: Judicial Review Under the Commerce Law*, 74 TEXAS L. REV. 719, 740 (1996).

[62] U.S. 514 U.S. 779, 838 (Kennedy, J., concurring).

[63] Maltz *supra* note 61, at 770.

[64] Compare Nat'l League of Cities v. Usury, 426 U.S. 833 (1976) (federal government cannot interfere with the integral governmental functions of the states) with Garcia v. San Antonio Metropolitan Transit Authority, 469 U.S. 528 (1985) (overruling Nat'l League of Cities v. Usury).

Most political leaders during this lengthy campaign to secure the adoption and ratification of the Seventeenth Amendment clearly did not appreciate the framers' understanding that the principal means of protecting federalism and preventing the transfer of the "residuary and inviolable sovereignty of the states" to the national government was the mode of electing the Senate. They did not worry about altering constitutional structure, because they embraced the Progressive dogma that the Constitution is a living organism that must constantly adapt to an ever changing environment. They did not worry that their alterations would break a Newtonian, clock-like mechanism; rather, they celebrated the Darwinian adaptability of the Constitution and the evolution of its principles.[65]

Professor Rossum thus sees the Court's sovereign immunity doctrine as an ill-advised and ineffective effort to plug a hole in a dike that has already been washed away. And even if that is not true, the narrow and continuing split within the Court underscores the insight of Bishop Hoadly that "he who has the power to declare the law is truly the lawgiver."[66] In a nine-person court, the majority is thus the lawgiver—as the late Justice Brennan's famous "Rule of Five" so bluntly reveals. Judge Noonan makes the same point: "If five members of the Supreme Court are in agreement on an agenda, they are mightier than five hundred members of Congress."[67] Consequently, the immediate future of state sovereignty depends more on the pattern of impending retirements and replacements than on the merits of the opposing positions.

That's the political reality. In any case, the longer term future of sovereign immunity will turn on broader political developments. Justice Frankfurter understood that these political trends ultimately transformed judicial doctrine:[68]

---

[65] Rossum at 220.

[66] In a recent article in the American Bar Association Journal, Rehnquist is characterized as an "impresario" rather than an "intellectual leader" who "is like the guy who deals the cards. He's skilled at seeing where he has five votes." RICHARD BURST, *Supreme Court Analysis*, AMERICAN BAR ASSOCIATION 43, 46 (May 2003).

[67] Noonan *supra* note 32 at 139.

[68] Larson v. Domestic and Foreign Commerce Corp., 337 U.S. 682, 709 (1949) (Frankfurter, J., dissenting).

> The course of decisions concerning sovereign immunity is a
> good illustration of the conflicting considerations that often
> struggle for mastery in the judicial process, at least implicitly.
> In varying degrees, at different times, the momentum of the
> historic doctrine is arrested or defected by an unexpressed
> feeling that governmental immunity runs counter to prevail-
> ing notions of reason and justice. Legal concepts are then
> found available to give effect to this feeling, and one of the
> results is the multitude of decisions in which this Court has
> refused to permit an agent of the government to claim that
> he is *pro tanto* the government and therefore sheltered by
> its immunity.

The Court's current state sovereign immunity doctrine may thus
prove to be one of Frankfurter's isolated "derelict[s] on the waters
of the law,"[69] and *Nevada v. Hibbs* may be the beginning of its demise.
To the extent that the American people, whether conservative or
liberal, increasingly look to the national government rather than to
their local and state governments to solve problems, federalism may
in fact be withering away.

As two astute scholars—one a political liberal and the other a
political conservative—have pointed out in recent books,[70] there are
decisive moments in American history when the people coalesce
around some new understanding of their constitutional principles
and enforce that understanding through their political institutions.
No Supreme Court majority, however determined to be the last
rather than the first to acquiesce in the jettisoning of federalism, can
long prevent the demise of America's compound republic if the
"sleeping sovereign" arises from its usual slumber and demands
that the federal government assume all policymaking for the nation.
When a conservative president insists on national standards to
ensure that "no child is left behind" and a liberal senator wins her
seat on a pledge to eliminate trailer classrooms across Washington
State, we may be perilously close to that moment. If it materializes,
the Justice Breyers of the world may well prove to have been the
oracles of a post-federal and liberty-lite America.

---

[69] Lambert v. California, 355 U.S. 225, 232 (1957) (Frankfurter, J., dissenting).

[70] BRUCE ACKERMAN, WE THE PEOPLE: FOUNDATIONS (1991); KEITH WHITTINGTON, CONSTITUTIONAL CONSTRUCTION (1999).

To prevent that unhappy event, the American people must act on their common sense and, like those who rallied to Paine's, demand that their state and national governments respect both the peoples' rights and the limits the people have imposed on governmental powers. In the specific context of the issue in *Hibbs v. Nevada*, they might well demand that they have the right to sue in state courts for the state's denial of rights guaranteed them by the national government. It ought never to be thought that a state's dignity is compromised when its citizen sovereigns ask it to appear in court and answer to the charge that it has violated their rights.

Found Money: IOLTA, *Brown v. Legal Foundation of Washington*, and the Taking of Property without the Payment of Compensation

Ronald D. Rotunda

Introduction

When James Madison drafted the Fifth Amendment, he included the "takings" clause, which provides that "private property [shall not] be taken for public use, without just compensation." Madison included this provision because he believed that property rights are a part of human rights. In an essay published after the states ratified the Bill of Rights, Madison explained:

> If there be a government then which prides itself in maintaining the inviolability of property; which provides that none shall be taken directly even for public use without indemnification to the owner, and yet directly violates the property which individuals have in their opinions, their religion, their persons, and their faculties; nay more, which indirectly violates their property, in their actual possessions, in the labor that acquires their daily subsistence, and in the hallowed remnant of time which ought to relieve their fatigues . . . such a government is not a pattern for the United States.[1]

Nearly two centuries later, Justice Stewart, speaking for the Court, echoed this theme, citing John Locke and Blackstone, two intellectual ancestors of Madison:

> [T]he dichotomy between personal liberties and property rights is a false one. Property does not have rights. People

---

[1] *Property*, Nat'l Gazette, Mar. 27, 1792, reprinted in 14 JAMES MADISON, THE PAPERS OF JAMES MADISON 266 (1983), quoted in Douglas W. Kmiec, *The Jurisprudence of Takings: The Original Understanding of the Taking Clause Is Neither Weak nor Obtuse*, COLUM. L. REV. 1630, 1661, n. 161 (1988).

> have rights. The right to enjoy property without unlawful deprivation, no less than the right to speak or the right to travel, is in truth a "personal" right, whether the "property" in question be a welfare check, a home, or a savings account. In fact, a fundamental interdependence exists between the personal right to liberty and the personal right in property. Neither could have meaning without the other.[2]

Initially, the takings clause applied only to the federal government. But, because a person's right to property is fundamental, the Court held that this clause applies to the states as well.[3]

The framers wanted limits on the power of government to use the people's money, and the takings clause is one of those limits. It provides a check on the government: the clause gives government the power to take a person's property, *if* the government (a) takes it for "public use," and (b) pays "just compensation." For example, if the government wants to build a road through my house, it can take my property, but first it must pay the fair market price for the land that it requires.[4] The purpose of the takings clause is "to bar Government from forcing some people alone to bear public burdens which, in all fairness and justice, should be borne by the public as a whole."[5] Thus, if the government wants the road badly enough so that it is willing to pay the market price for my land, the takings clause poses no roadblock.[6]

---

[2] Lynch v. Household Finance Corp., 405 U.S. 538, 552 (1972), citing, *inter alia*, JOHN LOCKE, OF CIVIL GOVERNMENT 82–85 (1924); JOHN ADAMS, A DEFENCE OF THE CONSTITUTIONS OF GOVERNMENT OF THE UNITED STATES OF AMERICA, in F. COKER, DEMOCRACY, LIBERTY, AND PROPERTY 121–32 (1942); and 1 WILLIAM BLACKSTONE, COMMENTARIES, *138–140.

[3] Chicago, B. & Q.R. Co. v. City of Chicago, 166 U.S. 226 (1897) (a state court judgment, although authorized by statute, that takes private property for public use without compensation, lacks due process of law. When the state court affirms such a judgment, it denies a right secured by the federal constitution).

[4] Roger Pilon, *Freedom, Responsibility, and the Constitution: On Recovering Our Founding Principles*, 68 NOTRE DAME L. REV. 507, 542–43 (1993).

[5] Armstrong v. United States, 364 U.S. 40, 49 (1960). *See also* Steven J. Eagle, *The Development of Property Rights in America and the Property Rights Movement*, 1 GEORGETOWN J. OF L. & PUBLIC POLICY 77 (2002).

[6] Ronald D. Rotunda, *The Impairments Clause and the Corporation*, 55 BROOKLYN L. REV. 809 (1989).

How is the government to determine what it must pay for the property it has taken? The Supreme Court tackled this takings issue in *Brown v. Legal Foundation of Washington.*[7] The issue in *Brown*[8] is, ultimately, this takings issue. The Court had to decide what the government owed, that is, what it had to pay, for property that the Washington State Supreme Court had taken. It is important to understand that all nine justices conceded that property had been "taken," but the five-person majority, surprisingly, found that the state government had to pay nothing for this property, although it was worth millions of dollars to the government.

Brown is a relatively short opinion that is much more complex than it first appears.[9] It is written so that lower courts could read it very narrowly, substantially limiting its applicability and growth. Granted, lower courts may ignore the caveats written throughout this opinion and simply see it as a green light for state courts and legislatures to "take," without compensation, the interest that grows out of the principal. But, the Court gives us many reasons why this case should be read narrowly, with the majority conceding that the government cannot take the principal (which belongs to the owners of that principal) unless it pays just compensation, and cannot even take the interest, except under the peculiar facts of this case.

The Court upheld the constitutionality of what is called "Interest on Lawyers' Trust Accounts" (IOLTA). The state court of Washington, by court rule, took the interest from these trust fund accounts. All nine justices agreed that what the state court had ordered was a "taking" of property. As Justice Stevens, for the Court, bluntly acknowledged, quoting an earlier decision, "the interest earned in the IOLTA accounts 'is the private property of the owner of the principal.' "[10] But then, five members concluded that the value of the money was worth zero to the owners of the principal out of which

---

[7] 123 S.Ct. 1406 (2003).

[8] 123 S.Ct. 1406 (2003).

[9] It could have been even more complex. Originally, the name of the case was "Washington Legal Foundation v. Legal Foundation of Washington," but a procedural ruling changed the name of the petitioner. *See* 123 S.Ct. at 1415 and n. 4. *See also* Brief of Petitioner, in Washington Legal Foundation v. Legal Foundation of Washington, 2002 WL 1974400 (Appellate Brief), (U.S. Pet. Brief Aug 22, 2002) (NO. 01-1325).

[10] Brown v. Legal Foundation of Washington, 123 S.Ct. 1406, 1419 (2003).

the interest grew, so, the majority concluded, the compensation that the state owed these people was also "zero."

Yet the Washington State Court and other IOLTA jurisdictions did not collect zero from IOLTA accounts. Washington IOLTA accounts generate between $2.5 and $4.0 million per year.[11] In the year 2000 alone, IOLTA programs throughout the United States generated more than $148 million through interest on nominal or short-term client funds.[12] By 2001, the figure had grown to more than $200 million.[13] The states treated this money as free money or found money, something akin to money you might find on the street corner: it just comes, like manna from heaven; one does not have to earn it. In this case, the state court collects this money without the necessity of imposing a tax, which is the normal way that the government "earns" money. The state court, in its view, created something out of nothing, a feat unrivaled since Genesis.

Before we turn to the decision, we must discuss the complicated historical and legal background.

The Historical Road Leading to IOLTA

IOLTA accounts are a relatively recent phenomenon made possible by a series of changes in trust law and tax law provisions.

As a matter of trust law, the general rule has long been that lawyers, who are fiduciaries of their clients, must not mix up, blend, or "commingle" their funds with their clients' funds.[14] Sometimes a client will have the lawyer hold a great deal of money in trust, and the lawyer will put that money in a trust fund established in that client's name. It is not necessary, however, that the lawyers establish a separate named trust account for each client. Lawyers typically combine small accounts from each client when the amounts from each client are small. These funds are usually held for only a

---

[11] Brief of Petitioners, Washington Legal Foundation v. Legal Foundation of Washington, 2002 WL 1974400 (Appellate Brief), (U.S. Pet. Brief, Aug 22, 2002)(NO. 01-1325), at 4.

[12] AMERICAN BAR ASSOCIATION, COMMISSION ON INTEREST ON LAWYERS' TRUST ACCOUNTS, IOLTA HANDBOOK 5 (2001).

[13] AMERICAN BAR ASSOCIATION, COMMISSION ON INTEREST ON LAWYERS' TRUST ACCOUNTS, IOLTA HANDBOOK 98, 208 (2002 update).

[14] See RONALD D. ROTUNDA, LEGAL ETHICS: THE LAWYER'S DESKBOOK ON PROFESSIONAL RESPONSIBILITY §16-1 (ABA-West Group, 2nd ed. 2002).

short time, and the amount only becomes substantial when all of the clients' deposits are aggregated.

Although the funds of each client are normally mingled together with the funds of other clients, there are records to detail what is each client's share of the pooled trust account.[15] In addition, these trust funds may not be commingled with the lawyer's personal funds.[16]

When lawyers establish trust funds for their clients, they traditionally place those funds in noninterest bearing accounts. First, the law governing lawyers' trust fund accounts forbids commingling and requires safekeeping and accounting; customarily, it does not require investing. IOLTA, as discussed below, requires that the funds be invested. In some unusual circumstances, trust law might require that funds be invested, but this rule does not apply when the trustee is merely under a duty to safeguard money, not to invest it.[17] Many lawyers' trust fund accounts fall in that category. In addition, before the advent of computers, it was administratively difficult to calculate how much interest should be assigned to a particular client when the funds were held for a short time and combined with the funds of other clients.

And then there was federal law. Until 1980, federal law did not allow federally insured banks to pay interest on checking accounts. If a lawyer held a large sum in trust for his client, he normally would place these funds in an interest-bearing savings account because the interest generated outweighed the inconvenience of not having the lack of immediate access to the fund via check-writing capabilities. But if the client's funds were small or only held for a short time,

---

[15] ABA Model Rule 1.15, Comment 1, advises that monies of clients or third persons should be kept "in one or more trust accounts. Separate trust accounts may be warranted when administering estate monies or acting in similar fiduciary capacities." The ABA Model Rules of Professional Conduct are not law but are "model" rules. The ABA urges state courts to adopt them as law governing the lawyers within the jurisdiction and most state courts have done that. *See* RONALD D. ROTUNDA, LEGAL ETHICS: THE LAWYER'S DESKBOOK ON PROFESSIONAL RESPONSIBILITY § 1.5.5.4 (ABA-West Group, 2nd ed. 2002).

[16] *See, e.g.*, Cincinnati Bar Association v. Stidham, 87 Ohio St.3d 455, 721 N.E.2d 977 (2000) (two year suspension on lawyer who, *inter alia*, delayed filing a matter for over a year, collected fees in probate matters before getting court permission, and wrote personal checks against his IOLTA account).

[17] 2 AUSTIN WAKEMAN SCOTT, THE LAW OF TRUSTS, §§ 180.3, 181 (3d ed. 1967).

the lawyer would pool this money with funds from other clients and put them in a single federally insured trust checking account, due to administrative convenience and ready access to the funds by check. Federal law prohibited federally insured banks and savings and loans from paying interest on these checking accounts.[18]

When Congress finally changed the law in 1980, it relaxed this prohibition on interest but did not eliminate it. Congress authorized federally insured banks to pay interest on a limited category of demand deposits referred to as negotiable order of withdrawal accounts or "NOW accounts."[19] The regulation governing NOW accounts allows the banks to pay interest on "deposits made by individuals and charitable organizations, but does not include those made by for-profit corporations or partnerships unless the deposits are made pursuant to a program under which charitable organizations have 'the exclusive right to the interest.'"[20] So, if lawyers pooled their clients' money held for safekeeping into one account, that account could be accessed by checking, and also earn interest as long as charitable programs have the exclusive right to the interest. Yet, the ethical rules governing lawyers required (until the advent of IOLTA) that any interest earned be given to the client under the age-old doctrine that interest on principal belongs to the owner of the principal.

If trust funds are placed in interest-bearing accounts, then, under standard trust rules, any interest would have to be credited to each client.[21] Under normal trust rules, the interest generated from the funds becomes the property of the client, not of the lawyer, because the client owns the principal from which the interest accrues. The general rule is that interest follows the principal. Consequently, the legal ethics rules provided that the lawyer could not use the interest earned on client funds to defray the lawyer's own operating expenses (such as bank handling fees, accounting costs, recordkeeping and

---

[18] See 12 U.S.C. §§ 371a, 1464(b)(1)(B), 1828(g).

[19] 12 U.S.C. § 1832, 87 Stat. 342.

[20] Legal Foundation, 123 S.Ct. at 1411 and n. 1, quoting Donald Middlebrooks, The Interest on Trust Accounts Program: Mechanics of Its Operation, 56 FLA. B.J. 115, 117 (1982) (Letter from Federal Reserve Board General Counsel Michael Bradfield to Donald Middlebrooks, Oct. 15, 1981).

[21] ABA Formal Opinion 348 (July 23, 1982).

notification expenses) unless the lawyer had "the specific and informed consent of the client."[22]

The response of the states was to change the law governing lawyers. The federal law governing NOW accounts changed in 1980. A year later, Florida became the first state to create an IOLTA program.[23] The Washington State Court created its IOLTA program by court order in 1984.[24] Now, every state in the union, plus the District of Colombia, has an IOLTA program. These programs, at a minimum, require lawyers to create accounts that earn interest and to give that interest to the charity that the state court stipulates. Many programs, like Washington State, are mandatory: the lawyer must deposit certain funds in IOLTA accounts.

In 1980, when Congress allowed interest to be paid on demand deposits for NOW accounts, it still prohibited for-profit corporations and partnerships from earning interest on demand deposits.[25] The Federal Reserve Board, however, later ruled that such funds could be held in NOW accounts *if* the funds were held in trust pursuant to which charitable organizations had the "exclusive right to the interest."[26] Further, the Internal Revenue Service ruled that it would not attribute the interest earned from such accounts to the income of the individual clients if they had no control over the decision to place the funds in the IOLTA account and did not designate who would receive the interest generated by the account.[27] A leading ABA Formal Opinion also approved IOLTA programs as permissible under the rules of ethics.[28]

---

[22] ABA Formal Opinion 348 (July 23, 1982). This principle is not new. ABA Informal Opinion 545 (1962) (lawyer may not keep interest earned on trust account even though it was "quite difficult to allocate" interest to particular clients, unless clients specifically authorize this action); ABA Informal Opinion 991 (1967) (law firm may not use interest earned on savings account to defray expenses of handling agency account unless clients specifically consent).

[23] The IOLTA concept originated in several Canadian provinces and British Commonwealth countries, THOMAS D. MORGAN & RONALD D. ROTUNDA, PROBLEMS AND MATERIALS ON PROFESSIONAL RESPONSIBILITY 574 (Foundation Press, 8th ed. 2003).

[24] The rule may be found at 101 Wn.2d 1242 (1984).

[25] 12 U.S.C.A. § 1832.

[26] *See* Donald Middlebrooks, *The Interest on Trust Accounts Program: Mechanics of Its Operations*, 56 FLA. BAR J. 115, 117 (Feb. 1982).

[27] *See* Revenue Ruling 81-209, 1981-2 Cum. Bull. 16; Revenue Ruling 87-2, 1987-1 Cum. Bull. 18.

[28] ABA Formal Opinion 348 (July 23, 1982).

Armed with this change in the law, bar associations and courts sought to capture this interest from the banks, and to use the money to fund various public service projects, such as legal services programs and similar pro bono activities. The shorthand word for all these programs is often called IOLTA.

The Legal Road Leading to IOLTA

The law governing the taking of property is complex, but one only need to understand three important points to comprehend *Brown*.

The first important point is that the government must pay for property that it takes by physical possession. But the Supreme Court has strayed from this principle and given the government a great deal of leeway in regulating property if it does not occupy the property. Zoning rules that limit the height of buildings are a typical example. In these cases, the Court does not require compensation unless the regulation is unusually excessive. For constitutional purposes, taking by regulation is different than taking by physical possession.

For example, *Penn Central Transportation Co. v. New York*[29] upheld state law that authorized the Landmark Preservation Commission to designate certain property as a "landmark." If such designation was upheld after judicial review, the landmark was subject to various restrictions, such as requiring that any proposed alterations to the building's external appearance have the prior approval of the commission. Penn Central claimed that the commission's refusal to allow it to build a multistory office building above the Grand Central Terminal was an unconstitutional "taking." Justice Brennan, for the divided Court, held that there was no taking, and said that a "taking" is more readily found "when the interference with property can be characterized as a physical invasion by government, than when interference arises from some public program adjusting the benefits and burdens of economic life to promote the common good."[30]

If there is, instead of a regulation, a physical intrusion, even a minor one, the normal rule is for the Court to find a "taking" and require compensation. Consider *Loretto v. Teleprompter Manhattan CATV Corp.*[31] Justice Thurgood Marshall, speaking for the Court,

[29] 438 U.S. 104 (1978).
[30] 438 U.S. at 124 (internal citation omitted).
[31] 458 U.S. 419 (1982).

described the issue as whether "a minor but permanent physical occupation of an owner's property authorized by government" is a "taking" of property for which just compensation is due."[32] New York law provides that a landlord must permit a cable television company to install its cable facilities on his property. In this case, the cable was about one-half inch in diameter, and its installation occupied a small portion of the appellant's roof and the side of her building. In addition, the cable and boxes in that case occupied only about one-eighth of a cubic foot of space on the roof of the appellant's Manhattan apartment building. The intrusion was minor and on the outside of the building. Nonetheless, Justice Marshall found a taking. This holding is part of a long judicial tradition. Thus, *Butler v. Frontier Telephone Co.*[33] held that an ejectment action would lie if a telephone wire was strung across the plaintiff's property without touching the soil.

Second, it is important to realize that the Court has held, as a constitutional matter, that interest is property that belongs to whoever owns the principal to which the interest has attached. The leading case is *Webb's Fabulous Pharmacies, Inc. v. Beckwith,*[34] where the Court found a taking of property when a Florida county took the interest earned on an interpleader fund while the fund was temporarily held by the county court. The value of the property taken was the interest that the county took.[35] Justice Blackmun, for the Court, ruled that neither the Florida Legislature by statute, nor the Florida courts by judicial decree, could accomplish this result by characterizing or deeming the principal of the deposited fund as "public money." The Court also rejected the argument that "the statute takes only what it creates."[36] Justice Blackmun, after citing

[32] 458 U.S. at 421.

[33] 186 N.Y. 486, 79 N.E. 716 (1906).

[34] 449 U.S. 155, 159 (1980) citing Chicago, Burlington & Quincy R.R. Co. v. Chicago, 166 U.S. 226 (1897).

[35] The general rule is that, when the government takes physical possession of money or property that otherwise would accrue to the benefit of a private person, the private person's claim for just compensation is established unless the government can demonstrate that its action in fact constituted only a regulation of the property use, or payment of an amount lawfully owed to the government. Because a state statute authorized a separate clerk's fee for services rendered, the taking of the interest could not be justified as payment of an obligation to the government.

[36] 449 U.S. at 158.

a long series of both state and federal court opinions, said, for a unanimous Court: "The usual and general rule is that any interest on an interpleaded and deposited fund follows the principal and is to be allocated to those who are ultimately to be the owners of that principal."[37]

Finally, it is important to understand that five years before it decided *Brown*, the Court issued its opinion in *Phillips v. Washington Legal Foundation*.[38] *Phillips* was the first Supreme Court case to ask whether state IOLTA plans constitute an unconstitutional taking of client funds. Under the Texas IOLTA program at issue in that case, an attorney who received client funds was required to deposit them in a separate, interest-bearing, account if he or she determined that the funds "could not reasonably be expected to earn interest for the client" or the interest that might be earned "is not likely to be sufficient to offset the cost of establishing and maintaining the account, service charges, accounting costs and tax reporting costs which would be incurred in attempting to obtain the interest."

The respondents in *Phillips* alleged that the Texas IOLTA program constituted a "taking" under the Fifth Amendment. The Court said that the question before it was narrow. The Court assumed that a lawyer was required to put funds into an IOLTA account only if the interest generated on the funds would be insufficient to offset bank service charges and accounting for the interest. The issue was whether the interest was nevertheless "property" of the lawyer or client so that the takings clause could apply. The Court held that the interest on client funds held in IOLTA accounts is property of the client for purposes of the takings clause of the Fifth Amendment.

Chief Justice Rehnquist, for the Court (5 to 4), adhered to the "interest follows principal" rule[39] and held that the interest on a client's funds in a lawyer's hands is "property" of the client even if bank charges would mean the client could never spend it. For example, the Court said, rental income would be the property of the owner of a building even if collecting the rent cost more than

[37] 449 U.S. at 162.

[38] 524 U.S. 156 (1998).

[39] This common law rule dates back hundreds of years. *See, e.g.,* Beckford v. Tobin, 1 Ves. Sen. 308, 310, 27 Eng. Rep. 1049, 1051 (Ch. 1749): "[I]nterest shall follow the principal, as the shadow the body."

the tenant had paid. The Court concluded that there is no traditional property law principal that allows the owners of funds temporarily deposited in an attorney's trust account to be deprived of the interest the funds generate.[40]

Although the decision in *Phillips* is narrow,[41] it raised significant constitutional doubt about the ultimate viability of IOLTA plans.

Then came *Brown*.

The Legal Road Leading to IOLTA

Brown v. Legal Foundation of Washington,[42] like ancient Gaul, may be divided into three parts.

In the first part, all nine justices agree that what the Washington State Court did was equivalent to a physical taking of the property rather than a regulatory taking in which the rules governing when compensation is due tend to be ad hoc.

On one level, this conclusion is unremarkable because the principal earned interest and the state took the interest. This is as much a physical intrusion as in *Teleprompter*. After *Phillips v. Washington Legal Foundation* it was clear that the interest on client funds held in IOLTA accounts is the property of the client for purposes of the takings clause. Nonetheless, the respondents, amici, and the lower court all argued that the ad hoc regulatory taking cases, such as *Penn Central Transportation Co. v. New York City*, should govern this taking.

Significantly, the Court rejected that argument and explicitly applied the per se rule of physical intrusions. There is a taking when IOLTA rules take the interest on clients' trust fund accounts and that taking is equivalent to a physical intrusion. The majority emphasizes:

[40]Because the questions had not been decided below, the Court left for another day whether the IOLTA program constituted an unconstitutional taking of the clients' property and what, if any, compensation might be due. 118 S.Ct. at 1934.

[41]Souter, J. (joined by Breyer, Stevens, & Ginsburg, JJ.) and Breyer, J. (joined by Stevens, Souter, & Ginsburg, JJ.) filed dissenting opinions in *Phillips*. They argued that the Court had reached out unnecessarily to decide an abstract issue, and that it could only properly decide the property issue in light of the issues that were not before the Court. They also believed, however, that it was meaningless to talk of "taking" or calling "property" an asset that had no practical value to the client. Under pre-existing federal law, the client's principal could not generate interest (because federal law prohibits for-profit corporations and partnerships from earning interest on demand deposits unless the interest is earned in an IOLTA account).

[42]123 S.Ct. 1406 (2003).

255

"As was made clear in *Phillips*, the interest earned in the IOLTA accounts 'is the "private property" of the owner of the principal.' If this is so, the transfer of the interest to the Foundation here seems more akin to the occupation of a small amount of rooftop space in *Loretto*."[43]

In the second part of *Brown*, the Court decided that the property had been taken for a "public use." Normally, the Court has not imposed a very high hurdle on the "public use" restriction and this case is no exception.

Before *Brown*, the leading modern case defining the scope of the public use limitation is the unanimous 1954 Supreme Court decision in *Berman v. Parker*.[44] This case involved the constitutionality of the 1945 District of Columbia Redevelopment Act. Under section 2 of that Act, Congress declared it the policy of the United States to eliminate all substandard housing in Washington, D.C., because such areas were "injurious to the public health, safety, morals, and welfare." The Act also created the District of Columbia Redevelopment Land Agency and granted that agency the power to assemble real property for the redevelopment of blighted areas of the city through the exercise of eminent domain. After assembling the necessary real estate, Congress authorized the Agency to lease or sell portions of the land to private parties upon an agreement that the purchasers would carry out the redevelopment plan.

The appellants in *Berman* owned property within the redevelopment area upon which a department store was located. They argued that their property could not constitutionally be taken for the project because the property was commercial and not residential or slum housing; and, by condemning the property for sale to a private agency for redevelopment, the land was being redeveloped for a private and not a public use as required by the Fifth Amendment. The Supreme Court, in an opinion by Justice Douglas, disagreed and upheld the use of the eminent domain power.

Berman does not treat the "public use" requirement as much of a constraint. Under that case, once the legislature has declared a

---

[43] 123 S.Ct. at 1419 (internal citations omitted).

[44] 348 U.S. 26 (1954), discussed further in 2 RONALD D. ROTUNDA & JOHN E. NOWAK, TREATISE ON CONSTITUTIONAL LAW: SUBSTANCE AND PROCEDURE § 15.13 ("The 'Public Use' Limitation") (West Group, 3rd ed., 1999).

condemnation to be for a public use, the role of the courts is an extremely narrow one. However, Justice Stevens, speaking for the *Brown* majority, seems to loosen those already loose restrictions when he appears to adopt a different test:

> [The public use] condition is unquestionably satisfied. If the State had imposed a special tax, or perhaps a system of user fees, to generate the funds to finance the legal services supported by the Foundation, there would be no question as to the legitimacy of the use of the public's money. The fact that public funds might pay the legal fees of a lawyer representing a tenant in a dispute with a landlord who was compelled to contribute to the program would not under-mine the public character of the "use" of the funds. Provided that she receives just compensation for the taking of her property, a conscientious pacifist has no standing to object to the government's decision to use the property she formerly owned for the production of munitions. Even if there may be occasional misuses of IOLTA funds, the overall, dramatic success of these programs in serving the compelling interest in providing legal services to literally millions of needy Americans certainly qualifies the Foundation's distribution of these funds as a "public use" within the meaning of the Fifth Amendment.[45]

The Court analogizes the state court's ethics rule setting up the IOLTA program to a tax. It is a tax, of sorts, because it takes away money (the interest on the IOLTA accounts) that would, but for the IOLTA program, go to the holders of the principal—the clients of the lawyers. Conversely, if the law did not allow interest to be earned, or if the lawyers holding the funds had placed them in a non-interest-bearing account, the banks would have captured this interest. In any event, before the IOLTA program, private parties earned the interest and after the program the state captured that interest. The effect of IOLTA is to allow the Washington Supreme Court to do what, normally, only the state legislature can do: impose a tax. Instead of a democratically elected legislature enacting a tax, the state court imposes its functional equivalent by enacting a rule of ethics governing lawyers. The rule, however, unlike most ethics rules, does not apply to conflicts of interest, or the attorney-client

---

[45] 123 S.Ct. at 1417 (footnote omitted).

privilege, or the assorted other matters that make up the bulk of the court's rules or rationales governing lawyers.

Justice Scalia's dissent, joined by Chief Justice Rehnquist and Justices Kennedy and Thomas, objected to Stevens's "ruminations" on the public use prong of the takings clause. The Court, Scalia wrote, appeared to be creating a new test that was even less restrictive than the broad public-use test employed since *Berman v. Parker.*

The Court said, "If the State had imposed a special tax, or perhaps a system of user fees, to generate the funds to finance the legal services supported by the Foundation, there would be no question as to the legitimacy of the use of the public's money." Scalia rejected this tax analogy. It—

> reduces the "public use" requirement to a negligible impediment indeed, since I am unaware of *any* use to which state taxes cannot constitutionally be devoted. The money thus derived may be given to the poor, or to the rich, or (insofar as the Federal Constitution is concerned) to the girl-friend of the retiring governor. Taxes and user fees, since they are not "takings," are simply not subject to the "public use" requirement, and so their constitutional legitimacy is entirely irrelevant to the existence *vel non* of a public use.[46]

It is difficult to know what to make of Stevens's effort to analogize the public-use limitation to the taxing power. On the one hand, the majority does not tell us that any case would come out differently under this new approach. It does not even argue that it is adopting a new approach. On the other hand, the Court did talk about the public-use issue. This is one of the instances in which lower courts might see this case as broadening the power of states to take property for "public use." Yet, the Court does not purport to overrule any case or even question the reasoning of any of its prior decisions relating to the already-relaxed public-use requirement. None of the parties briefed, or even raised, the public-use issue, nor was it part of the question presented to the Court for review. In a real sense, Stevens's discussion is dictum. No one argued that the IOLTA program failed the public-use test. Given the context in which the discussion is presented, it seems likely that this leg of the case will have no growing power.

---

[46]123 S.Ct. at 1423, n. 2 (Scalia, J., dissenting), citing United States v. Sperry Corp., 493 U.S. 52, 63 (1989).

Then there is the third part of *Brown*. This portion of the case relates to the issue of how one values the property that the state court has taken. All nine justices agreed that the property has been taken. None of the nine justices disputed the issue of whether the taking is for a public use. What is left then is the final issue: how does one measure "just compensation"?

Before this case, the short answer was that the compensation is the fair market value of the property taken at the time of the taking. The Court in *Brown* repeated Justice Holmes' oft-quoted dictum that the test is "what the owner lost, not what the taker has gained."[47] Holmes was known for his pithy statements, but the actual statement is not quite as pithy as the above quotation suggests:

> But the Constitution does not require a disregard of the mode of ownership,—of the state of the title. It does not require a parcel of land to be valued as an unencumbered whole when it is not held as an unencumbered whole. It merely requires that an owner of property taken should be paid for what is taken from him. It deals with persons, not with tracts of land. And the question is, What has the owner lost? not, What has the taker gained? We regard it as entirely plain that the petitioners were not entitled, as matter of law, to have the damages estimated *as if* the land was the sole property of one owner, and therefore are not entitled to $60,000 under their agreement.[48]

In context, Holmes meant that the taker only has to pay the fair market value of the land (the typical item that is taken), even if the particular parcel of land is very crucial to the plans of the taker— for example, if the farm that the state takes is crucial because it allows the state to avoid a more costly alternative for that leg of the highway that the state is constructing, the state does not have to pay more than the fair market value of the farm as farmland simply because the state wants to use that farmland to construct a crucial bridge for a crucial route in the road.[49]

---

[47]Boston Chamber of Commerce v. Boston, 217 U.S. 189, 195 (1910).

[48]217 U.S. at 195 (emphasis added).

[49]Holmes' introduction to the *Boston Chamber of Commerce* case shows that the factual background of this case is a bit more complex than the hypothetical in the text. In spite of this factual complexity, the principle is the same. Holmes said:

> This is a petition for the assessment of damages caused by the laying out of a public street over 2,955 square feet of land at the apex of a triangle between India street and Central Wharf street, in Boston, the latter being a private way between Milk street and Atlantic

A long series of prior Supreme Court cases have summarized "just compensation" as the "market value of the property at the time of the taking."[50] This statement reflects how commentators recapitulated the general rule before this decision: "Here the courts normally look to the market value of the property that has been taken."[51]

In determining what the market value is, the court will look to the value of the property as if land were applied to its "highest and

---

avenue, laid out by the same order, as part of the same street. The chamber of commerce had a building at the base of the triangle, and owned the fee of the land taken. The Central Wharf & Wet Dock Corporation, which owned other land abutting on the new street, had an easement of way, light, and air over the land in question, and the Boston Five Cents Savings Bank held a mortgage on the same, subject to the easement. These three were the only parties having any interests in the land. They filed an agreement in the case that the damages might be assessed in a lump sum, the city of Boston refusing to assent, and they contended that it was their right, as matter of law, under the Massachusetts statute, Rev. Laws chap. 48, §§ 20-22, and the 14th Amendment, to recover the full value of the land taken, considered as an unrestricted fee. The city, on the other hand, offered to show that the restriction being of great value to the Central Wharf & Wet Dock Corporation, the damage to the market value of the estate of the chamber of commerce was little or nothing, and contended that the damages must be assessed according to the condition of the title at act date of the order laying out the street. It contended that the jury could consider the improbability of the easement being released, as it might affect the mind of a possible purchaser of the servient estate, and that the dominant owner could recover nothing, as it lost nothing by the superposition of a public easement upon its own. The parties agreed that if the petitioners were right, the damages should be assessed at $60,000, without interest; but, if the city was right, they should be $5,000.

217 U.S. at 193.

[50] *See, e.g.,* United States v. 50 Acres of Land, 469 U.S. 24, 29 (1984) (holding that just compensation is "market value of the property at the time of the taking"), *see also* Olson v. United States, 292 U.S. 246, 255 (1934); Kirby Forest Industries, Inc. v. United States, 467 U.S. 1, 10 (1984); United States v. 564.54 Acres of Monroe and Pike County Land, 441 U.S. 506, 511, (1979); Almota Farmers Elevator & Warehouse Co. v. United States, 409 U.S. 470, 474 (1973); United States v. Commodities Trading Corp., 339 U.S. 121, 130 (1950); United States v. New River Collieries Co., 262 U.S. 341, 344 (1923).

[51] 2 RONALD D. ROTUNDA & JOHN E. NOWAK, TREATISE ON CONSTITUTIONAL LAW: SUBSTANCE AND PROCEDURE § 15.14 (West Group, 3rd ed., 1999), at p. 752. *Accord, e.g.,* Note, *Valuation of Conrail Under the Fifth Amendment,* 90 HARV. L. REV. 596, 598 (1977).

best" use. The highest and best use of a piece of property is determined by the value of the property in light of its present and potential uses if those uses can be anticipated with reasonable certainty.[52]

The majority in *Brown*, however, rejects the market value test. It quotes the short form of Holmes's dictum and language from several other cases that did not discuss the issue before the Court. For example, Stevens quotes Frankfurter's statement that an owner's nonpecuniary losses attributable to "his unique need for property or idiosyncratic attachment to it," are not compensable,[53] a noncontroversial statement that is not relevant to the facts of *Brown*.

Stevens, in a weak effort to muster support, even relies on language in a dissent. Quoting the dissent from a 1940 case, Stevens says that it stands for the proposition that the government should pay "not for what it gets but for what the owner loses."[54] The dissent, of course, is the part of a decision in which one is least likely to find the holding.

---

[52]Super–Power Co. v. Sommers, 352 Ill. 610, 618, 186 N.E. 476, 479 (1933). The market value test is not, however, a definitive test. *See* United States v. Fuller, 409 U.S. 488 (1973), which stated that the overall standard is governed by basic equitable principles of fairness. *Fuller* held that the government as a condemnor was not required to pay for elements of the property's market value that the government had created by granting the landowner a revocable permit to graze his animals on adjoining Federal lands. The Court also does not use market value if it is too difficult to ascertain, or if paying of market value would result in "manifest injustice" to the owner or the public. *See also* United States v. Commodities Trading Corp., 339 U.S. 121, 123 (1950).

The Court explained this matter further in Kirby Forest Industries, Inc. v. United States, 467 U.S. 1, 10 n.15 (1984). Note that even here the Court reaffirmed the fair market value measure:

> We have acknowledged that, in some cases, this standard fails fully to indemnify the owner for his loss. Particularly when property has some special value to its owner because of its adaptability to his particular use, the fair-market-value measure does not make the owner whole. United States v. 564.54 Acres of Land, 441 U.S. 506, 511–12 (1979). We are willing to tolerate such occasional inequity because of the difficulty of assessing the value an individual places upon a particular piece of property and because of the need for a clear, easily administrable rule governing the measure of "just compensation."

[53]123 S.Ct. at 1419, quoting Kimball Laundry Co. v. United States, 338 U.S. 1, 5 (1940).

[54]*See* 123 S.Ct. at 1419, quoting Kimball Laundry, 338 U.S. 1, 23 (1940) (Douglas, J., dissenting), stating that the government should pay "not for what it gets but for what the owner loses."

Stevens then announces that just compensation should be "measured by the property owner's loss rather than the government's gain. This conclusion is supported by consistent and unambiguous holdings in our cases."[55] But are these prior cases really so clear? Their fact patterns do not match the present case, the language that Stevens quotes does not come from holdings, and there is abundant Supreme Court precedent that adopts a different rule—that the proper measurement of just compensation is the market value of the property taken on the date it is appropriated.[56] His statement that these earlier cases are both consistent and unambiguous is unconvincing.

In any event, given the Court's statement of the rule—just compensation is the market value of what the taker receives, not what the property owner has lost—the final question is, what has the property owner lost? One would think that the measure of loss should be easy: if the IOLTA account turns over one million dollars in interest to the state, then the various property owners who own the principal from which that interest came would have suffered the loss of one million dollars and the market value of what the taker receives or the property owner loses is the same. But the *Brown* rule is not that simple.

Stevens concluded that the owners of the money deposited in the IOLTA accounts—the owners of the money that draws interest that is taken by the state—have suffered *no* loss. Remember that Washington IOLTA accounts generate between $2.5 and $4.0 million per year of interest, and that, nationwide, these accounts in 2001 generated more than $200 million in interest payments.[57] We should remember that Stevens also concluded that the state has engaged

---

[55] 123 S.Ct. at 1419.

[56] *See, e.g.,* United States v. 50 Acres of Land, 469 U.S. 24, 29 (1984); Olson v. United States, 292 U.S. 246, 255 (1934); Kirby Forest Industries, Inc. v. United States, 467 U.S. 1, 10 (1984); United States v. 564.54 Acres of Monroe and Pike County Land, 441 U.S. 506, 511, (1979); Almota Farmers Elevator & Warehouse Co. v. United States, 409 U.S. 470, 474 (1973); United States v. Commodities Trading Corp., 339 U.S. 121, 130 (1950); United States v. New River Collieries Co., 262 U.S. 341, 344 (1923).

[57] Brief of Petitioners, Washington Legal Foundation v. Legal Foundation of Washington, 2002 WL 1974400 (Appellate Brief), (U.S. Pet. Brief, Aug 22, 2002) (NO. 01-1325), at 4; AMERICAN BAR ASSOCIATION, COMMISSION ON INTEREST ON LAWYERS' TRUST ACCOUNTS, IOLTA HANDBOOK 98, 208 (2002 update).

in a per se taking of these interest payments.[58] How can one conclude that the owners of the principal from which the interest was taken have suffered zero loss?

Stevens answers by making a factual assumption on the way he believes that law firms conduct business. Because of this factual assumption, a future court can interpret this case to apply to IOLTA accounts as they operate in the present and not as they must operate in the near future. Let us examine this factual assumption about the way law firms engage in business or administer IOLTA accounts. Stevens quotes a hypothetical factual scenario presented in the lower court:

> Suppose $2,000 is deposited into a lawyer's trust account paying 5% and stays there for two days. It earns about $.55, probably well under the cost of a stamp and envelope, along with clerical expenses, needed to send the $.55 to the client. In that case, the client's financial loss from the taking, if a reasonable charge is made for the administrative expense, is nothing. The fair market value of a right to receive $.55 by spending perhaps $5.00 to receive it would be nothing.[59]

That is not the way one would expect a law firm to do business. Let us say that the client's interest amounted to fifty-five cents. The law firm would not cut a check for that amount and mail it. When the next billing cycle came around, the law firm would merely deduct fifty-five cents from the amount that the client owed the law firm. The cost of rebating the fifty-five cents to the client is zero in administrative expense. When you deposit money in a NOW account, and the bank tells you that you earned fifty-five cents in interest that month, it also does not send you a check. This would only impose unnecessary administrative expenses that would eat up the minor interest that an account earns, particularly in the present day when checking accounts pay less than one-half percent interest. The bank just adds the miniscule amount of interest, such

---

[58] 123 S.Ct. at 1419 (internal citations omitted).

[59] Brown v. Legal Foundation of Washington, 123 S.Ct. 1406, 1420 (2003), *quoting* Washington Legal Foundation v. Legal Foundation of Washington, 271 F.3d 835, 833 (9th Cir. 2001) (Judge Kleinfeld, dissenting), affirmed in part, vacated in part, and remanded in, Washington Legal Foundation v. Legal Foundation of Washington, 271 F.3d 835 (9th Cir. 2001), affirmed, Brown v. Legal Foundation of Washington, 123 S.Ct. 1406 (2003).

as fifty-five cents, to your account. Given modern computers, the marginal cost of calculating and rebating the interest for one month on an account that varies in amount from day to day is zero.

Stevens presents a slightly different hypothetical fact situation immediately after the one I have just quoted. He also quotes from the Ninth Circuit opinion:

> On the other hand, suppose, hypothetically, that the amount deposited into the trust account is $30,000, and it stays there for 6 days. The client's loss here would be about $29.59 if he does not get the interest, which may well exceed the reasonable administrative expense of paying it to him out of a common fund. It is hard to see how just compensation could be zero in this hypothetical taking, even though it would be in the $2,000 for 2 days hypothetical taking. It may be that the difference between what a pooled fund earns, and what the individual clients and escrow companies lose, adds up to enough to sustain a valuable IOLTA program while not depriving any of the clients and customers of just compensation for the takings. This is a practical question entirely undeveloped on this record. We leave it for the parties to consider during the remedial phase of this litigation.[60]

Stevens rejected the idea that a remand is necessary because of the way he characterizes the IOLTA program. His description is lengthy, and he repeats it in different phraseology several times. In short, he concludes that, by definition, if the client could earn interest, then the lawyer should not deposit the funds in the IOLTA account, and if the lawyer did deposit funds, the lawyer would be liable to the client for the interest. There are several features of the Washington State IOLTA plan that Stevens regards as crucial and that he therefore discusses and reiterates several times in his opinion.

First: "*All* client funds paid to any Washington lawyer or law firm must be deposited in identifiable interest-bearing trust accounts separate from any accounts containing non-trust money of the lawyer or law firm. The program is mandatory for all Washington lawyers."[61] This provision, alone, raises no takings issue. It simply requires lawyers to keep the clients' funds in interest-bearing

---

[60] 123 S.Ct. at 1420 (footnote omitted), *quoting Brown,* 271 F.3d at 893.
[61] 123 S.Ct. at 1413.

accounts. It says nothing about what accounts the lawyer uses. That provision comes next.

Second:

> The new rule provides for two kinds of interest-bearing trust accounts. The first type of account bears interest to be paid, net of any transaction costs, to the client. This type of account may be in the form of either separate accounts for each client or a single pooled account with subaccounting to determine how much interest is earned for each client. The second type of account is a pooled interest-bearing account with the interest to be paid directly by the financial institution to the Legal Foundation of Washington (hereinafter the Foundation), a nonprofit entity [that the Washington Supreme Court established by court rule.][62]

Thus, says Stevens, there is no taking of principal (as opposed to interest on that principal) when the client's money is put in an interest-bearing account because the client still owns the principal. If the client's funds are too small to justify its own account, the Washington Supreme Court rule allows funds from various clients to be pooled into one account and earn interest for the various clients.

That leads us to the third point and the crucial issue: When must the lawyer put the client's money in a pooled fund to earn interest for the various clients and when must it be paid to the Legal Foundation of Washington?

On that point, Stevens quotes again from the court rule:

> Determining whether client funds should be deposited in accounts bearing interest for the benefit of the client or the Foundation is left to the discretion of each lawyer, but the new rule specifies that the lawyer shall base his decision *solely* on whether the funds could be invested to provide a positive net return to the client. This determination is made by considering several enumerated factors: the amount of interest the funds would earn during the period they are expected to be deposited, the cost of establishing and administering the account, and the capability of financial institutions to calculate and pay interest to individual clients.[63]

[62]123 S.Ct. at 1413.
[63]123 S.Ct. at 1413–14 (emphasis added).

In other words, Stevens says, if the funds could earn "net interest" for the client, the money must be deposited in a *non*-IOLTA fund— even if it is a pooled fund—where the interest inures to the benefit of the client. At another point he quotes from the state court opinion creating IOLTA: "Can the client's money be invested so that it will produce a net benefit for the client? *If so, the attorney must invest it to earn interest for the client.* Only if the money cannot earn net interest for the client is the money to go into an IOLTA account."[64] Later he reemphasizes the same point, where he explained that the state court said that—

> *as cost-effective subaccounting services become available*, making it possible to earn net interest for clients on increasingly smaller amounts held for increasingly shorter periods of time, more trust money will have to be invested for the clients' benefit under the new rule. *The rule is therefore self-adjusting and is adequately designed to accommodate changes in banking technology* without running afoul of the state or federal constitutions.[65]

To reemphasize the fact that the Court assumes that the clients had lost no money, Stevens quotes the lower court, which found, as a factual matter, that the clients could not have made any net returns from their investments.[66] Because of certain procedural rulings, Stevens limited his discussion to "the claims asserted by petitioners Allen Brown and Greg Hayes."[67] He quoted from the trial transcript to show that Brown, one of the individual plaintiffs, "did not claim that he would have received any interest if the IOLTA Rules had not been in place."[68] With respect to both litigants, Stevens admitted that "the facts are not crystal clear," but it "seems" that the petitioners' funds generated some interest that was paid to IOLTA. Stevens assumed the "net interest" was zero and that therefore, as "a factual matter," the clients' net interest was zero.[69]

[64] *Id.* at 1414 (emphasis added).
[65] *Id.* at 1415 (emphasis added).
[66] 123 S.Ct. at 1416.
[67] *Id.* at 1415.
[68] *Id.* at 1416 & n.5.
[69] *Id.* at 1416.

Stevens is always speaking of "net interest," and he seems to assume that the cost of refunding the money to the client, when the money may be less than one dollar, is prohibitive, or an administrative nightmare.[70] No; it is only the cost of subtracting the twenty-five cents from the client's bill, and the marginal cost of doing that is also zero because, to the computer, once it goes about figuring out the bill, there is no extra effort for it to add or subtract twenty-five cents from the client's bill.

The petitioners also argued that the lawyers may inadvertently place clients funds in an IOLTA account instead of a pooled account from which the client can earn some interest. Stevens's response is that if funds are inadvertently deposited, the lawyer will have violated the requirements of IOLTA and will be liable in tort to the client.[71]

There is another reason to read this case quite narrowly. In addition to the qualifying remarks that pepper his opinion, Stevens does not purport to overrule any prior decision. Instead, he constantly emphasizes that the clients' net interest gain was zero, and that, if the net interest were higher than zero, the money belongs to the clients according to the Washington Court rules. Finally, if the lawyer inadvertently gives this money to IOLTA instead of to the client, the lawyer will be liable to the client for damages. The net interest to the client is always zero, "whenever the Washington law is obeyed,"[72] because the Washington law requires that client funds that generate net interest—that is, interest after subtracting the cost of administration—must be given to the client. "IOLTA funds are only those funds that cannot, under any circumstances, earn net interest (after deducting transaction and administrative costs and bank fees) for the client."[73]

---

[70] *Id.* at 1420. In the twenty-first century computers engage in complicated mathematical computations with lightning speed. Once the law firm buys the computer program, the marginal cost to the firm is zero. The cost of refunding the money, even if the refund is twenty-five cents, is not the cost of a postage stamp—that is what Stevens appeared to have assumed earlier.

[71] 123 S.Ct. at 1421.

[72] *Id.* at 1421.

[73] *Id.* 1421 n.10 (internal quotation marks omitted, quoting Washington IOLTA adoption order).

Conclusion

When one looks closely at this case, there is much less than meets the eye. On one level, many commentators may argue that *Brown* gives the green light to IOLTA programs to take the interest earned from private clients' funds and pay no compensation for that interest. Perhaps one or more members of the five-person majority would embrace that view of the law, but that is not what the language of the majority conveys.

Stevens turned this case into one that invites further dispute in IOLTA matters. Computer programs already exist that allow banks to compute interest on money left in NOW accounts for very short periods of time. Although computers are very good for playing solitaire or watching movies on DVD, they were, after all, originally designed to compute. And, the marginal cost of their computing is zero, just like the marginal, out-of-pocket cost of my typing this sentence on the computer is zero. Typing the sentence on a computer uses no paper and no ink.

The future should see more suits over IOLTA accounts. First, the Court did not approve any IOLTA programs that lack the limiting language found in the Washington program. That language demands that "IOLTA funds are only those funds that *cannot, under any circumstances*, earn *net* interest (after deducting transaction and administrative costs and bank fees) for the client."—a phrase that Justice Stevens quotes with emphasis added *twice* in his opinion.[74]

Second, if the cost of apportioning the interest from a pooled account, after deducting transaction and administrative costs and bank fees is zero, *Brown* holds that the IOLTA program is invalid, because that interest then belongs to the client. The marginal cost of apportioning the interest among the various accounts all deposited in a pooled interest account is either zero or soon will be zero. Bank fees will be more than zero, but they have to be apportioned over all the accounts deposited in a pool interest account. We know that Washington IOLTA accounts generate between $2.5 and $4.0 million per year. We can safely assume that the bank fees on IOLTA are substantially less than the $4 million in interest generated by these accounts.

[74] *Id.* at 1414; 123 S.Ct. at 1420.

There is another reason that we should expect to see more IOLTA suits in court. The petitioners in this case raised not only a takings issue but a free speech issue. The Court did not reach that question, but Justice Kennedy's separate dissent noted:

> Had the State, with the help of Congress, not acted in violation of its constitutional responsibilities by taking for itself property which all concede to be that of the client, the free market might have created various and diverse funds for pooling small interest amounts. These funds would have allowed the true owners of the property the option to express views and policies of their own choosing. Instead, as these programs stand today, the true owner cannot even opt out of the State's monopoly.
>
> The First Amendment consequences of the State's action have not been addressed in this case, but the potential for a serious violation is there. Today's holding, then, is doubly unfortunate. One constitutional violation (the taking of property) likely will lead to another (compelled speech). These matters may have to come before the Court in due course.[75]

The *Brown* case did not end the litigation over IOLTA. Like its predecessor, *Phillips*, the case is written narrowly and suggests that five or more members of the Court would not approve an IOLTA program that did not, as a legal and factual matter, contain all the caveats found in the majority opinion.

---

[75]*Id.* at 1428 (Kenney, J., dissenting) (internal citations omitted).

Coming Up: October Term 2003

Michael A. Carvin

Following the Supreme Court's dramatic decisions this June, including the *Grutter v. Bollinger*, 123 S. Ct. 2325 (2003), and *Gratz v. Bollinger*, 123 S. Ct. 2411 (2003), affirmative action cases and the *Lawrence v. Texas*, 123 S. Ct. 2472 (2003), decision striking down a state sodomy law, the Court's docket for the October 2003 Term appears less likely to result in quite as many high-profile and groundbreaking decisions. Nonetheless, the Court has before it several cases raising significant legal issues, particularly the challenge to the new campaign finance statute and an important case involving the discriminatory funding of educational scholarships based on religion. Moreover, additional grants in the course of the Term could result in further significant cases.

Campaign Finance

In September, the Court will hear argument in eleven cases consolidated with *McConnell v. FEC*, No. 02-1784, involving challenges to the constitutionality of the Bipartisan Campaign Reform Act (BCRA).[1] The most significant provisions of the statute are those imposing stringent new limitations on "soft money" contributions to, and expenditures by, participants in the political process, and those imposing broad new restraints upon issue advocacy before elections. Both of those categories of regulation imposed by the BCRA dramatically change the rules governing the financing of elections and raise the most fundamental constitutional concerns.

The BCRA's ban on political parties' receipt and use of "soft" money, that is, any money outside of the narrowly defined federal

---

[1] The author is cocounsel for the Republican National Committee, which is challenging the constitutionality of the statute in this case. Although the argument will be held in September 2003, technically at the end of the October 2002 Term, the decision will be issued during the October 2003 Term.

"hard" money regulations, is significantly different from the sorts of campaign finance regulations upheld by the Court in *Buckley v. Valeo*, 425 U.S. 946 (1976), and other cases. Whereas the previous cases primarily involved limits on contributions to political *candidates*, the BCRA's soft-money ban drastically limits contributions to, and independent *spending* by, political *parties* that do not hold office and cannot themselves be subject to political corruption. The Court has recognized that parties, like individuals, enjoy the basic First Amendment right to participate in the political process. Yet BCRA prevents national political parties from spending money on grass-roots voter mobilization at the state and local levels, which is the essence of the democratic process and which has been the parties' traditional function throughout our history. The fact that this spending limitation is stated as a restriction on the *source* of money that can be spent, rather than the *amount*, is of no moment, since the Court has recognized that such source restrictions have the same draconian effect on political participation as a straightforward expenditure ceiling. See *Austin v. Michigan Chamber of Commerce*, 494 U.S. 652 (1990); *FEC v. Massachusetts Citizens for Life, Inc.*, 479 U.S. 238 (1986).

Moreover, the government's primary justification for the soft-money ban, the rationale of preventing political corruption, has significant weaknesses. The Supreme Court has already held that "soft money" contributions to political parties have, "at best," an "attenuated" link to the appearance of corruption. See *Colorado Republican Fed. Campaign Comm. v. FEC*, 518 U.S. 604, 616 (1996). It is difficult to see why, as presupposed by the BCRA regime, a $2,000 contribution to a political candidate (which remains legal) would be *less* corrupting than an identical donation to the candidate's political party (which the BCRA makes unlawful), particularly given that the candidate will not receive, or even be aware of, the money given to the party. BCRA is particularly overbroad with respect to state and local elections because, for example, the Act makes it a felony for the national political parties to even solicit money for local mayor's races, or for state parties to spend unregulated money on state or local candidates or for voter mobilization or even ballot initiatives. This effort to close an alleged "loophole" for state electoral activity is wholly unsupported by any evidence that such grassroots politics has ever "appeared" to "corrupt" any *federal* candidate.

The BCRA's soft-money ban is also subject to a significant Equal Protection challenge. The statute's rigorous soft-money restrictions apply to political parties but not to similarly situated interest groups. For example, the BCRA restricts parties, but not other interest groups such as Emily's List or the League of Conservation Voters, from raising or spending soft money to engage in nonfederal activities, from engaging in generic campaign activities like "get out the vote" drives, and from other significant political activities. Thus, BCRA is premised on the inherently contradictory notions that it is corrupting for a political party to spend "special interest" money but not corrupting for the special interest group itself to spend the same money *directly* for the same purpose. BCRA's discrimination in favor of special interest groups in this fashion is ironic in light of its stated goal of eliminating undue special interest influence over federal candidates.

The issue advocacy provisions of the BCRA are subject to similarly serious First Amendment challenges. Here, Congress has passed a law prohibiting unions and corporations from sponsoring ads criticizing (or supporting or *mentioning*) candidates for Congress. Needless to say, restrictions on the expression of ideas in core political debates cut at the heart of the Free Speech Clause. And the Court has struck restrictions on expenditures made independently of candidates except where they expressly advocate the election or defeat of a specifically identified candidate. Since corporations have First Amendment rights, particularly nonprofit corporation groups focusing on issues, it is difficult to perceive any legitimate, much less compelling, government interest in so limiting political speech.

College Scholarships for Religious Studies

Locke v. Davey, No. 01-1315, raises some very interesting issues relating to the unconstitutional conditions doctrine and the Free Exercise Clause. The case involves a challenge to a Washington state statute that prohibits any awards of public scholarships to students studying theology at either public or private institutions. The Ninth Circuit held that the Washington law violated theology students' Free Exercise rights by facially discriminating against them.

The Washington statute would appear to be quite vulnerable to the constitutional challenge the Court will consider. In its previous cases under the Free Exercise Clause, the Court has generally declined to draw distinctions between the withholding of funding and other sorts of burdens imposed on religious exercise. For example, *Sherbert v. Verner*, 374 U.S. 398 (1963), held that a state cannot deny unemployment *compensation* based on a religious refusal to work on Saturdays. However difficult it may be to reconcile *Employment Division v. Smith*, 496 U.S. 913 (1990), with *Sherbert* in other respects, *Smith* too applied normal free-exercise analysis to the withholding of funding involved there. Moreover, the Court has held that states cannot discriminate in funding on the basis of religious viewpoint. Thus, *Rosenberger v. Rector & Visitors, Univ. of Va.*, 515 U.S. 819 (1995), held that a denial of funds to a student organization publishing a Christian newspaper was unconstitutional viewpoint discrimination. Together, these principles would seem to cast serious doubt on the propriety of the funding distinction drawn by the Washington statute in this case.

Locke will also present the Court with the opportunity, following *Zelman v. Simmons-Harris*, 536 U.S. 639 (2002), the Ohio school vouchers case, to move somewhat toward reconciling its historically disparate approaches to the First Amendment religion clauses. *Zelman*, of course, held that states are *permitted* under the Establishment Clause to fund religious education on a neutral, evenhanded basis. Just as the criterion of "neutrality" has played an increasingly important role in the Court's Establishment Clause jurisprudence, *Smith* seemed to establish neutrality as the touchstone for Free Exercise analysis. Thus, invalidating the sort of religious discrimination embodied in the Washington statute would help establish a harmonious interpretation of the Religion Clauses.

Eleventh Amendment

The Court has granted review in two significant cases involving the states' sovereign immunity. *Frew v. Hawkins*, No. 02-628, raises an issue of great practical importance involving the scope of sovereign immunity in the context of enforcing consent decrees. The plaintiff in *Frew* filed suit against Texas for alleged violations of a federal Medicaid program. The parties entered a consent decree, which the district court approved. The first issue is whether state officials waived their sovereign immunity by urging the district court to adopt the consent decree, which was based on federal law and which provides that the court will supervise the state official for compliance.

The second, and potentially more significant, issue involves whether the Eleventh Amendment precludes a district court from enforcing a consent decree entered by state officials that is not directed to remedying a violation of a federal right that can be the subject of a lawsuit under 42 U.S.C. § 1983. The Court's ruling on this issue could have a significant impact on the enforcement of consent decrees entered by states, particularly in prison and desegregation cases in which elaborate consent decrees often dictate detailed funding and operational requirements for state facilities. The states have a strong interest in cabining the scope of such decrees to provisions actually directed to remedying violations of identified rights.

In *Tennessee v. Lane*, No. 02-1667, the Court will decide whether Title II of the Americans with Disabilities Act (ADA) validly abrogates the states' sovereign immunity from private damages claims. The Court held in *Board of Trustees of University of Alabama v. Garrett*, 531 U.S. 356 (2001), that Title I of the ADA is not a valid exercise of the congressional power to enforce the Fourteenth Amendment and thus does not validly abrogate the states' sovereign immunity. In *Lane*, two plaintiffs sued Tennessee, claiming that they were denied access to courthouses due to lack of accommodation of their physical disabilities. Although the circuits have split as to whether the reasoning of *Garrett* extends to Title II, there would be little reason to expect the Court to rule that Title II is valid Enforcement Clause legislation while Title I is not. The congressional findings supporting the two titles do differ somewhat at the margins, but the essential conclusions of *Garrett* would appear to apply with equal force to Title II.

The wrinkle in *Lane* is that the Sixth Circuit held that while Title II does not validly abrogate sovereign immunity as legislation enforcing the Equal Protection Clause, the statute nonetheless is a valid exercise of the power to enforce the Due Process Clause (and hence validly abrogates the states' sovereign immunity on that independent ground). The Sixth Circuit's reliance on due process stemmed from the unique facts of *Lane*, which happened to involve a claimed inability to access to a courthouse. Access to the courts can implicate the Due Process Clause. This analysis is surprising, however, and the Supreme Court may be unlikely to accept it, given that Title II is not specific to courts, but rather is a general law that happened to be applied to court buildings in the unique context of this case. The Sixth Circuit in effect treated the abrogation inquiry on an "as applied" basis because the due process rationale would not have been available with respect to other Title II claims. This approach appears to be in significant tension with *Garrett* and other recent sovereign immunity cases, which have analyzed whether *statutes* were validly enacted under the Enforcement Clause, an inquiry that does not depend on the facts of the case at hand, and thus appears to rule out case-specific, "as applied" abrogations of sovereign immunity.

Miranda Warnings

The Court will also consider three cases in the upcoming Term involving the effects of violating *Miranda v. Arizona*, 396, U.S. 868 (1969). The Term could well produce the most significant developments in this area since the Court held that *Miranda* survived the enactment of 18 U.S.C. § 3501 in *Dickerson v. United States*, 530 U.S. 428 (2000). Clearly, *Dickerson* has not ended the confusion in the lower courts regarding the scope of, and basis for, the *Miranda* requirements, and the cases that the Court will address this term highlight the continuing uncertainty as to whether *Miranda* is a constitutional requirement under the Fifth Amendment or a policy-based, extraconstitutional prophylactic measure.

In *Missouri v. Seibert*, No. 02-1371, the Court will revisit an issue it decided in *Oregon v. Elstad*, 470 U.S. 298 (1985), which held that waivers of *Miranda* rights can be valid even if the defendant had previously undergone improper questioning without having been given *Miranda* warnings. Seibert was arrested and charged with second-degree murder for participating in setting fire to a mobile home while someone was inside it. Initially, a police officer questioned Seibert without reading her the *Miranda* warnings, but at the beginning of a subsequent session, the officer did give the *Miranda* warnings. After hearing the warnings in the second session, Seibert waived her *Miranda* rights and repeated incriminating statements she had made during the earlier session. The Missouri Supreme Court held that the post-*Miranda* statements should have been suppressed, distinguishing *Elstad* on the ground that the *Miranda* violation in *Seibert* appeared to be a deliberate tactic to elicit a confession.

The Court will address the significance of police officers' tactical use of non-*Miranda* questioning to the rule in *Elstad*. The Missouri Supreme Court's distinction might be difficult to maintain if the *Miranda* right is a constitutional rule under the Fifth Amendment because looking to the subjective motivations of the police officers would move the analysis even further from the text of the Amendment than is authorized under the existing precedents. To the extent that *Miranda* announces a general prophylactic measure, however, the Court might decide that a policy discouraging tactical *Miranda* violations is sufficient to justify the outcome below.

United States v. Patane, No. 02-1183, involves the suppression of physical evidence obtained by police questioning in violation of *Miranda*. Patane was charged with possession of a firearm by a convicted felon in violation of 18 U.S.C. § 922(g)(1). After his arrest, a police detective questioned him without giving the *Miranda* warnings. As a result of this improper questioning, the police were able to retrieve a firearm that the government introduced against Patane at trial. The Tenth Circuit held that the firearm should have been suppressed as the "fruit of the poisonous tree." The Supreme Court will decide whether physical evidence derived from noncoerced questioning without *Miranda* warnings must be suppressed. This case presents the tension between the constitutional and prophylactic strands of the Court's *Miranda* jurisprudence particularly clearly because, if *Miranda* is a constitutional rule, it only protects a *testimonial* privilege and would not appear to support an exclusionary rule with regard to nontestimonial evidence, regardless of how it is obtained. If *Miranda* is treated as prophylaxis, of course, there is little basis to predict the outcome in *Patane*.

Finally, *Fellers v. United States*, No. 02-6320, involves the effect of a *Miranda* violation on the Sixth Amendment right to counsel. Fellers, who was arrested and charged with conspiracy to possess with intent to distribute methamphetamine, made incriminating statements in response to questions without receiving his *Miranda* warnings. After police officers brought Fellers to the jail and informed him of his *Miranda* rights, Fellers waived those rights and repeated statements he had made earlier. Fellers argues that the inculpatory statements made at the jail should be suppressed as improperly elicited because he first spoke to the police before they presented him his *Miranda* rights, and that the failure to administer his *Miranda* warning violated his Sixth Amendment right to counsel because the encounter constituted a post-indictment interview. The Court will consider (1) whether the police violated Fellers' Sixth Amendment right to counsel, and (2) whether Fellers' post-warning statements should have been suppressed as the fruit of an illegal post-indictment interview outside of the presence of counsel.

Fourth Amendment

The Court has granted certiorari in no fewer than five Fourth Amendment cases so far, an unusually large number for a single Term. The cases will present several close issues relating to the propriety of searches.

In *Indianapolis, Inc. v. Edmond*, 531 U.S. 32 (2000), the Supreme Court held that checkpoint roadblocks for the purpose of nonspecific drug interdiction violated the Fourth Amendment. The Court will return to the issue of checkpoint roadblocks in *Illinois v. Lister*, No. 02-1060, which involves the constitutionality of checkpoints designed to investigate specific offenses. Law enforcement agents set up a checkpoint at the location of a specific automobile accident that had occurred at the same time of day, one week before the roadblock. The agents were trying to solicit information from anyone who may have witnessed the hit-and-run accident. Lister, a motorist stopped at the roadblock, was arrested for an unrelated offense, driving under the influence. The Illinois Supreme Court held that the search of Lister's vehicle violated the Fourth Amendment in light of *Edmond*. The Court will determine the constitutionality of checkpoint roadblocks for the purpose of investigating specific offenses. The added nexus to a specific criminal investigation might well be sufficient for the Court to distinguish the case from *Edmond*, and to hold that the search of Lister's automobile was lawful.

The Supreme Court held in *New York v. Belton*, 453 U.S. 454 (1981), that a police officer may search the passenger compartment of a vehicle as a contemporaneous incident of a lawful arrest of the occupant. In *Arizona v. Gant*, No. 02-1019, the Court will decide whether the rule announced in *Belton* applies when the occupant had no knowledge (either actual or constructive) of the presence of the police officer before leaving the vehicle. Gant was arrested on an outstanding warrant after parking his car in a driveway and exiting the vehicle on his own initiative. Police officers thereupon arrested Gant, then searched his car, and found contraband. The

Arizona Court of Appeals ruled that this evidence should have been suppressed, and distinguished *Belton* on the ground that Gant lacked any knowledge of the officers' presence before leaving the car. *Gant* thus raises the issue of whether the *Belton* rule that allows incidental searches of automobiles is limited to situations in which the arrest is effected by instructing the defendant to exit the vehicle that is then searched, or whether the mere presence of the vehicle is sufficient to trigger the "contemporaneous incident" exception.

In another, more fact-specific automobile case, *Maryland v. Pringle*, No. 02-809, the Court will clarify the application of the Fourth Amendment in the area of vehicle searches. Pringle was a passenger in the front seat of an automobile when it was stopped by a police officer. The propriety of the stop is not at issue in the case. The officer observed a roll of cash in the glove compartment when the driver opened it to retrieve the vehicle registration, and the officer asked permission to search the car. The driver consented to the search, and the officer discovered cocaine as well as the money he had previously observed. Pringle and the driver of the car disclaimed ownership of the cocaine and money, and the officer arrested both of them. The Court of Appeals of Maryland held that Pringle's arrest was improper, finding no probable cause and no facts sufficient to establish that Pringle had either knowledge or control of the cocaine. The case obviously will have to balance the interests of individuals being arrested for riding in a car in which, unbeknownst to them, illegal substances are present against a rule that prohibits prosecution whenever more than one person is in the car.

In *Groh v. Ramirez*, No. 02-811, the Court will address two issues arising from executing a deficient search warrant related to the "good faith" exception to the exclusionary rule. Police officers executed a warrant to search a home, but the warrant mistakenly printed the description of the home in the space provided for identifying the items to be seized. The homeowner sued the officers, and the Ninth Circuit ruled that the officer in charge of the operation was not entitled to qualified immunity from the suit because he had an obligation to proofread the warrant before executing it. The Supreme Court will review the qualified immunity issue, and will also determine whether the warrant stated in sufficient detail the places to be searched and the items to be seized pursuant to the Fourth Amendment particularity requirement. Whatever the virtues of the "exclusionary rule" in deterring police *misconduct*, applying it to "failures to proofread" would not seem to really protect *serious* Fourth Amendment rights and would further convert criminal prosecution into a game of judicial "gotcha." The Ninth Circuit's recent Supreme Court track record suggests that the chances of affirmance here are less than robust.

The Court will consider in *United States v. Banks*, No. 02-473, whether law enforcement officers violated either the Fourth Amendment or the "knock-and-announce" statute, 18 U.S.C. § 3109, when they forcibly entered an apartment approximately twenty seconds after knocking on the front door and announcing their presence. The statute requires that officers wait a reasonable period before forcibly entering a residence when executing a search warrant and specifically stipulates that an officer may forcibly enter into a home to execute the search warrant if he is refused admittance after the officer has announced his authority and his purpose. The Ninth Circuit held that the conduct of the officers violated both the Constitution and the statute and required suppression of the evidence, observing that no occupant of the house had denied the officers admission and that there were no exigent circumstances.

Freedom of Information Act

In *Office of Independent Counsel v. Favish*, No. 09-954, the Supreme Court will consider exemption 7(C) of the Freedom of Information Act (FOIA), which exempts from disclosure records or information collected for law enforcement purposes if their disclosure could constitute an invasion of privacy. Exemption 7(C) requires courts to weigh the public interest in requested documents against the intrusion on privacy that disclosure could be expected to cause. Favish submitted a FOIA request to the Office of Independent Counsel requesting photographs related to the death of former Deputy White House Counsel Vincent Foster. The Ninth Circuit affirmed the district court's conclusion that the materials fell under exemption 7(C), and thus did not need to be disclosed. The Court will consider whether the Foster materials were properly withheld on the grounds that autopsy pictures would seem to invade one's privacy.

Future Cases

Predicting future grants is difficult, but the most significant cases of a Term often include some in which the Court granted certiorari during the course of the Term. Indeed, both *Lawrence* and *Grutter*, arguably the most important cases of the 2002 Term, were taken by the Court during the Term. Several cases in which the Supreme Court has not yet granted certiorari raise issues that might warrant the Court's attention.

In *Alvarez-Machain v. United States*, 331 F.3d 604 (9th Cir. 2003), the Drug Enforcement Agency (DEA) recruited Mexican citizens to kidnap a Mexican national and bring him to the United States to face charges stemming from his alleged involvement in the kidnapping of a DEA agent. Alvarez was eventually acquitted and later brought suit, inter alia, under the Federal Tort Claims Act (FTCA) and the Alien Tort Claims Act (ATCA), asserting that his abduction was a violation of his civil rights. The Ninth Circuit held that the alleged extraterritorial tortious conduct by Mexican citizens gave rise to a civil claim under U.S. law, and that the complaint stated a violation to the law of nations, a predicate to federal court jurisdiction under the ATCA. The case presents the certiorari-worthy issue of whether the ATCA creates a private right of action for torts committed (anywhere in the world) in violation of customary international law. This decision could have ramifications for American corporations, which are increasingly being sued in the United States for "participating" in a foreign country's "torts" against foreign citizens.

In *United States v. McCoy*, 323 F.3d 1114 (9th Cir. 2003), the Ninth Circuit held unconstitutional the application of a federal child pornography statute, 18 U.S.C. § 2252, to noncommercial possession of such materials wholly within a single state, even if the pornography was created with materials that traveled interstate. McCoy was charged with possession of pornographic photographs of herself with her underage daughter, but was not alleged to have engaged in commercial activity with regard to the materials. The Ninth Circuit, in an opinion written by Judge Stephen Reinhardt (an unlikely champion of federalism principles), applied *United States v. Lopez*, 514 U.S. 549 (1995) and *United States v. Morrison*, 529 U.S. 598 (2000), to hold that an application of the statute to McCoy's conduct exceeded Congress's lawmaking power under the Commerce Clause. The case could provide another opportunity for the Court to address the scope of the congressional commerce power, an area of significant development in recent years. A negative decision could invalidate a number of other federal statutes, which justify regulating wholly intrastate activity exclusively on the grounds that materials relevant to the activity traveled between states.

Contributors

Randy E. Barnett is the Austin B. Fletcher Professor at Boston University School of Law where he has taught cyberlaw, contracts, constitutional law, and torts. Previously, he tried many felony cases as a criminal prosecutor for the Cook County State's Attorney's Office in Chicago. Professor Barnett's book, *The Structure of Liberty: Justice and the Rule of Law*, published by Oxford University Press appeared in paperback in 2000 and is available on Amazon.com. His latest book, *Restoring the Lost Constitution: The Presumption of Liberty*, will be published in February 2004 by Princeton University Press. A graduate of Northwestern University and Harvard Law School, he delivered the Kobe 2000 Lectures on Legal Philosophy at the University of Tokyo and Doshisha University in Kyoto. Currently, Professor Barnett is one of the lead attorneys for the Oakland Cannabis Cooperative in its pending case with the federal government and for the plaintiffs in the medical cannabis case of *Raich v. Ashcroft*. On behalf of the Institute for Justice, he coauthored an amicus brief to the Supreme Court in *Lawrence v. Texas* contending that the Texas antisodomy law was unconstitutional. Professor Barnett is a senior fellow of the Cato Institute.

James E. Bond is University Professor at Seattle University where he teaches in the Law School and the College of Arts and Sciences and where he served as Dean for twelve years. He has also taught at Washington and Lee and Wake Forest. Professor Bond is a graduate of Wabash College and the Harvard and Virginia Schools of Law. His most recent book, *No Easy Walk to Freedom: Reconstruction and the Ratification of the 14th Amendment*, concludes that those Southerners who favored ratification (including the freedmen) generally understood the 14th Amendment to nationalize the protection of individual liberty within the federal structure ordained by the original Constitution. They did not think, however, that it supported a more general democratization and nationalization of the American

Republic. In particular, he finds no evidence that they believed that the 14th Amendment incorporated the Bill of Rights. In his current writing and speaking, Professor Bond is thus very critical of much of the Supreme Court's post-New Deal 14th Amendment jurisprudence.

Michael A. Carvin is a partner in the D.C. office of Jones Day and specializes in constitutional, appellate, civil rights, and civil litigation against the federal government. During the Reagan administration, Mr. Carvin was Deputy Assistant Attorney General in both the Justice Department's Civil Rights Division and the Office of Legal Counsel. In those positions, he was involved in the department's leading civil rights, separation-of-powers, and other constitutional law controversies. In private practice, he has argued numerous cases in the U.S. Supreme Court and in virtually every federal appeals court. These cases include the decisions overturning the federal government's plan to statistically adjust the census, limiting the Justice Department's ability to create "majority-minority" districts, upholding Proposition 209's ban on racial preferences in California, holding the government liable in *Winstar* for breaching contracts in the thrift bailout legislation, and upholding a Cincinnati referendum barring special gay rights laws.

Mr. Carvin was one of the lead lawyers, and argued before the Florida Supreme Court, on behalf of George W. Bush in the 2000 election Florida recount controversy. He has also represented numerous state governments, financial institutions, and telecommunications and energy companies in "takings," First Amendment, civil rights, and statutory challenges to federal government actions.

Robert Corn-Revere is a partner in the Washington, D.C., office of Davis Wright Tremaine LLP, specializing in First Amendment, Internet, and communications law. He has served as counsel in First Amendment litigation involving the Communications Decency Act, the Child Online Protection Act, Internet content filtering in public libraries, public broadcasting regulations, and export controls on encryption software. In 1999 Mr. Corn-Revere was listed on a 30th Anniversary Roll of Honor by the American Library Association Office of Intellectual Freedom and Freedom to Read Foundation for his role as lead counsel in *Mainstream Loudoun v. Board of Trustees* *of the Loudoun County Library.* He successfully argued *United States v. Playboy Entertainment Group, Inc.,* 529 U.S. 803 (2000), in which the U.S. Supreme Court struck down Section 505 of the Telecommunications Act of 1996 as a violation of the First Amendment. Mr. Corn-Revere also served as lead counsel in *Motion Picture Association v. FCC,* 309 F.3d 796 (D.C. Cir. 2002), in which the U.S. Court of Appeals for the District of Columbia Circuit vacated video description rules imposed on networks by the Federal Communications Commission.

Before joining Davis Wright Tremaine L.L.P. in March 2003, Mr. Corn-Revere was a partner at Hogan & Hartson L.L.P. in Washington, D.C., from 1994 to 2003. Previously, he served as Chief Counsel to Interim Chairman James H. Quello of the FCC. From 1990 until 1993, he was Commissioner Quello's Legal Adviser. He has written extensively on First Amendment, Internet, and communications-related issues and is a frequent speaker at professional conferences. Mr. Corn-Revere is coauthor of a three-volume treatise, *Modern Communications Law,* published by West Group, and is editor and coauthor of *Rationales & Rationalizations* published in 1997. He is a member of the Editorial Advisory Board of Pike & Fischer's *Internet Law & Regulation.* From 1987 to 2001, Mr. Corn-Revere taught at the Communications Law Institute of the Columbus School of Law, Catholic University of America. He is Chairman of the Media Institute's First Amendment Advisory Council and is a member of the Institute's Board of Trustees. From 2000 to 2002, Mr. Corn-Revere served on the Board of Trustees of the Freedom to Read Foundation, affiliated with the American Library Association. He also is an Adjunct Scholar to the Cato Institute in Washington, D.C.

Douglas H. Ginsburg received his undergraduate degree from Cornell University and his law degree from the University of Chicago. After clerking for Judge Carl McGowan on the U.S. Court of Appeals for the District of Columbia Circuit, and Justice Thurgood Marshall on the Supreme Court of the United States, in 1975 he joined the faculty of Harvard Law School, where he became a tenured professor. Beginning in 1985, he held a series of posts in the Reagan administration, including Deputy Assistant Attorney General for Regulatory Affairs in the antitrust division of the U.S. Department of Justice; Administrator for Information and Regulatory Affairs at the Office of Management and Budget, Executive Office of the President; and finally Assistant Attorney General for Antitrust. Appointed by President Reagan in 1986 to the U.S. Court of Appeals for the District of Columbia Circuit, he became Chief Judge in July 2001. Judge Ginsburg has taught law at Columbia, Harvard, the University of Chicago, and George Mason University.

Thomas C. Goldstein is the founder and a partner of the Washington, D.C., law firm of Goldstein & Howe, P.C. The firm specializes in litigation before the Supreme Court of the United States and almost all of its cases are in that forum. Mr. Goldstein will argue his ninth Supreme Court case, *Lamie v. U.S. Trustee*, in November 2003. His previous arguments involved an array of federal law questions, including the First Amendment, ERISA, and civil procedure. He was cocounsel to Nike in the Supreme Court proceedings in *Nike v. Kasky*. Mr. Goldstein has also taken a lead role, serving second chair, in a number of leading Supreme Court cases, including *Bush v. Gore* and *New York Times v. Tasini*. He recently was named one of the top 45 lawyers under the age of 45 by *American Lawyer* magazine, which also profiled him as one of the nation's half-dozen leading Supreme Court advocates. He also was named one of the top 40 lawyers under the age of 40, and one of a half-dozen attorneys to take note of in the 21st century in Washington, D.C. Before founding Goldstein & Howe, he was an attorney with Boies & Schiller, LLP (now Boies, Schiller & Flexner, LLP). His practice focused on Supreme Court litigation as well as commercial litigation and arbitration. Before that, he was an associate with Jones Day Reavis & Pogue, where his practice focused on Supreme Court litigation and appellate litigation generally. Previously, Mr. Goldstein was a law clerk to Judge Patricia M. Wald of the U.S. Court of Appeals for the District of Columbia Circuit. He graduated law school summa cum laude from the Washington College of Law of American University. Among other honors, he graduated first in his class, was editor-in-chief of the law review, was named the outstanding graduate student of the university, and won the first-year and upperclass moot court competitions. His law review Note on *Shaw v. Reno* received the Judge John R. Brown Award as the best article by a law student in the nation. This year Mr. Goldstein will teach Supreme Court litigation at Stanford Law School.

Erik S. Jaffe is a solo appellate attorney in Washington, D.C., whose practice emphasizes First Amendment and other constitutional issues. He is a 1986 graduate of Dartmouth College and a 1990 graduate of Columbia Law School. Following law school he clerked for Judge Douglas II. Ginsburg on the U.S. Court of Appeals for the District of Columbia Circuit, practiced for five years at Williams & Connolly in Washington, D.C., clerked for Justice Clarence Thomas on the U.S. Supreme Court during October Term 1996, and then began his solo appellate practice in 1997. Since 1999 Mr. Jaffe has been involved in more than a dozen cases at the merits stage before the U.S. Supreme Court. He represented one of the successful respondents in the First Amendment case of *Bartnicki v. Vopper*, 532 U.S. 514 (2001), and authored amicus briefs for such organizations as the Cato Institute and the Center for Individual Freedom in constitutional cases such as *Republican Party of Minnesota v. Kelly*, 122 S. Ct. 2528 (2002) (judicial speech); *Zelman v. Simmons-Harris*, 122 S. Ct. 2460 (2002) (vouchers); *Watchtower Bible and Tract Society v. Village of Stratton*, 122 S. Ct. 2080 (2002) (anonymous speech); *United States v. United Foods, Inc.*, 533 U.S. 405 (2001) (compelled advertising); *Boy Scouts of America v. Dale*, 530 U.S. 640 (2000) (freedom of expressive association); and *United States v. Morrison*, 529 U.S. 598 (2000) (Commerce Clause).

Robert A. Levy joined Cato in 1997 after 25 years in business. He is an adjunct professor at the Georgetown University Law Center, a director of the Institute for Justice, and a trustee of the Objectivist Center. Mr. Levy received his Ph.D. in business from American University in 1966. During 1966 he founded CDA Investment Technologies, Inc., a major provider of financial information and software. Levy was chief executive officer of CDA until 1991. He then earned his J.D. in 1994 from George Mason University, where he was chief articles editor of the law review. For the next two years Mr. Levy clerked for Judge Royce C. Lamberth on the U.S. District Court in Washington, D.C., and for Judge Douglas H. Ginsburg on the U.S. Court of Appeals for the District of Columbia Circuit. Among Levy's publications are a book, dozens of articles on investments, and, more recently, numerous papers on law and public policy. His work has been published in the *New York Times, Wall Street Journal, USA Today, Washington Post, National Review, Weekly*

Standard, Journal of the American Medical Association, and numerous other media. He also has discussed public policy on many national radio and TV programs, including CNN's "Crossfire," ABC's "Nightline," "Geraldo," "Hardball," and NBC's "Today Show."

Roger Pilon is vice president for legal affairs at the Cato Institute. He holds Cato's B. Kenneth Simon Chair in Constitutional Studies and is the founder and director of Cato's Center for Constitutional Studies. Established in 1989 to encourage limited constitutional government at home and abroad, the Center has become an important force in the national debate over constitutional interpretation and judicial philosophy. Mr. Pilon's work has appeared in the *New York Times, Washington Post, Wall Street Journal, Los Angeles Times, Legal Times, National Law Journal, Harvard Journal of Law & Public Policy, Notre Dame Law Review, Stanford Law & Policy Review, Texas Review of Law & Politics,* and elsewhere. He has appeared, among other places, on ABC's "Nightline," CBS's "60 Minutes II," National Public Radio, Fox News Channel, CNN, MSNBC, and CNBC. He lectures and debates at universities and law schools across the country and testifies often before Congress. Before joining Cato, Pilon held five senior posts in the Reagan administration, including at State and Justice. He has taught philosophy and law and was a national fellow at Stanford's Hoover Institution. Mr. Pilon holds a B.A. from Columbia University, an M.A. and a Ph.D. from the University of Chicago, and a J.D. from the George Washington University School of Law. In 1989 the Bicentennial Commission presented him with the Benjamin Franklin Award for excellence in writing on the U.S. Constitution. In 2001 Columbia University's School of General Studies awarded him its Alumni Medal of Distinction.

Ronald D. Rotunda became the George Mason University Foundation Professor of Law in 2002. Previously, he was the Albert E. Jenner Jr. Professor at the University of Illinois. He graduated magna cum laude from Harvard College and Harvard Law School, clerked on the Second Circuit, practiced law in Washington, D.C., and was assistant majority counsel for the Senate Watergate Committee. He coauthored the most widely used course book on legal ethics, *Problems and Materials on Professional Responsibility* (Foundation Press, 7th ed. 2000); a five-volume *Treatise on Constitutional Law* (3rd ed.

1999), and a one-volume *Treatise on Constitutional Law* (6th ed. 2000). He authored *Modern Constitutional Law* (West Group., 6th ed. 2000) and *Legal Ethics: The Lawyer's Deskbook on Professional Responsibility* (ABA-West Group, 2nd ed. 2002). Professor Rotunda has written several other books and more than 200 articles. He was Constitutional Law Adviser to the Supreme National Council of Cambodia and the Supreme Constitutional Court of Moldova. He advised the Constitutional Convention that created the Ukrainian Constitution. In 1996, he assisted the Czech Republic in drafting the first Rules of Ethics for lawyers in that country. In 2000, he was Visiting Senior Fellow in Constitutional Studies at the Cato Institute. In November–December 2002, he was Visiting Scholar, Katholieke Universiteit Leuven, Belgium. In May 2000 American Law Media, publisher of *The American Lawyer*, chose Professor Rotunda as one of the ten most influential Illinois Lawyers. Also in 2000, the University of Chicago Press published a study that rated Professor Rotunda as the seventeenth most influential law professor over the last several decades. The 2002–2003 New Educational Quality Ranking of U.S. Law Schools (EQR) ranked Professor Rotunda as the eleventh most cited of all law faculty in the United States.

Bradley A. Smith was appointed to the Federal Election Commission by President William Jefferson Clinton in 2000 for a term expiring in 2005. He was elected Vice Chairman of the Commission in 2003. While he is serving on the FEC, Vice Chairman Smith is on leave from his position as Professor of Law at Capital University in Columbus, Ohio, where he taught Election Law, Jurisprudence, Law & Economics, and Civil Procedure from 1993 to 2000. He is also an Adjunct Professor of Law at George Mason University School of Law. His writings have appeared in a variety of popular and academic publications, including the *Wall Street Journal*, *USA Today*, *Commentary*, *National Review*, the *Yale Law Journal*, the *Georgetown Law Journal*, and the *University of Pennsylvania Law Review*. His 2001 book, *Unfree Speech: The Folly of Campaign Finance Reform*, was praised by George Will as "the year's most important book on governance," and by the *Times Literary Supplement* as "a much needed dose of realism which has relevance far beyond America." Vice Chairman Smith earned his B.A. in economics and political science, cum laude, from Kalamazoo College in Kalamazoo, Michigan, and his J.D., cum laude, from Harvard Law School. The views expressed in his article are those of Bradley Smith and not those of the Federal Election Commission.

James L. Swanson is a senior fellow in constitutional studies at the Cato Institute and editor in chief of the *Cato Supreme Court Review*. A graduate of the University of Chicago and the UCLA School of Law, he was a member of the law review and recipient of a moot court distinguished advocate award. Mr. Swanson served as a legal adviser to Chairman Susan Liebeler at the U.S. International Trade Commission, clerked for Judge Douglas H. Ginsburg on the U.S. Court of Appeals for the District of Columbia Circuit, and was a special assistant in the Office of Legal Counsel at the Department of Justice, where he worked on Supreme Court nominations. Swanson is the founding and current editor of the *First Amendment Law Handbook* (West Group), an annual volume on recent developments in constitutional law and freedom of speech. He has written articles on intellectual property, the First Amendment, and other topics, and his work has appeared in the *Chicago Tribune*, *Los Angeles Times*, *Weekly Standard*, *American Heritage*, and other publications. A member of the National Book Critics Circle, he covers books on law, politics, the presidency, war, and African American history. Mr. Swanson's latest book, *Lincoln's Assassins: Their Trial and Execution*, was reviewed widely, including in the *New York Times*, the *Sunday Times* of London, *Wilson Quarterly*, and elsewhere. His next book, *Manhunt: The Twelve Day Chase for Lincoln's Killers*, will be published by William Morrow. As an adjunct professor at the John Marshall Law School in 2000 and 2001, he taught First Amendment law. In 2003 he was appointed to the advisory committee of the Congressionally mandated Abraham Lincoln Bicentennial Commission.

ABOUT THE CATO INSTITUTE

The Cato Institute is a public policy research foundation dedicated to the principles of limited government, individual liberty, free markets, and private property. It takes its name from *Cato's Letters*, popular libertarian pamphlets that helped to lay the philosophical foundation for the American Revolution.

Despite the Founders' libertarian values, today virtually no aspect of life is free from government encroachment. A pervasive intolerance for individual rights is shown by government's arbitrary intrusions into private economic transactions and its disregard for civil liberties.

To counter that trend, the Cato Institute undertakes an extensive publications program that addresses the complete spectrum of policy issues. It holds major conferences throughout the year, from which papers are published thrice yearly in the *Cato Journal*, and also publishes the quarterly magazine *Regulation*.

The Cato Institute accepts no government funding. It relies instead on contributions from foundations, corporations, and individuals and revenue generated from the sale of publications. The Institute is a nonprofit, tax-exempt educational foundation under Section 501(c)(3) of the Internal Revenue Code.

ABOUT THE CENTER FOR CONSTITUTIONAL STUDIES

Cato's Center for Constitutional Studies and its scholars take their inspiration from the struggle of America's founding generation to secure liberty through limited government and the rule of law. Under the direction of Roger Pilon, the center was established in 1989 to help revive the idea that the Constitution authorizes a government of delegated, enumerated, and thus limited powers, the exercise of which must be further restrained by our rights, both enumerated and unenumerated. Through books, monographs, conferences, forums, op-eds, speeches, congressional testimony, and TV and radio appearances, the center's scholars address a wide range of constitutional and legal issues—from judicial review to federalism, economic liberty, property rights, civil rights, criminal law and procedure, asset forfeiture, tort law, and term limits, to name just a few. The center is especially concerned to encourage the judiciary to be "the bulwark of our liberties," as James Madison put it, neither making nor ignoring the law but interpreting and applying it through the natural rights tradition we inherited from the founding generation.

CATO INSTITUTE
1000 Massachusetts Ave., N.W.
Washington, D.C. 20001